Take the Next Step in Your IT Career

Save 10%
on Exam Vouchers*
(up to a $35 value)

CompTIA.

Get details at
sybex.com/go/comptiavoucher

*Some restrictions apply. See web page for details.

CompTIA® Linux+
Practice Tests
Exam XK0-004
Second Edition

Steven Suehring

Senior Acquisitions Editor: Kenyon Brown
Development Editor: Tom Cirtin
Technical Editor: Kevin Ryan
Production Editor: Amy Odum
Copy Editor: Tiffany Taylor
Editorial Manager: Pete Gaughan
Production Manager: Kathleen Wisor
Executive Editor: Jim Minatel
Proofreader: Kathryn Duggan
Indexer: Ted Laux
Project Coordinator, Cover: Brent Savage
Cover Designer: Wiley
Cover Image: © Jeremy Woodhouse/Getty Images, Inc.

Copyright © 2019 by John Wiley & Sons, Inc., Indianapolis, Indiana

Published simultaneously in Canada

ISBN: 978-1-119-55596-4
ISBN: 978-1-119-55602-2 (ebk.)
ISBN: 978-1-119-55610-7 (ebk.)

Manufactured in the United States of America

No part of this publication may be reproduced, stored in a retrieval system or transmitted in any form or by any means, electronic, mechanical, photocopying, recording, scanning or otherwise, except as permitted under Sections 107 or 108 of the 1976 United States Copyright Act, without either the prior written permission of the Publisher, or authorization through payment of the appropriate per-copy fee to the Copyright Clearance Center, 222 Rosewood Drive, Danvers, MA 01923, (978) 750-8400, fax (978) 646-8600. Requests to the Publisher for permission should be addressed to the Permissions Department, John Wiley & Sons, Inc., 111 River Street, Hoboken, NJ 07030, (201) 748-6011, fax (201) 748-6008, or online at http://www.wiley.com/go/permissions.

Limit of Liability/Disclaimer of Warranty: The publisher and the author make no representations or warranties with respect to the accuracy or completeness of the contents of this work and specifically disclaim all warranties, including without limitation warranties of fitness for a particular purpose. No warranty may be created or extended by sales or promotional materials. The advice and strategies contained herein may not be suitable for every situation. This work is sold with the understanding that the publisher is not engaged in rendering legal, accounting, or other professional services. If professional assistance is required, the services of a competent professional person should be sought. Neither the publisher nor the author shall be liable for damages arising herefrom. The fact that an organization or Web site is referred to in this work as a citation and/or a potential source of further information does not mean that the author or the publisher endorses the information the organization or Web site may provide or recommendations it may make. Further, readers should be aware that Internet Web sites listed in this work may have changed or disappeared between when this work was written and when it is read.

For general information on our other products and services or to obtain technical support, please contact our Customer Care Department within the U.S. at (877) 762-2974, outside the U.S. at (317) 572-3993 or fax (317) 572-4002.

Wiley publishes in a variety of print and electronic formats and by print-on-demand. Some material included with standard print versions of this book may not be included in e-books or in print-on-demand. If this book refers to media such as a CD or DVD that is not included in the version you purchased, you may download this material at http://booksupport.wiley.com. For more information about Wiley products, visit www.wiley.com.

Library of Congress Control Number: 2019938095

TRADEMARKS: Wiley, the Wiley logo, and the Sybex logo are trademarks or registered trademarks of John Wiley & Sons, Inc. and/or its affiliates, in the United States and other countries, and may not be used without written permission. CompTIA is a registered trademark of Computing Technology Industry Association, Inc. All other trademarks are the property of their respective owners. John Wiley & Sons, Inc. is not associated with any product or vendor mentioned in this book.

C10010866_060619

To Tim Krause

Acknowledgments

Thank you to the team that helped put this title together: Pete Gaughan, editorial manager; Kenyon Brown, the acquisitions editor; Kevin Ryan, technical editor; Tom Cirtin, the project editor; Amy Odum, production editor; copyeditor Tiffany Taylor; and the compositors at Aptara.

Thank you also to all of those individuals who support me throughout book-writing and project endeavors, including my family, Patti, Rob, and Jim at Partners, Kent and everyone at Soundworks, and my colleagues at UWSP.

About the Author

Steve Suehring is an assistant professor of computing and new media technologies at University of Wisconsin—Stevens Point. Prior to joining the faculty in 2015, Steve gained 20 years of field experience in a variety of technical engineering, system and network administration, and system architectural roles. Steve has written several books and has served as an editor for *LinuxWorld* magazine.

Contents at a Glance

Introduction   *xv*

Chapter 1   Hardware and System Configuration   1
Chapter 2   System Operations and Maintenance   37
Chapter 3   Security   87
Chapter 4   Linux Troubleshooting and Diagnostics   123
Chapter 5   Automation and Scripting   159
Chapter 6   Practice Exam   185
Appendix   Answers and Explanations   201

Index   *277*

Contents

Introduction *xv*

Chapter 1	**Hardware and System Configuration**	**1**
Chapter 2	**System Operations and Maintenance**	**37**
Chapter 3	**Security**	**87**
Chapter 4	**Linux Troubleshooting and Diagnostics**	**123**
Chapter 5	**Automation and Scripting**	**159**
Chapter 6	**Practice Exam**	**185**
Appendix	**Answers and Explanations**	**201**
	Chapter 1: Hardware and System Configuration	202
	Chapter 2: System Operations and Maintenance	216
	Chapter 3: Security	233
	Chapter 4: Linux Troubleshooting and Diagnostics	246
	Chapter 5: Automation and Scripting	259
	Chapter 6: Practice Exam	268

Index *277*

Introduction

This book is a companion volume to *CompTIA Linux+ Study Guide: Exam XK0-004* (4th ed.). The book will help you prepare for the certification exams by testing your knowledge using questions derived directly from the exam objectives. There are 1,000 questions within this book, divided into chapters based on the objectives.

Each of the chapters will test your knowledge on a given exam objective along with its subobjectives. There is also a practice exam at the end covering all exam objectives. The questions are a mix of easy to difficult and will help you prepare for the types of knowledge needed to demonstrate that you can work with Linux systems.

To achieve maximum benefit, the book should be used with the corresponding certification study guide. You can also use the book to identify areas where additional study is needed.

Objective Map

The following table lists each of the five objective domains in the CompTIA Linux+ exam and the percentage of the exam of each domain. The subobjectives are also listed for each domain. Because each chapter in this book focuses on a specific domain, the mapping is easy: for Domain 1.0, refer to Chapter 1; for Domain 2.0, refer to Chapter 2, and so on.

Objective Domain	Percentage of Exam	Chapter
Domain 1.0 Hardware and System Configuration	21%	1
1.1 Explain Linux boot process concepts		
1.2 Given a scenario, install, configure, and monitor kernel modules		
1.3 Given a scenario, configure and verify network connection parameters		
1.4 Given a scenario, manage storage in a Linux environment		
1.5 Compare and contrast cloud and virtualization concepts and technologies		
1.6 Given a scenario, configure localization options		

Objective Domain	Percentage of Exam	Chapter
Domain 2.0 Systems Operation and Maintenance	**26%**	**2**
2.1 Given a scenario, conduct software installations, configurations, updates, and removals		
2.2 Given a scenario, manage users and groups		
2.3 Given a scenario, create, modify, and redirect files		
2.4 Given a scenario, manage services		
2.5 Summarize and explain server roles		
2.6 Given a scenario, automate and schedule jobs		
2.7 Explain the use and operation of Linux devices		
2.8 Compare and contrast Linux graphical user interfaces		
Domain 3.0 Security	**19%**	**3**
3.1 Given a scenario, apply or acquire the appropriate user and/or group permissions and ownership		
3.2 Given a scenario, configure and implement appropriate access and authentication methods		
3.3 Summarize security best practices in a Linux environment		
3.4 Given a scenario, implement logging services		
3.5 Given a scenario, implement and configure Linux firewalls		
3.6 Given a scenario, backup, restore, and compress files		

Objective Domain	Percentage of Exam	Chapter
Domain 4.0 Linux Troubleshooting and Diagnostics	20%	4
4.1 Given a scenario, analyze system properties and remediate accordingly		
4.2 Given a scenario, analyze system processes in order to optimize performance		
4.3 Given a scenario, analyze and troubleshoot user issues		
4.4 Given a scenario, analyze and troubleshoot application and hardware issues		
Domain 5.0 Automation and Scripting	14%	5
5.1 Given a scenario, deploy and execute basic Bash scripts		
5.2 Given a scenario, carry out version control using Git		
5.3 Summarize orchestration processes and concepts		

Chapter 1

Hardware and System Configuration

THE FOLLOWING COMPTIA LINUX+ EXAM OBJECTIVES ARE COVERED IN THIS CHAPTER:

✓ **1.1 Explain Linux boot process concepts.**

- The following is a partial list of the used files, terms, and utilities:
  - Boot loaders such as GRUB and GRUB2
  - Boot options such as UEFI/EFI, PXE, NFS, and booting from ISO and HTTP/FTP
  - `/etc/default/grub`
  - `/etc/grub2.cfg`
  - `/boot`
  - `mkinitrd`
  - `dracut`
  - `grub2-install`
  - `grub2-mkconfig`
  - `initramfs`
  - `linux.efi`
  - `vmlinuz`
  - `vmlinux`

✓ **1.2 Given a scenario, install, configure, and monitor kernel modules**

- The following is a partial list of the used files, terms, and utilities:
  - lsmod
  - insmod

- modprobe
- dmesg
- rmmod
- depmod
- /usr/lib/[kernelversion]
- /usr/lib/modules
- /etc/modprobe.conf
- /etc/modprobe.d/

✓ 1.3 Given a scenario, configure and verify network connection parameters

- The following is a partial list of the used files, terms, and utilities:
  - ping
  - netstat
  - nslookup
  - dig
  - host
  - route
  - ip
  - ethtool
  - ss
  - iwconfig
  - nmcli
  - brctl
  - nmtui
  - /etc/sysconfig/network
  - /etc/sysconfig/network-scripts/
  - /etc/hosts
  - /etc/network
  - /etc/resolv.conf
  - /etc/netplan

- /etc/sysctl.conf
- /etc/dhcpd.conf
- Bonding aggregation, active/passive, load balancing

✓ 1.4 Given a scenario, manage storage in a Linux environment

- The following is a partial list of the used files, terms, and utilities:
  - Basic partitions including raw devices, GPT, and MBR
  - File system hierarchy including real file systems, virtual filesystems, relative paths, and absolute paths
  - Device mappers including lvm, mdadm, and Multipath
  - XFS tools
  - LVM tools
  - EXT tools
  - fdisk
  - parted
  - mkfs
  - iostat
  - df
  - du
  - mount
  - umount
  - tune2fs
  - fsck
  - /etc/fstab
  - /etc/cryptab
  - /dev/
  - /dev/mapper
  - /dev/disk/by-id
  - /etc/mtab
  - /sys/block
  - Filesystem types including ext3, ext4, xfs, nfs, smb, cifs, and ntfs

✓ **1.5 Compare and contrast cloud and virtualization concepts and technologies**

- The following is a partial list of the used files, terms, and utilities:
  - Templates including VM, OVA, OVF, JSON, YAML, and container images
  - Bootstrapping, including Cloud-init, Anaconda, and Kickstart
  - Storage such as thin vs. thick provisioning, persistent volumes, blob, and block
  - Network considerations including bridging, overlay networks, NAT, local, and dual-homed
  - Types of hypervisors
  - Tools such as `libvirt`, `virsh`, and `vmm`

✓ **1.6 Given a scenario, configure localization options**

- The following is a partial list of the used files, terms, and utilities:
  - `/etc/timezone`
  - `/usr/share/zoneinfo`
  - `localectl`
  - `timedatectl`
  - `date`
  - `hwclock`
  - `time`
  - Environment variables such as LC_*, LC_ALL, LANG, and TZ
  - Character sets such as UTF-8, ASCII, and Unicode

Chapter 1 ▪ Hardware and System Configuration

1. Which command is used to load a module and its dependencies automatically?
   A. modprobe
   B. lsmod
   C. insmod
   D. rmmod

2. Which option given at boot time within the GRUB configuration will boot the system into single-user mode?
   A. single-user
   B. su
   C. single
   D. root

3. During boot of a system with GRUB2, which key can be pressed to display the GRUB menu?
   A. Shift
   B. E
   C. V
   D. H

4. Which command can be used to view the kernel ring buffer in order to troubleshoot the boot process?
   A. lsboot
   B. boot-log
   C. krblog
   D. dmesg

5. Which command can be used to obtain a list of currently loaded kernel modules?
   A. insmod
   B. modlist
   C. ls --modules
   D. lsmod

6. Within which partition will the EFI system partition typically be mounted?
   A. /etc/efi
   B. /efi
   C. /sys/efi
   D. /boot/efi

7. Assuming that a USB disk contains a single partition and is made available on /dev/sdb, which command mounts the disk in /media/usb?
   A. mount /dev/sdb1 /media/usb
   B. usbconnect /dev/sdb0 /media/usb
   C. mount /dev/sdb0 /media/usb
   D. usbmount /dev/sdb1 /media/usb

8. What is one reason a device driver does not appear in the output of lsmod, even though the device is loaded and working properly?
   A. The use of systemd means drivers are not required for most devices.
   B. The use of initramfs means support is enabled by default.
   C. The system does not need a driver for the device.
   D. Support for the device has been compiled directly into the kernel.

9. Which option to rmmod will cause the module to wait until it's no longer in use to unload the module?
   A. -test
   B. -b
   C. -w
   D. -unload

10. Which command will output a new GRUB2 configuration file and send the output to the correct location for booting?
    A. update-grub > /boot/grub/grub.cfg
    B. update-grub boot > /boot/grub.cfg
    C. grub-rc.d
    D. grub-boot

11. What is the maximum number of primary partitions available on an MBR partitioning system?
    A. 2
    B. 4
    C. 1
    D. 5

12. When working with disk partitions through a tool like fdisk, you see the type 0x82. Which type of partition is this?
    A. Linux
    B. Linux swap
    C. NTFS
    D. FAT

13. Which file should you edit when using GRUB2 in order to set things like the timeout?
    A. /etc/default/grub
    B. /etc/grub/boot
    C. /etc/boot/grub.d
    D. /grub.d/boot

14. Which option for the grub2-mkconfig command sends output to a file instead of STDOUT?
    A. -stdout
    B. --fileout
    C. -o
    D. -f

15. Of the following choices, which size would be most appropriate for the /boot partition of a Linux system?
    A. Between 100 MB and 500 MB
    B. Between 1 GB and 10 GB
    C. /boot should not be partitioned separately.
    D. Less than 5 MB

16. Which of the following commands initializes a physical disk partition for use with LVM?
    A. lvmcreate
    B. pvcreate
    C. fvcreate
    D. lvinit

17. Which of the following commands installs GRUB into the MBR of the second SATA disk?
    A. grub2-install /dev/hdb2
    B. grub2-install /dev/sda2
    C. grub2-config /dev/sda
    D. grub2-install /dev/sdb

18. Which command is used to create a logical volume with LVM?
    A. pvcreate
    B. lvmcreate
    C. lvcreate
    D. volcreate

19. What is the logical order for creation of an LVM logical volume?
   A. Physical volume creation, volume group creation, logical volume creation
   B. Physical volume creation, logical volume creation, volume group creation
   C. Logical volume creation, physical volume creation, volume group creation
   D. LVM creation, format, partition

20. Which command should be run after making a change to the /etc/default/grub file?
   A. grub
   B. grub-mkconfig
   C. grub-inst
   D. reboot

21. Which command is used to search for physical volumes for use with LVM?
   A. lvmcreate
   B. pvcreate
   C. lvmdiskscan
   D. lvmscan

22. A hard drive is reported as hd(0,0) by the GRUB Legacy configuration file. To which of the following disks and partitions does this correspond?
   A. /dev/hdb2
   B. /dev/hda0
   C. /dev/disk1
   D. /dev/sda1

23. Which of the following commands installs GRUB into the master boot record (MBR) of the first SATA drive?
   A. grub-install /dev/hda
   B. grub-install /dev/sda
   C. grub-install /dev/hd0,0
   D. grub -i /dev/hda

24. When running fsck on an ext3 filesystem, the process is taking longer than expected and requiring input from the administrator to fix issues. What option could be added to fsck next time so that the command will automatically attempt to fix errors without intervention?
   A. -o
   B. -V
   C. -y
   D. -f

25. After inserting a new hard drive into the system, what is the correct order to make the drive ready for use within Linux?

   A. Use `fdisk` to create partitions, and then mount the partitions.

   B. Mount the partitions.

   C. Use `fdisk` to create partitions and mount -a to mount all the newly created partitions.

   D. Use `fdisk` to create partitions, then format the partitions using a command such as `mkfs`, and then mount the partitions.

26. You are using a storage area network (SAN) that keeps causing errors on your Linux system due to an improper kernel module created by the SAN vendor. When the SAN sends updates, it causes the filesystem to be mounted as read-only. Which command and option can you use to change the behavior of the filesystem to account for the SAN bug?

   A. `mount --continue`

   B. `tune2fs -e continue`

   C. `mkfs --no-remount`

   D. `mount -o remount`

27. Which of the following describes a primary difference between `ext2` and `ext3` filesystems?

   A. `ext3` was primarily a bug-fix update to `ext2`.

   B. `ext3` includes journaling for the filesystem.

   C. `ext3` completely changed the tools needed for management of the disks.

   D. `ext3` has no significant differences.

28. According to the Filesystem Hierarchy Standard (FHS), what is the correct location for site-specific data for a server?

   A. `/etc`

   B. `/var`

   C. `/tmp`

   D. `/srv`

29. Which option to the `mount` command will mount all filesystems that are currently available in `/etc/fstab`?

   A. `-f`

   B. `-d`

   C. `-a`

   D. `-m`

30. Which command and option are used to display the number of times a filesystem has been mounted?
   A. `tune2fs -h`
   B. `cat /etc/fstab`
   C. `mount -a`
   D. `less /etc/fsmnt`

31. Which option to `xfs_metadump` displays a progress indicator?
   A. `-g`
   B. `-p`
   C. `-f`
   D. `-v`

32. The system is running out of disk space within the home directory partition, and quotas have not been enabled. Which command can you use to determine the directories that might contain large files?
   A. `du`
   B. `df`
   C. `ls`
   D. `locate`

33. Which file contains information about the filesystems to mount, their partitions, and the options that should be used to mount them?
   A. `/etc/filesystems`
   B. `/etc/mounts`
   C. `/etc/fstab`
   D. `/srv/mounts`

34. According to the FHS, what is the proper mount point for removable media?
   A. `/etc`
   B. `/srv`
   C. `/tmp`
   D. `/media`

35. Which file contains information on currently mounted filesystems, including their mount options?
   A. `/etc/mtab`
   B. `/etc/fstab`
   C. `/tmp/files`
   D. `/etc/filesystems`

36. Which option to umount will cause the command to attempt to remount the filesystem in read-only mode if the unmounting process fails?
   A. -o
   B. -r
   C. -f
   D. -v

37. Which of the following represents the correct format for the /etc/fstab file?
   A. <directory> <device> <type> <options>
   B. <device> <type> <options>
   C. <device> <type> <options> <directory> <dump> <fsck>
   D. <device> <directory> <type> <options> <dump> <fsck>

38. Which of the following commands is used to identify the UUID for partitions?
   A. blkid
   B. ls
   C. find
   D. cat

39. The xfs_info command is functionally equivalent to which command and option?
   A. xfs_test -n
   B. xfs_list
   C. tunexfs -i
   D. xfs_growfs -n

40. Which of the following commands will create a btrfs filesystem on the first SATA drive?
   A. mkfs /dev/sda1
   B. mkfs.btrfs /dev/sda
   C. mkfs.btr2fs /dev/sda1
   D. mkfs -b /dev/sda

41. Which command and option are used to set the maximum number of times a filesystem can be mounted between running fsck?
   A. tune2fs -c
   B. dumpe2fs
   C. tune2fs -m
   D. setmount

42. Which command can be used to change the partitioning scheme for a disk, such as to change the size of existing partitions without deleting them?
    A. resize2fs
    B. parted
    C. mkfs
    D. rfdisk

43. Which of the following commands will mount a USB device at /dev/sdb1 into the /media/usb directory, assuming a VFAT filesystem for the USB drive?
    A. mount -t vfat /dev/sdb1 /mnt
    B. usbmount /dev/sdb1 /mnt/usb
    C. mount -t vfat /dev/sdb1 /mnt/usb
    D. mount -t usb /dev/sdb1 /mnt/usb

44. Which option within gdisk will change the partition name?
    A. n
    B. b
    C. v
    D. c

45. Which option to the dumpe2fs command can be used to display blocks that are reserved because of being marked as bad?
    A. -v
    B. -f
    C. -b
    D. -m

46. Which options to fsck can be used to check all filesystems listed in /etc/fstab while excluding the root partition?
    A. -NR
    B. -AM
    C. -X
    D. -C

47. Which option in /etc/fstab sets the order in which the device is checked at boot time?
    A. options
    B. dump
    C. fsck
    D. checkorder

48. Which file is used to indicate the local time zone on a Linux server?
   A. /etc/timez
   B. /etc/timezoneconfig
   C. /etc/timezone
   D. /etc/localtz

49. Within which directory will you find files related to the time zone for various regions?
   A. /etc/timezoneinfo
   B. /etc/zoneinfo
   C. /var/zoneinfo
   D. /usr/share/zoneinfo

50. Which command within `virsh` obtains information about a domain?
   A. info
   B. dominfo
   C. domainlist
   D. infodom

51. Which environment variable controls the format of dates and times, such as a 12-hour or 24-hour formatted clock?
   A. LOCALE_DATE
   B. DATE_FORMAT
   C. LC_TIME
   D. LC_DATE

52. Which of the following encodings provides a multibyte representation of characters?
   A. ISO-8859
   B. UTF-8
   C. ISO-L
   D. UFTMulti

53. Which command can be used to view the available time zones on a system?
   A. tzd
   B. /etc/locale
   C. timedatectl
   D. tzsel

54. Which of the following lines added to `.profile` in a user's home directory will set their time zone to Central time?
   A. `TZ=/Central ; export TZ`
   B. `TIMEZONE='America/Chicago' ; export TIMEZONE`
   C. `set TZ=/Central`
   D. `TZ='America/Chicago'; export TZ`

55. Which of the following values for the `LANG` variable will configure the system to bypass locale translations where possible?
   A. `LANG=COMPAT`
   B. `LANG=NONE`
   C. `LANG=C`
   D. `LANG=END`

56. If you need to temporarily reconfigure all locale variables and settings for a given session, which environment variable can be used?
   A. `LC_LIST`
   B. `LC_GLOBAL`
   C. `LC_ALL`
   D. `ALL_LOCALE`

57. Which of the following commands will set the systemwide time zone to `'America/Los_Angeles'`?
   A. `ln -sf /usr/share/zoneinfo/America/Los_Angeles /etc/localtime`
   B. `ln -sf America/Los_Angeles ; /etc/localtime`
   C. `ln -sd /etc/localtime /usr/share/timezone/America/Los_Angeles`
   D. `ln -sf /etc/localtime /usr/share/zoneinfo/America/Los_Angeles`

58. Which locale-related variable is used for currency-related localization?
   A. `LC_MONE`
   B. `LC_CURRENCY`
   C. `LC_MONETARY`
   D. `LC_CURR`

59. Which command is used to query and work with the hardware clock on the system?
   A. `hwc`
   B. `ntpdate`
   C. `systime`
   D. `hwclock`

60. Which option to the date command can be used to set the date and time?
    A. date -f
    B. date -t
    C. date --change
    D. date -s

61. Which function of the hwclock command will set the hardware clock to the current system time?
    A. -w
    B. -s
    C. -a
    D. -m

62. Which of the following commands sets the hardware clock to UTC based on the current system time?
    A. hwclock --systohc --utc
    B. hwclock --systohc --localtime
    C. hwclock --systohc
    D. hwclock --systoutc

63. Which of the following commands shows the current default route without performing DNS lookups on the IP address(es) involved?
    A. netstat -rn
    B. netstat -n
    C. netstat -r
    D. netstat -f

64. Which of the following is not used as a private address for local, non-Internet, use?
    A. 172.16.4.2
    B. 192.168.40.3
    C. 10.74.5.244
    D. 143.236.32.231

65. Which of the following commands adds a default gateway of 192.168.1.1 for interface eth0?
    A. route add default gateway 192.168.1.1 eth0
    B. eth0 --dg 192.168.1.1
    C. route add default gw 192.168.1.1 eth0
    D. route define eth0 192.168.1.1

66. Which option for the host command will query for the authoritative name servers for a given domain?
   A. -t ns
   B. -t all
   C. -ns
   D. -named

67. Which option for the ping command enables you to choose the interface from which the ICMP packets will be generated?
   A. -i
   B. -I
   C. -t
   D. -a

68. Which of the following commands queries for the mail servers for the domain example.com?
   A. dig example.com mx
   B. dig example.com
   C. host -t smtp example.com
   D. dig example.com smtp

69. Which of the following addresses represents the localhost in IPv6, such as you might find in /etc/hosts?
   A. 0:1
   B. ::1
   C. 127:0:1
   D. :127:0:0:1

70. Which command can be used to listen for netlink messages on a network?
   A. ip monitor
   B. netlink -a
   C. ip netlink
   D. route

71. Which of the following configuration lines in /etc/nsswitch.conf causes a lookup for group information to first use local files and then use LDAP?
   A. group: files ldap
   B. lookup: group [local ldap]
   C. group: [local ldap]
   D. group: localfiles ldap

72. Which of the following dig commands sends the query for example.com directly to the server at 192.168.2.5 rather than to a locally configured resolver?
    A. dig example.com @192.168.2.5
    B. dig -t 192.168.2.5 example.com
    C. dig -s 192.168.2.5 example.com
    D. dig server=192.168.2.5 example.com

73. Which of the following commands will enumerate the hosts database?
    A. getent hosts
    B. gethosts
    C. nslookup
    D. host

74. Which of the following configuration lines will set the DNS server to 192.168.1.4 using /etc/resolv.conf?
    A. dns 192.168.1.4
    B. dns-server 192.168.1.4
    C. nameserver 192.168.1.4
    D. name-server 192.168.1.4

75. Which of the following commands adds a route to the server for the network 192.168.51.0/24 through its gateway 192.168.51.1?
    A. route add -net 192.168.51.0 netmask 255.255.255.0 gw 192.168.51.1
    B. route add -net 192.168.51/24 gw 192.168.1.51
    C. route -net 192.168.51.0/24 192.168.51.1
    D. route add 192.168.51.1 -n 192.168.51.0//255.255.255.0

76. Which of the following commands shows network services or sockets that are currently listening along with sockets that are not listening?
    A. netstat -a
    B. netlink -a
    C. sockets -f
    D. opensock -l

77. Which of the following represents a correct configuration line for /etc/hosts?
    A. 192.168.1.4 cwa.braingia.org cwa
    B. cwa.braingia.org cwa 192.168.1.4
    C. cwa.braingia.org 192.168.1.8 alias cwa
    D. alias cwa.braingia.org cwa 192.168.1.4

78. Which of the following commands will change the default gateway to 192.168.1.1 using eth0?

   A. `ip route default gw 192.168.1.1`
   B. `ip route change default via 192.168.1.1 dev eth0`
   C. `ip route default gw update 192.168.1.1`
   D. `ip route update default 192.168.1.1 eth0`

79. Which of the following commands displays the Start of Authority information for the domain `example.com`?

   A. `dig example.com soa`
   B. `dig example.com authority`
   C. `dig example.com -auth`
   D. `dig -t auth example.com`

80. Assume that you want to enable local client services to go to hosts on the network without needing to fully qualify the name by adding the domain for either `example.com` or `example.org`. Which option in `/etc/resolv.conf` will provide this functionality?

   A. `search`
   B. `domain`
   C. `local-domain`
   D. `local-order`

81. Which of the following commands prevents traffic from reaching the host 192.168.1.3?

   A. `route add -host 192.168.1.3 reject`
   B. `route -nullroute 192.168.1.3`
   C. `route add -null 192.168.1.3`
   D. `route add -block 192.168.1.3`

82. Which of the following commands will emulate the `ping` command in Microsoft Windows, where the ping is sent for four packets and then the command exits?

   A. `ping -n 4`
   B. `ping -t 4`
   C. `ping -p 4`
   D. `ping -c 4`

83. You need to prevent local clients from going to a certain host, www.example.com, and instead redirect them to localhost. Which of the following is a method to override DNS lookups for the specified host?

   A. Add a firewall entry for the IP address of www.example.com to prevent traffic from passing through it.
   B. Delete www.example.com from the route table using the `route` command.
   C. Add a null route to prevent access to the IP address for www.example.com.
   D. Add an entry for www.example.com in `/etc/hosts` to point to 127.0.0.1.

84. Which of the following commands should be executed after running `ip route change`?
   A. `ip route flush cache`
   B. `ip route reload`
   C. `ip route cache reload`
   D. `ip route restart`

85. Which option should be used to send a DNS query for an SPF record with `dig`?
   A. `-t txt`
   B. `-t spf`
   C. `-t mx`
   D. `-t mailspf`

86. When viewing the available routes using the `route` command, one route contains flags UG while the others contain U. What does the letter G signify in the route table?
   A. The G signifies that the route is good.
   B. The G signifies that the route is unavailable.
   C. The G signifies that this is a gateway.
   D. The G signifies that the route is an aggregate.

87. Which of the following commands requests a zone transfer of `example.org` from the server at 192.168.1.4?
   A. `dig example.org @192.168.1.4 axfr`
   B. `dig example.org @192.168.1.4`
   C. `dig example.org @192.168.1.4 xfer`
   D. `dig example.org #192.168.1.4 xfer`

88. When using `iostat` to assess performance, which option displays information on a per-partition basis for block devices?
   A. `-a`
   B. `-c`
   C. `-d`
   D. `-p`

89. Which of the following commands can be used to display the current disk utilization?
   A. `df`
   B. `du`
   C. `diskutil`
   D. `diskuse`

90. You are working with a legacy CentOS 5 system and need to re-create the initial RAM disk. Which of the following commands is used for this purpose?
   A. `mkinitrd`
   B. `mkramdisk`
   C. `mkdisk --init`
   D. `mkfs.init`

91. Which of the following commands is used to display the currently loaded modules on a running system?
   A. `ls -mod`
   B. `lsmod`
   C. `listmod`
   D. `mod --list`

92. Which of the following commands creates a list of modules and their dependencies?
   A. `lsmod`
   B. `depmod`
   C. `modlist`
   D. `listmod`

93. Which option to `sysctl` displays all values and their current settings?
   A. `-a`
   B. `-b`
   C. `-d`
   D. `-c`

94. Which of the following commands installs a kernel module, including dependencies?
   A. `lsmod`
   B. `modprobe`
   C. `modinst`
   D. `instmod`

95. Which command is used to determine the modules on which another module depends?
   A. `modinfo`
   B. `modlist`
   C. `modprobe`
   D. `tracemod`

96. Which of the following commands inserts a module into the running kernel but does not resolve dependencies?
    A. `lsmod`
    B. `modinstall`
    C. `insmod`
    D. `moduleinst`

97. Which option to `modprobe` will remove a module and attempt to remove any unused modules on which it depends?
    A. `-v`
    B. `-r`
    C. `-d`
    D. `-f`

98. Within which of the following directories will you find blacklist information for modules loaded with `modprobe`?
    A. `/etc/blacklist`
    B. `/etc/modprobe.d`
    C. `/etc/blacklist.mod`
    D. `/etc/modprobe`

99. When working with a CentOS 6 system, which command is used to create the initial RAM disk?
    A. `mkinit`
    B. `dracut`
    C. `mkraminit`
    D. `mkinitfs`

100. If you'd like a value set with the `sysctl` command to take effect on boot, within which file should you place the variable and its value?
    A. `/etc/sysctl.cfg`
    B. `/etc/sysctl.conf`
    C. `/lib/sysctl`
    D. `/var/sysctl.conf`

101. Which of the following options to `modprobe` will show the dependencies for a module?
    A. `--show-deps`
    B. `--show-depends`
    C. `--deps`
    D. `--list-depends`

102. Which of the following commands mounts /dev/sda1 in the /boot partition?
   A. mount /dev/sda /boot
   B. mount /boot /dev/sda1
   C. mount /dev/sda1 /boot
   D. mount -dev sda1 /boot

103. Which of the following commands changes the boot order for the next boot?
   A. efibootmgr -c
   B. efibootmgr -b -B
   C. efibootmgr -o
   D. efibootmgr -n

104. Which bootloader can be used to boot from ISO with ISO9660 CD-ROMs?
   A. ISOLINUX
   B. EFIBOOT
   C. ISOFS
   D. BOOTISO

105. When using UEFI, which of the following files can be used as a bootloader?
   A. shim.uefi
   B. shim.efi
   C. shim.fx
   D. efi.shim

106. Which of the following commands, executed from within the UEFI shell, controls the boot configuration?
   A. bootcfg
   B. bcfg
   C. grub-install
   D. grcfg

107. Which of the following can be identified as an initial sector on a disk that stores information about the disk partitioning and operating system location?
   A. Minimal Boot Record (MBR)
   B. Master Boot Record (MBR)
   C. Init Sector
   D. Master Partition Table (MPT)

108. When using PXE boot, which file must exist within /tftpboot on the TFTP server for the system that will use PXELINUX for its bootloader?
    A. pxelinux.tftp
    B. pxelinux.boot
    C. pxelinux.conf
    D. pxelinux.0

109. Which option to grub-install will place the GRUB images into an alternate directory?
    A. --boot-dir
    B. -b
    C. -boot
    D. --boot-directory

110. When using a shim for booting a UEFI-based system, which of the following files is loaded after shim.efi?
    A. grubx64.cfg
    B. grub.conf
    C. grubx64.efi
    D. efi.boot

111. Part of the EXT tools, which option to the mke2fs command sets the type of filesystem to be created?
    A. -f
    B. -a
    C. -t
    D. -e

112. Which file is used to store a list of encrypted devices that are to be mounted at boot?
    A. /etc/cryptdev
    B. /etc/crypttab
    C. /etc/encrtab
    D. /etc/fsencrypt

113. Which option to dumpe2fs displays the bad blocks for a given partition?
    A. -bb
    B. -C
    C. -b
    D. -f

114. Which option to `xfs_check` is used to verify a filesystem that is stored in a file?
  A. -v
  B. -a
  C. -f
  D. -d

115. You are performing an `xfsrestore`. The `xfsdump` was executed with a block size of 4M. Which option do you need to invoke on `xfsrestore` in order for it to successfully use this dump?
  A. -b 4M
  B. -g 1M
  C. -i 1M
  D. -k 1028K

116. You see the word `defaults` within `/etc/fstab`. Which options are encompassed within the defaults?
  A. ro, exec, auto
  B. rw, suid, dev, exec, auto, nouser, async
  C. rw, exec, auto, nouser, async
  D. rw, exec, nouser, async, noauto, suid

117. Which of the following options to `xfsdump` sets the maximum size for files to be included in the dump?
  A. -p
  B. -s
  C. -z
  D. -b

118. Which partition type is used to indicate a software RAID array, such as an array built with mdadm?
  A. 0xmd
  B. -x-
  C. 0xRD
  D. 0xFD

119. When working with World Wide Identifiers (WWIDs), within which directory on a Red Hat server will you find symlinks to the current `/dev/sd` device names?
  A. /dev/disk/wwid
  B. /dev/wwid
  C. /dev/disk/by-id
  D. /dev/sd.wwid

120. Which of the following commands displays information about a given physical volume in an LVM setup?
    A. pvdisp
    B. pvlist
    C. pvdisplay
    D. pvl

121. When viewing information in /dev/disk/by-path using the command ls -l, which of the following filenames represents a LUN from Fibre Channel?
    A. /dev/fc0
    B. pci-0000:1a:00.0-fc-0x500601653ee0025f:0x0000000000000000
    C. pci-0000:1a:00.0-scsi-0x500601653ee0025f:0x0000000000000000
    D. /dev/fibre0

122. Which of the following commands displays path information for LUNs?
    A. luninfo -a
    B. ls -lun
    C. multipath -l
    D. dm-multi

123. Which command is used to remove unused filesystem blocks from thinly provisioned storage?
    A. thintrim
    B. thtrim
    C. fstrim
    D. fsclean

124. When using tune2fs to set an extended option such as stripe_width, which command-line option is needed to signify that an extended option follows?
    A. -extend
    B. -E
    C. -e
    D. -f

125. Which option to mdadm is used to create a new array?
    A. --create
    B. --start
    C. --begin
    D. --construct

126. Information about logical volumes can be found in which of the following directories?
   A. /dev/lvinfo
   B. /dev/map
   C. /dev/mapper
   D. /dev/lvmap

127. Which option to mdadm watches a RAID array for anomalies?
   A. --mon
   B. --watch
   C. --monitor
   D. --examine

128. When running mdadm in monitor mode, which option within /etc/mdadm.conf sets the destination for email if an issue is discovered?
   A. MAILTO
   B. MAILADDR
   C. MAILFROM
   D. MAILDEST

129. When using the ip command, which protocol family is used as the default if not otherwise specified?
   A. tcpip
   B. ip
   C. inet
   D. arp

130. Which command is used for setting parameters such as the essid, channel, and other related options for a wireless device?
   A. ifconfig
   B. iwconfig
   C. wlancfg
   D. iconf

131. Which of the following commands shows network sockets and their allocated memory?
   A. ss -m
   B. mpas
   C. mem
   D. free

132. Which option to the ss command shows the process IDs associated with the socket?
   A. -l
   B. -a
   C. -p
   D. -f

133. On a Debian system, within which directory hierarchy will you find configuration information and directories to hold scripts to be run when an interface is brought up or taken down?
   A. /etc/netconf
   B. /etc/netconfig
   C. /etc/net.conf.d
   D. /etc/network

134. Which of the following characters are valid for hostnames in /etc/hosts?
   A. Alphanumerics, minus, underscore, and dot
   B. Alphanumerics, minus, and dot
   C. Alphanumerics and dot
   D. Alphanumerics

135. Which of the following configuration lines in /etc/resolv.conf enables debugging?
   A. debug
   B. options debug
   C. option debug
   D. enable-debug

136. The system contains an NFS mounted filesystem that has become unreachable. Which option should be passed to umount in order to force the unmounting of the filesystem?
   A. -nfs
   B. --fake
   C. -f
   D. -n

137. Which of the following commands will send the output of the grub2-mkconfig command to the correct location for booting?
   A. grub2-mkconfig --output=/boot/grub2/grub.cfg
   B. grub2-mkconfig --file=/boot/grub2.menu
   C. grub2-mkconfig --file=/boot/grub.lst
   D. grub2-mkconfig --output=/boot/menu.lst

138. Which PXE Linux binary file is required for booting from HTTP or FTP?
   A. lpxelinux.0
   B. pxelinux.http
   C. netpxlinux.0
   D. netpxe.0

139. The file /etc/grub2.cfg is typically a symbolic link to which file?
   A. /boot/grub.conf
   B. /boot/grub2/grub.cfg
   C. /boot/grub2.conf
   D. /etc/sysconfig/grub2.cfg

140. Which of the following describes a difference between vmlinuz and vmlinux?
   A. vmlinuz is used for zOS systems, and vmlinux is used for x86 architecture.
   B. vmlinuz is used for 64-bit systems, and vmlinux is used for 32-bit systems.
   C. vmlinuz is compressed, whereas vmlinux is not.
   D. vmlinuz contains additional binary code for certain systems.

141. Which of the following is the location in which kernel modules are stored?
   A. /usr/modules
   B. /modules
   C. /usr/lib/modules/{kernel-version}
   D. /usr/modules/{kernel-version}

142. After recovering from kernel panic, you would like to look at what might have happened. Which of the following files contains the kernel ring buffer messages?
   A. /var/log/dmesglog
   B. /var/log/dmesg.log
   C. /var/log/kern.log
   D. /var/log/bootlog.txt

143. You have been asked to create a template for virtualization. The template will be in JSON format. Which of the following is the correct name for JSON?
   A. Just Simple Object Nodes
   B. JavaScript Object Notation
   C. Java Standard Object Notation
   D. JavaScript Standard Object Notation

144. You are using a container image for a cloud deployment and are building a stateful application that must store data between deployments. Which type of storage should be used?
    A. Ephemeral volume
    B. Bridged volume
    C. Container image
    D. Persistent volume

145. When working with a network configuration, which of the following terms refers to a computer with two network interfaces?
    A. Bridging
    B. Dual-homed
    C. Overlay
    D. Forwarding

146. Which of the following commands is used to change the keyboard layout settings?
    A. keybrdctl
    B. keyctl
    C. localectl
    D. localemap

147. Which of the following directories contains configuration files related to networking?
    A. /etc/netdevices/
    B. /etc/netcfg/
    C. /etc/config/network/
    D. /etc/sysconfig/network-scripts/

148. You need to change the label that has been applied to a filesystem. The filesystem is formatted as EXT4. Which EXT tool can be used to change the label?
    A. e2label
    B. e4label
    C. fslabel.ext4
    D. fslabel

149. The default format for an OVF template uses which document standard?
    A. YML
    B. XML
    C. OVFMeta
    D. HTML

150. Which of the following describes the difference between NAT and bridging in a virtualization environment?
   A. NAT uses the host adapter IP address for all network activity, while bridging enables the virtual machine to get its own IP.
   B. NAT enables the virtual machine to get its own IP, while bridging uses the host adapter IP address for all network activity.
   C. NAT is used to enable external clients to access the virtual machine, and bridging joins two virtual machines together.
   D. NAT and bridging refer to the same thing in virtualization.

151. Assume you need to add a kernel module with a custom command, such as to specify options at load time. Within which file could you add this configuration?
   A. /etc/modprobe-cfg
   B. /etc/modprobe.conf
   C. /etc/modprobe.cf
   D. /etc/modprobe.cfg

152. Which mode of network bonding is used for an active/passive configuration?
   A. active-passive
   B. active-balance
   C. active-backup
   D. active-back

153. Which command is used to install a kernel into the /boot directory, using the files from /usr/lib/kernel?
   A. kernel-ins
   B. ins-kernel
   C. install-kernel
   D. kernel-install

154. When troubleshooting a file that is not found, you notice that the file location is linked as ../file.txt. Which type of path has been used for this file?
   A. Virtual
   B. Symbolic
   C. Relative
   D. Absolute

155. When using fdisk to partition a disk, you have two partitions created for the system but still have leftover space, also called unallocated space, on the drive. What is another name used to refer to unallocated space?
   A. Highly available
   B. Redundant
   C. Raw device
   D. Partition forward

156. Which of the following values to `LIBVIRT_DEBUG` is used to enable debug logging for libvirt?

   A. 1
   B. 2
   C. 3
   D. 4

157. Which of the following describes the relationship between anaconda and kickstart?

   A. Anaconda is used to script an installation, while kickstart is used to boot the system.
   B. Kickstart is used to script an installation, while anaconda is used to install the system.
   C. Anaconda is used to install the system, while kickstart is used to boot the system.
   D. Kickstart is used to install the system, while anaconda is used to boot the system.

158. Which command can be used to determine how much time a Linux command takes?

   A. `time`
   B. `cmdtime`
   C. `timeproc`
   D. `proctime`

159. Which type of storage would be the most appropriate format to store a large object as a single file in a cloud environment?

   A. Block
   B. ext2
   C. cifs
   D. Blob

160. Which layer is used to enable client applications to work with disk devices in a standard way, regardless of disk architecture?

   A. Virtual filesystem
   B. Redundant filesystem
   C. Physical filesystem
   D. ICE

161. Which of the following real filesystems can be resized using `resize2fs`?

   A. nfs
   B. ext2
   C. ext3
   D. cifs

162. Which subcommand to the `virsh` command is used to connect to the hypervisor?
   A. plug
   B. hypervisorconnect
   C. conhyper
   D. connect

163. You need to determine if ASCII and Unicode are supported on the system. Which option to the `iconv` command shows the available character sets on a given system?
   A. --showchar
   B. --show
   C. --list
   D. --all

164. Which of the following best describes the /dev/ filesystem?
   A. The /dev/ filesystem is used for storing device information for connected devices.
   B. The /dev/ filesystem is used for configuration files.
   C. The /dev/ filesystem is used for development.
   D. The /dev/ filesystem is used to list devices for compilation into the kernel.

165. Which of the following files shows the currently mounted filesystems?
   A. /etc/fstab
   B. /proc/mounts
   C. /fs
   D. /root/mounts

166. When working with a Microsoft Windows-based filesystem, you see that it is mounted as a CIFS mount. What does CIFS stand for?
   A. Common Information File Sharing
   B. Common Internet File System
   C. Cloned Internet File Sharing
   D. Created In Five Seconds

167. When using `cloud-init` for deployment of an EC2 instance, which format should be used for the configuration files?
   A. XML
   B. YAML
   C. HTML
   D. JS

168. Which option to the `blkid` command purges the cache to remove devices that do not exist?

   A. -p
   B. -a
   C. -g
   D. -m

169. While you can use `blkid` to obtain the UUIDs for filesystems, which location on the filesystem also shows this information?

   A. /dev/diskbyuuid
   B. /dev/uuid
   C. /dev/fs/uuid
   D. /dev/disk/by-uuid

170. In a scripting scenario, you need to enable legacy locations for things like networking. Which file can be used for storing network configuration?

   A. /etc/netdev
   B. /etc/networking
   C. /etc/sysconfig/network
   D. /etc/sysconfig/netdev

171. You are building a configuration that requires bonded-link aggregation on the Linux server. Which protocol should the switch support in order to take advantage of aggregation?

   A. 802.11
   B. LACP
   C. LinkAG
   D. 802.3ag

172. Which of the `vmm` (`virt-manager`) tools is used to install a virtual machine?

   A. `virt-install`
   B. `vm-install`
   C. `install-virt`
   D. `virt-launch`

173. When checking filesystems with the `fsck` command, which option skips checking of the root filesystem?

   A. -A
   B. -M
   C. -R
   D. -S

174. Which type of virtualization hypervisor is considered a Type 1 hypervisor?
    A. Bare-metal
    B. Hosted
    C. Hypervisor on Linux
    D. Virtualized cloud

175. Which file contains the current list of partitions along with their major and minor numbers and number of blocks?
    A. /dev/disk
    B. /dev/partitions
    C. /proc/disk
    D. /proc/partitions

176. Assuming a block storage device used for virtualization of sda, which file can be used to view the number of read I/O requests for the device?
    A. /proc/sys/sda
    B. /proc/sys/sda/stat
    C. /sys/block/sda/stat
    D. /sys/disk/sda/stat

177. Which of the following best describes an OVA file?
    A. It is a virtualization appliance file.
    B. It is an open virtualization configuration file in YAML format.
    C. It is an open virtualized application file.
    D. It is an open virtual asset.

178. Files found within the /etc/netplan directory should be formatted using which syntax?
    A. JSON
    B. YAML
    C. XML
    D. Key=Value

179. When using the du command to diagnose which directories are large, you would like to summarize the output in a more human-friendly format. Which option(s) should be used?
    A. --summarize
    B. -uh
    C. -h
    D. -sh

180. When using a multipath device, found in /dev/disk/by-multipath, what is the name given to the identifier for that device that is globally unique?
    A. UUID
    B. WWID
    C. GUID
    D. DISKID

181. Which of the following is not a valid option for booting when using kickstart?
    A. CD-ROM
    B. NFS
    C. HTTP
    D. SFTP

182. Which of the following modes are used for load balancing in a bonding scenario on Linux?
    A. balance
    B. lb
    C. balance-rr
    D. balance-load

183. While troubleshooting a kernel issue and using the console, you are having difficulty working with the console due to continual messages being displayed on the console itself. Which option to dmesg can be used to disable logging to the console?
    A. -o "no logging console"
    B. -D
    C. -Q
    D. -F

184. Which option to rmmod forces the module to be unloaded?
    A. -f
    B. -a
    C. -w
    D. -h

185. Which command-line option modifies the behavior of depmod such that only newer modules are added when comparing modules.dep?
    A. -A
    B. -B
    C. -C
    D. -D

186. Which command prints device and partition information in a tree-like structure, including partition size and current mount status?
    A. fsck
    B. lsblk
    C. blkshow
    D. shblk

187. You need to create a script for use with the `parted` command. When using the `parted` command to obtain a list of partitions, which additional option formats the output such that it can be more easily parsed by a script?
    A. -p
    B. -S
    C. -m
    D. -v

188. Which command is used to create an ethernet bridge?
    A. bridgecon
    B. brctl
    C. bridgeman
    D. BridgeManager

189. Which file is used to maintain the configuration for DHCP?
    A. /etc/dhcpd.conf
    B. /etc/DHCP.cfg
    C. /etc/DHCPconf.txt
    D. /sys/dhcp.conf

190. You are working with a network interface called ens3 and would like to determine which driver is being used for this device. Which command is valid for this purpose?
    A. ip list ens3
    B. netstat ens3
    C. ethtool -i ens3
    D. ethlist ens3

191. When using `nslookup` interactively, which of the following commands changes the destination to which queries will be sent?
    A. dest
    B. server
    C. queryhost
    D. destination

Chapter 2

System Operations and Maintenance

THE FOLLOWING COMPTIA LINUX+ EXAM OBJECTIVES ARE COVERED IN THIS CHAPTER:

✓ **2.1 Given a scenario, conduct software installations, configurations, updates, and removals**

- Package types
  - rpm
  - deb
  - tar
  - tgz
  - gz
- Installation tools
  - RPM
  - Dpkg
  - APT
  - YUM
  - DNF
  - Zypper
- Build tools
  - Commands
    - `make`
    - `make install`
    - `ldd`
  - Compilers
  - Shared libraries

- Acquisition commands
  - wget
  - curl

✓ 2.2 Given a scenario, manage users and groups

- Creation
  - useradd
  - groupadd
- Modification
  - usermod
  - groupmod
  - passwd
  - chage
- Deletion
  - userdel
  - groupdel
- Queries
  - id
  - whoami
  - who
  - w
  - last
- Quotas
  - User quota
  - Group quota
- Profiles
  - Bash parameters
    - User entries
      - .bashrc
      - .bash_profile
      - .profile

- Global entries
    - /etc/bashrc
    - /etc/profile.d/
    - /etc/skel
    - /etc/profile
- Important files and file contents
    - /etc/passwd
    - /etc/group
    - /etc/shadow

✓ **2.3 Given a scenario, create, modify, and redirect files**

- Text editors
    - nano
    - vi
- File readers
    - grep
    - cat
    - tail
    - head
    - less
    - more
- Output redirection
    - <
    - >
    - |
    - <<
    - >>
    - 2>
    - &>
    - stdin
    - stdout

- stderr
- /dev/null
- /dev/tty
- xargs
- tee
- Here documents
- Text processing
  - grep
  - tr
  - echo
  - sort
  - awk
  - sed
  - cut
  - printf
  - egrep
  - wc
  - paste
- File and directory operations
  - touch
  - mv
  - cp
  - rm
  - scp
  - ls
  - rsync
  - mkdir
  - rmdir
  - ln
    - Symbolic (soft)
    - Hard

- unlink
- inodes
- find
- locate
- grep
- which
- whereis
- diff
- updatedb

✓ **2.4 Given a scenario, manage services**

- Systemd management
  - Systemctl
    - Enabled
    - Disabled
    - Start
    - Stop
    - Mask
    - Restart
    - Status
    - Daemon-reload
  - Systemd-analyze blame
  - Unit files
    - Directory locations
    - Environment parameters
    - Targets
    - Hostnamectl
    - Automount
- SysVinit
  - chkconfig
    - on
    - off
    - level

- Runlevels
  - Definitions of 0–6
  - `/etc/init.d`
  - `/etc/rc.d`
  - `/etc/rc.local`
  - `/etc/inittab`
  - Commands:
    - `runlevel`
    - `telinit`
- Service
  - Restart
  - Status
  - Stop
  - Start
  - Reload

✓ **2.5 Summarize and explain server roles.**

- NTP
- SSH
- Web
- Certificate authority
- Name server
- DHCP
- SNMP
- File servers
- Authentication server
- Proxy
- Logging
- Containers
- VPN
- Monitoring
- Database

- Print server
- Mail server
- Load balancer
- Clustering

✓ **2.6 Given a scenario, automate and schedule jobs**
- cron
- at
- crontab
- fg
- bg
- &
- kill
- Ctrl+C
- Ctrl+Z
- nohup

✓ **2.7 Explain the use and operation of Linux devices**
- Types of devices
  - Client devices
  - Bluetooth
  - WiFi
  - USB
  - Monitors
  - GPIO
  - Network adapters
  - PCI
  - HBA
  - SATA
  - SCSI
  - Printers
  - Video
  - Audio

- Monitoring and configuration tools
  - lsdev
  - lsusb
  - lspci
  - lsblk
  - dmesg
  - lpr
  - lpq
  - abrt
  - CUPS
  - udevadm
    - add
    - reload-rules
    - control
    - trigger
- File locations
  - /proc
  - /sys
  - /dev
  - /dev/mapper
  - /etc/X11
- Hot pluggable devices
  - /etc/rc5/udev
  - /etc/udev/rules.d

✓ **2.8 Compare and contrast Linux graphical user interfaces**

- Servers
  - Wayland
  - X11
- GUI
  - Gnome
  - Unity

- Cinnamon
- MATE
- KDE
- Remote desktop
  - VNC
  - XRDP
  - NX
  - Spice
- Console redirection
  - SSH port forwarding
    - Local
    - Remote
    - X11 forwarding
    - VNC
- Accessibility

1. Which command enables you to view the current IRQ assignments?
   A. view /proc/irq
   B. cat /proc/interrupts
   C. cat /dev/irq
   D. less /dev/irq

2. Configuration of udev devices is done by working with files in which directory?
   A. /udev/devices
   B. /devices/
   C. /udev/config
   D. /etc/udev

3. Which command is used to obtain a list of USB devices?
   A. usb-list
   B. lsusb
   C. ls-usb
   D. ls --usb

4. During the initialization process for a Linux system using SysVinit, which runlevel corresponds to single user mode?
   A. Runlevel 5
   B. Runlevel SU
   C. Runlevel 1
   D. Runlevel 6

5. On a system using SysVinit, in which directory are startup and shutdown scripts for services stored?
   A. /etc/init-d
   B. /etc/init
   C. /etc/sysV
   D. /etc/init.d

6. Which command can be used to reboot a system?
   A. init 6
   B. shutdown -h -t now
   C. init 1
   D. refresh-system

7. When working with a SysV system, which `chkconfig` option will display all services and their runlevels?
   A. `--reload`
   B. `--list`
   C. `--all`
   D. `--ls`

8. A drive connected to USB will be considered to be which type of device?
   A. Medium
   B. Coldplug
   C. Hotplug
   D. Sideplug

9. Which option within a `systemd` service file indicates the program to execute?
   A. `StartProgram`
   B. `ShortCut`
   C. `ExecStart`
   D. `Startup`

10. What is the command to display the default target on a computer running `systemd`?
    A. `systemctl defaults`
    B. `update-rc.d defaults`
    C. `systemctl runlevel`
    D. `systemctl get-default`

11. Which option of the `systemctl` command will change a service so that it runs on the next boot of the system?
    A. `enable`
    B. `startonboot`
    C. `loadonboot`
    D. `start`

12. Which of the following best describes the `/proc` filesystem?
    A. `/proc` contains information about files to be processed.
    B. `/proc` contains configuration files for processes.
    C. `/proc` contains information on currently running processes, including the kernel.
    D. `/proc` contains variable data such as mail and web files.

13. Which command is used to update the links and cache for shared libraries on the system?
    A. ldcache
    B. cache-update
    C. link-update
    D. ldconfig

14. Which command and option are used to update a Debian system to the latest software?
    A. apt-update
    B. apt-get upgrade
    C. dpkg -U
    D. apt-cache clean

15. Which option given to a yum command will install a given package?
    A. update
    B. configure
    C. install
    D. get

16. When working with an rpm package file and using rpm2cpio, by default the output is sent to which location?
    A. STDOUT
    B. The file cpio.out
    C. The file a.out
    D. The file /tmp/cpi.out

17. Which command is used to determine the libraries on which a given command depends?
    A. ldconfig
    B. librarylist
    C. listdeps
    D. ldd

18. Which command will retrieve information about the USB connections on a computer in a tree-like format?
    A. lsusb -tree
    B. lsusb --tree
    C. lsusb -t
    D. usblist --tree

19. How many SCSI devices are supported per bus?
    A. 7 to 15
    B. 2 to 4
    C. 12
    D. 4

20. Which command and option can be used to determine whether a given service is currently loaded?
    A. `systemctl --ls`
    B. `telinit`
    C. `systemctl status`
    D. `sysctl -a`

21. Which command on a `systemd`-controlled system would place the system into single-user mode?
    A. `systemctl one`
    B. `systemctl isolate rescue.target`
    C. `systemctl single-user`
    D. `systemctl runlevel one`

22. Which command would you use if you make changes to the `/etc/inittab` file and want those changes to be reloaded without a reboot?
    A. `init-refresh`
    B. `init 6`
    C. `telinit`
    D. `reload-inittab`

23. Which command displays the current runlevel for a system?
    A. `show-level`
    B. `init --level`
    C. `sudo init`
    D. `runlevel`

24. Within which folder are `systemd` unit configuration files stored?
    A. `/etc/system.conf.d`
    B. `/lib/system.conf.d`
    C. `/lib/systemd/system`
    D. `/etc/sysconfd`

25. Which option best describes the following, gathered with the `ls -la` command?
    `lrwxrwxrwx. 1 root root 35 Jul 8 2014 .fetchmailrc -> .configs/fetchmail/.fetchmailrc`
    A. It is a file called `.fetchmailrc` that is linked using a symbolic link.
    B. It is a file called `.configs/fetchmail/.fetchmailrc` that is owned by `lrwxrwxrwx`.
    C. It is a directory called `.fetchmailrc` that is owned by user Jul.
    D. It is a local directory called `.configs/fetchmail/.fetchmailrc`.

26. Which command is used with `systemd` in order to list the available service units?
    A. `systemd list-units`
    B. `systemctl list-units`
    C. `systemd unit-list`
    D. `systemctl show-units`

27. Which option to `lspci` is used to display both numeric codes and device names?
    A. `-numdev`
    B. `-n`
    C. `-nn`
    D. `-devnum`

28. Within which directory is information about USB devices stored?
    A. `/etc/usbdevices`
    B. `/var/usb`
    C. `/lib/sys/usb`
    D. `/proc/bus/usb`

29. A Serial ATA (SATA) disk will use which of the following identifiers?
    A. `/dev/hdX`
    B. `/dev/sataX`
    C. `/dev/sdX`
    D. `/disk/sataX`

30. When partitioning a disk for a mail server running Postfix, which partition/mounted directory should be the largest in order to allow for mail storage?
    A. `/etc`
    B. `/usr/bin`
    C. `/mail`
    D. `/var`

31. Which yum option displays the dependencies for the package specified?
   A. list
   B. deplist
   C. dependencies
   D. listdeps

32. Which options for the `rpm` command will display verbose output for an installation along with progress of the installation?
   A. -ivh
   B. -wvh
   C. --avh
   D. --ins-verbose

33. Which command will search for a package named zsh on a Debian system?
   A. apt-cache search zsh
   B. apt-get search zsh
   C. apt-cache locate zsh
   D. apt search zsh

34. Within which directory will you find the repositories used by yum?
   A. /etc/yum.conf
   B. /etc/repos
   C. /etc/yum.conf.d
   D. /etc/yum.repos.d

35. Which rpm option can be used to verify that no files have been altered since installation?
   A. -V
   B. -v
   C. --verbose
   D. --filesum

36. Which of the following is not typically used to store shared libraries?
   A. /lib
   B. /etc/lib
   C. /usr/lib
   D. /usr/local/lib

37. Which of the following commands updates the package cache for a Debian system?
    A. apt-get cache-update
    B. apt-cache update
    C. apt-get update
    D. apt-get upgrade

38. You need to update the configuration files for package repositories. Within which file are details of the current package repositories stored on a Debian system?
    A. /etc/apt.list
    B. /etc/sources.list
    C. /etc/apt/sources.list
    D. /etc/apt.d/sources.list

39. Which command should be used to make changes to the choices made when a Debian package was installed?
    A. dpkg-reconfigure
    B. dpkg -r
    C. dpkg --reconf
    D. apt-get reinstall

40. Which option for yum performs a search of the package cache?
    A. seek
    B. query
    C. --search
    D. search

41. Which command option for rpm can be used to show the version of the kernel?
    A. rpm kernel
    B. rpm -q kernel
    C. rpm search kernel
    D. rpm --list kern

42. Which option in /etc/yum.conf is used to ensure that the kernel is not updated when the system is updated?
    A. exclude=kernel*
    B. exclude-kernel
    C. updatekernel=false
    D. include-except=kernel

43. Which command searches for and provides information on a given package on a Debian system, including whether the package is currently installed?

   A. dpkg -i
   B. dpkg -s
   C. apt-cache
   D. apt-info

44. Which of the following installs a previously downloaded Debian package?

   A. dpkg -i <package name>
   B. apt-install <package name>
   C. apt-slash <package name>
   D. dpkg -U <package name>

45. You need to download source code for a package to install. The package has a .tgz file extension. Which of the following commands decompresses and unarchives the package?

   A. tar -xvf
   B. tar -zcvpf
   C. tar -zxvf
   D. tar -xf

46. You need to obtain information about a package installed on an OpenSUSE system that uses the zypper command. Which of the following options to the zypper command displays information about the package?

   A. inf
   B. getInfo
   C. info
   D. i

47. You need to find available packages on a Fedora system managed by the dnf package system. Which option to the dnf command looks for a given package?

   A. search
   B. info
   C. find
   D. locate

48. When using sed for a substitution operation, which option must be included so that the substitution applies to the entire line rather than just the first instance?

   A. g
   B. a
   C. r
   D. y

49. Which option for the wc command prints the number of lines given as input?
  A. -f
  B. -a
  C. -l
  D. -o

50. What is the default number of lines printed by the head and tail commands, respectively?
  A. 10 for head, 5 for tail
  B. 5 for head, 10 for tail
  C. 10 for both head and tail
  D. 3 for both head and tail

51. You are attempting to use rmdir to remove a directory, but there are still multiple files and other directories contained within it. Assuming that you're sure you want to remove the directory and all of its contents, what are the command and arguments to remove the directory and all of its contents?
  A. rm -f
  B. rm -rf
  C. rmdir -a
  D. rmdir -m

52. Which command will find directories with names beginning with 2019 located beneath the current directory?
  A. find ./ -name "2019"
  B. find ./ -type d -name "2019"
  C. find / -type d "2019"
  D. find ./ -type d -name "2019*"

53. Which of the following commands will provide the usernames in a sorted list gathered from the /etc/passwd file?
  A. cat /etc/passwd | awk -F : '{print $1}' | sort
  B. sort /etc/passwd | cut
  C. echo /etc/passwd
  D. cat /etc/passwd | awk '{print $1}' | sort

54. Which options to ls will produce output, including hidden (dot) files, in a list that is ordered such that the newest files are at the end of the output?
  A. -la
  B. -lat
  C. -latr
  D. -ltr

55. What will be the result if the touch command is executed on a file that already exists?
    A. The access timestamp of the file will change to the current time when the touch command was executed.
    B. The file will be overwritten.
    C. There will be no change.
    D. The file will be appended to.

56. Which option to both mv and cp will cause the command to prompt before overwriting files that already exist?
    A. -f
    B. -Z
    C. -r
    D. -i

57. Which of the following commands will send the contents of /etc/passwd to both STDOUT and a file called passwordfile?
    A. cat /etc/passwd > passwordfile
    B. var /etc/passwd | passwordfile
    C. cat /etc/passwd | tee passwordfile
    D. echo /etc/passwd | stdout > passwordfile

58. The current hierarchy on the server contains a directory called /usr/local. You need to create an additional directory below that called /usr/local/test/october. Which command will accomplish this task?
    A. mkdir -p /usr/local/test/october
    B. mkdir /usr/local/test/october
    C. mkdir -r /usr/local/test/october
    D. mkdir -f /usr/local/test/october

59. Which option to the cp command will copy directories in a recursive manner?
    A. -v
    B. -R
    C. -Z
    D. -i

60. What is the default delimiter used by the cut command?
    A. Colon
    B. Tab
    C. Space
    D. Comma

61. What command is used to bring a command to foreground processing after it has been backgrounded with an &?
    A. bg
    B. fore
    C. 4g
    D. fg

62. You are using the Vi editor to change a file, and you need to exit. You receive a notice indicating "No write since last change." Assuming you want to save your work, which of the following commands will save your work and exit Vi?
    A. :wq
    B. :q!
    C. dd
    D. x

63. What option is used to change the number of lines of output for the head and tail commands?
    A. -l
    B. -f
    C. -g
    D. -n

64. You have attempted to stop a process using its service command and also using the kill command. Which signal can be sent to the process using the kill command in order to force the process to end?
    A. -15
    B. -f
    C. -9
    D. -stop

65. When working in the bash shell, you need to redirect both STDOUT and STDERR. Which of the following commands will redirect both STDOUT and STDERR?
    A. 1>2
    B. >2
    C. 2>&1
    D. >>

66. Which of the following egrep commands will examine /etc/passwd to find users that are using either /bin/bash or /usr/bin/zsh for their shell environment?
    A. grep sh /etc/passwd
    B. egrep '/*/.sh$' /etc/passwd
    C. grep '/*/.=sh$' /etc/passwd
    D. egrep '/*/..?sh$' /etc/passwd

67. When editing with Vi, which command changes into insert mode and opens a new line below the current cursor location?
   A. f
   B. a
   C. o
   D. i

68. Which kill signal can be sent in order to restart a process?
   A. -HUP
   B. -RESTART
   C. -9
   D. -SIG

69. Which of the following commands searches each user's .bash_history file to determine if the user has invoked the sudo command?
   A. find /home -name "bash_history" | grep sudo
   B. find /home -name ".bash_history" | xargs grep sudo
   C. find /home/.bash_history | xargs grep sudo
   D. find /home -type history | xargs grep sudo

70. Which find command will locate files within the current directory that have been modified within the last 24 hours?
   A. find ./ -type f -mtime 1
   B. find ./ -type f -mtime 24
   C. find ./ -type f -mtime +1
   D. find ./ type -f time 24

71. Which command will move all files with a .txt extension to the /tmp directory?
   A. mv txt* tmp
   B. move *txt /temp
   C. mv *.txt /tmp
   D. mv *.txt tmp

72. Assume that you have a file called zips.txt that contains several postal zip codes, and you need to determine how many unique zip codes there are in the file. Which of the following commands can be used for that purpose?
   A. sort zips.txt | uniq -c
   B. uniq zips.txt
   C. count zips.txt
   D. cat zips.txt | uniq -c

73. You're working with a file using the `less` command and need to search for instances of a string earlier in the file. Which key will search backward in the file?

  A. /

  B. H

  C. ?

  D. C

74. Which command can be used to determine the location of a given executable that would be run if typed from your current environment and location?

  A. which

  B. what

  C. whatis

  D. when

75. Another administrator made a change to one of the local scripts stored in /usr/local/bin and used for administrative purposes. The change was also immediately reflected in the copy of the script in your home directory. However, when you examine the file with `ls`, it appears to be a normal file. What is the likely cause of such a scenario?

  A. The file was executed after edit.

  B. The administrator copied the file to yours.

  C. Your file is a hard link to the original.

  D. The file has been restored from backup.

76. Which command can be used to print the inode index number of files?

  A. in -l

  B. ln -i

  C. ls -i

  D. inodelist

77. Which option to `ln` creates a symlink to another file?

  A. -sl

  B. -s

  C. -l

  D. --ln

78. Which of the following commands can be used if you need to locate various elements of a given command, such as its binaries and man pages?

  A. whatis

  B. find

  C. whereis

  D. ls

79. Which command is used to execute a check of user quotas on the filesystem?
   A. quota -u
   B. runquota -u
   C. qcheck -u
   D. quotacheck -u

80. When using ls -la to obtain a directory listing, you see an object with permissions of lrwxrwxrwx. What type of object is this?
   A. It is a directory.
   B. It is a symlink.
   C. It is a temporary file.
   D. It is a local file.

81. Which command and option will output a summary of quota usage across all filesystems that are currently read-write with quotas enabled?
   A. repq -a
   B. repquota -a
   C. quotarun -a
   D. quota -u

82. The locate command is reporting out-of-date information. Which command should be run in order to have the locate command update its database?
   A. locatedb -u
   B. locate -u
   C. updatedb
   D. updatelocate

83. You need to enable the web server (running as the www-data user and group) to write into a directory called /home/webfiles. Which commands will accomplish this task in the most secure manner?
   A. chgrp www-data /home/webfiles ; chmod 775 /home/webfiles
   B. chmod 777 /home/webfiles
   C. chgrp www-data /home/webfiles ; chmod 711 /home/webfiles
   D. chmod 707 /home/webfiles

84. Which option to the find command will search for files by their inode number?
   A. -inode
   B. -type
   C. -in
   D. -inum

85. What is the order in which user configuration files are located on login to a bash shell?
    A. .bash_login, .profile, /etc/profile
    B. .bash_profile, .bash_login, .profile
    C. .profile, .bash_login, .bash_profile
    D. .bash_login, .bash_profile, .profile

86. Within which directory should you place files to have them automatically copied to a user's home directory when the user is created?
    A. /etc/userhome
    B. /etc/templateuser
    C. /etc/skel
    D. /home/skel

87. Which bash parameter or option will cause the shell to be executed without reading the initialization files?
    A. --no-rc
    B. --no-init
    C. --norc
    D. --rc-none

88. You need to create a function that will be available each time that you log in to the system. Within which file should this function be placed?
    A. .bash_profile
    B. .rc
    C. /etc/profile
    D. .bash_run

89. Which section in /etc/X11/xorg.conf is used to describe configurations for a given graphics card and monitor pair?
    A. Server
    B. Screen
    C. VidMode
    D. Video

90. Assuming X forwarding has been enabled on the SSH server, which environment variable is used to set the location for newly spawned windows from within an SSH session?
    A. DISPLAY
    B. XTERMINAL
    C. XTERM
    D. XDISP

91. Within the greeter section of a display manager such as GDM in Gnome, which option sets the welcome message for users logging in locally?
    A. LoginMessage
    B. Login
    C. WinGreet
    D. Welcome

92. Within Gnome, you need to add the accessibility option known as sticky keys. Which key should be pressed five times in a row to enable sticky keys?
    A. Ctrl
    B. Enter
    C. Shift
    D. Tab

93. Which program is used in a Gnome environment as a screen reader?
    A. Orca
    B. Screed
    C. Screen
    D. Reader

94. When using KDE, which program provides magnification functionality?
    A. xmag
    B. mag
    C. pmag
    D. kmag

95. Which of the following options in the SSH configuration file needs to be enabled so that X sessions can be sent over an SSH connection?
    A. X11Connect yes
    B. X11Forwarding yes
    C. ForwardX yes
    D. XForward yes

96. Which file contains user information such as username and real name and is readable by all users of the system?
    A. /etc/pass
    B. /etc/shadow
    C. /etc/passwd
    D. /etc/userinfo

97. Which of the following will execute a job through cron at 12:15 a.m. and 12:15 p.m. every day?
    A. 0,12 15 * * *
    B. 15 0,12 * * *
    C. 15 * * * 0/12
    D. */12 * * * 15

98. Which file is used to provide a list of users that can add and delete cron jobs?
    A. /etc/cron.job
    B. /etc/cron.allow
    C. /etc/cron.users
    D. /etc/crontab

99. Which of the following commands schedules a series of commands to execute one hour from now?
    A. atq +1hr
    B. at now + 1 hour
    C. atq
    D. at -1

100. You need to delete a user from the system, including their home directory. Which of the following commands accomplishes this task?
    A. userdel
    B. userdel -r
    C. userdel -R
    D. deluser

101. Which of the following commands changes a group called DomainAdmins to DomainUsers?
    A. groupmod -n DomainAdmins DomainUsers
    B. groupchg DomainAdmins DomainUsers
    C. chgroup DomainAdmins DomainUsers
    D. group -N DomainAdmins DomainUsers

102. Within which directory would you find a list of files corresponding to the users who have current cron jobs on the system?
    A. /var/spool/cron/crontabs
    B. /var/spool/jobs
    C. /etc/cron
    D. /etc/cron.users

103. Which command deletes an at job with an ID of 3?
    A. atq
    B. at -l
    C. atrm 3
    D. rmat 3

104. Which of the following is used as a system-wide cron file?
    A. /etc/cron.d
    B. /etc/cron.sys
    C. /etc/crontab
    D. /etc/cron.tab

105. Within which directory will you find scripts that are scheduled to run through cron every 24 hours?
    A. /etc/cron.daily
    B. /etc/cron.weekly
    C. /etc/cron.hourly24
    D. /etc/crontab

106. When running useradd, which option needs to be specified in order for the user's home directory to be created?
    A. -h
    B. -m
    C. -x
    D. -a

107. Which of the following commands locks out password-based login for a user but does not prevent other forms of login?
    A. usermod -L
    B. userdel -r
    C. useradd -h
    D. userlock

108. Which of the following will run a command called /usr/local/bin/changehome.sh as the www-data user when placed in /etc/crontab?
    A. 1 1 * * * www-data /usr/local/bin/changehome.sh
    B. www-data changehome.sh
    C. */1 www-data changehome.sh
    D. * * */www-data /usr/local/bin/changehome.sh

109. Which of the following commands produces a report listing the last password change date for all users on the system?
    A. passwd -a
    B. passwd -S
    C. passwd -a -S
    D. passwd --all

110. Which file contains a list of usernames, UIDs, and encrypted passwords?
    A. /etc/passwd
    B. /etc/shadow
    C. /etc/encpass
    D. /etc/grouppass

111. When configuring an authentication server, which of the following best describes the relationship between UIDs and GIDs on a Linux system?
    A. The UID and GID are the same across the system for a given user.
    B. Each user has a UID and GID that are the same and are created when the user is created.
    C. The UID represents the user, while the GID is a globally unique user id.
    D. There is no direct relationship between UID and GID.

112. Which command is used to change a user's home directory to /srv/data/username and move the contents at the same time?
    A. usermod -d /srv/data/username -m
    B. homedir -m /srv/data/username
    C. userex -m /srv/data/username
    D. userchg /m /srv/data/username -d

113. Which option to useradd will add groups for a user?
    A. -g
    B. -x
    C. -l
    D. -G

114. Assume that passwords must be changed every 60 days. Which command will change the date of the user's last password change without the user actually changing the account password?
    A. chage -f
    B. chage -W
    C. chage -l
    D. chage -d

115. Which command will list the cron entries for a given user as denoted by <username>?
    A. crontab -l -u <username>
    B. crontab -u <username>
    C. cron -u <username>
    D. cronent -u <username>

116. Which option to useradd creates a system user rather than a normal user?
    A. -r
    B. -s
    C. -a
    D. -S

117. Which file contains encrypted password information for groups?
    A. /etc/group
    B. /etc/gshadow
    C. /etc/gsecure
    D. /etc/group.conf

118. Which of the following best describes the use of the groupdel command?
    A. You may force group deletion with the -f option.
    B. If a user's primary group is to be deleted, that user must be deleted first or have their primary group changed.
    C. Groupdel can be run at any time, regardless of group membership.
    D. The -r option for groupdel will recursively change users' GIDs after group deletion.

119. Which of the following commands displays the UID, primary group, and supplemental groups for a given user?
    A. id
    B. getid
    C. passwd
    D. chage

120. Which option to the usermod command is used to change a given user's real name?
    A. -R
    B. -n
    C. -d
    D. -c

121. Assume that you have deleted a user account with UID 1501, including the -r option. Which command should you also run to look for other files that might have been owned by the user?

    A. find -id 1501
    B. grep 1501 *
    C. grep -u 1501 *
    D. find / -uid 1501

122. When configuring a local NTP server role, to what server address can you set the server's NTP client?

    A. 127.0.0.1
    B. 192.168.1.100
    C. ntp.example.com
    D. pool.ntp.org

123. When configuring a server for a mail server role, which command must you run after making a change to email aliases, assuming the server is running Postfix?

    A. service postfix restart
    B. newaliases
    C. alias -n
    D. postfix -e

124. Within which directory hierarchy will you find configuration files related to printing with the CUPS printing system on a print server?

    A. /etc/cupsd
    B. /etc/cups.d
    C. /etc/CUPS
    D. /etc/cups

125. Within which directory will you find the mail queue on a Qmail server?

    A. /var/spool/qmail
    B. /var/qmail/queue
    C. /var/spool/mailq
    D. /var/spool/qmail/queue

126. You are creating a logging server. Which syslog level is used to provide informational messages?

    A. kern
    B. emerg
    C. debug
    D. info

127. When running the NTP daemon, which command can you execute to work with the NTP server in an interactive mode?
   A. ntpd
   B. ntpdate
   C. ntpq
   D. ntp-interactive

128. Which of the following commands places a file into the print queue?
   A. lpr
   B. lpd
   C. lpq
   D. lpx

129. What is the default port for the CUPS administrative web interface?
   A. tcp/53
   B. tcp/8080
   C. udp/456
   D. tcp/631

130. Which of the following URLs can be used to view a list of completed print jobs in CUPS?
   A. http://localhost:631/jobs?which_jobs=completed
   B. http://localhost:631?completed
   C. http://localhost:631/?completed
   D. http://cups/jobs=completed

131. Which of the following commands causes the mail queue to be processed on a Postfix server?
   A. postqueue -f
   B. postqueue -D
   C. postfix -q
   D. postsuper -q

132. A developer has created an application and wants to take advantage of syslog for logging to a custom log file. Which facility should be used for an application such as this?
   A. syslog
   B. kern
   C. local#
   D. user

133. A user needs to work with printers and printer-related items. Which of the following commands adds the user (called username in the options) to the appropriate group for this purpose?

  A. `usermod -aG printerusers username`
  B. `usermod -aG lpadmin username`
  C. `usermod -gA lpadm username`
  D. `usermod -a lpadm username`

134. Which command can be used to gather and display statistics about mail processed on a server running sendmail?

  A. `mailq`
  B. `mailstats`
  C. `statmail`
  D. `sendmailstats`

135. Which of the following commands can be used to restart CUPS on a server running systemd?

  A. `systemctl restart cups.service`
  B. `systemctl restart cups`
  C. `systemctl reboot cups.target`
  D. `systemctl restart cups.target`

136. When configuring a server for an SNMP server role, which ports need to be allowed through the firewall for SNMP traffic?

  A. Ports 23 and 25
  B. Ports 110 and 143
  C. Ports 80 and 443
  D. Ports 161 and 162

137. You need to look at information on logins beyond what was captured by the current log file for the last command. Which option to the last command can be used to load information from an alternate file?

  A. `-a`
  B. `-t`
  C. `-e`
  D. `-f`

138. You need to examine who is currently logged in to the system. Which of the following commands will display this information?

  A. `listuser`
  B. `fuser`

C. ls -u

D. w

139. When expiring a user account with usermod -e, which of the following represents the correct date format?
    A. YYYY-MM-DD
    B. MM/DD/YYYY
    C. DD/MM/YY
    D. MM/DD/YY HH:MM:SS

140. Which of the following commands can be used to stop a given service, such as httpd.service, from starting on boot with a systemd-based system?
    A. systemctl disable httpdservice
    B. systemctl stop httpd.service
    C. systemd disable httpd.service
    D. systemd enable httpd.service boot=no

141. Within the following entry in /etc/shadow, to what does the number 15853 refer?
    mail:*:15853:0:99999:7:::
    A. The UID of the mail user
    B. The number of files owned by mail
    C. The date of the last password change (since 1/1/1970)
    D. The number of days until the account expires

142. You need to deploy a monitoring solution that enables alerts along with advanced scripted responses based on configurable performance conditions. Which of the following software packages performs these tasks?
    A. MySQL
    B. ntop
    C. mrtg
    D. nagios

143. You are upgrading the kernel that has been previously compiled on the same server. Which of the following commands incorporates the contents of the existing kernel configuration into the new kernel?
    A. config --merge
    B. make oldconfig
    C. merge config
    D. int configs

Chapter 2 ▪ System Operations and Maintenance

144. Which of the following commands is used to view kernel-related udev events in real-time?
    A. `udevls all`
    B. `lsudev -f`
    C. `udevmon -a`
    D. `udevadm monitor`

145. Which of the following commands should you execute after making changes to `systemd` service configurations in order for those changes to take effect?
    A. `systemd reload`
    B. `reboot`
    C. `systemctl daemon-reload`
    D. `systemctl reboot`

146. Which of the following files contains the runlevels for the system along with a reference to the corresponding `rc` file?
    A. `/etc/runlevels`
    B. `/etc/inittab`
    C. `/etc/rc`
    D. `/etc/runlevel`

147. Within which hierarchy are files from `/etc/init.d` linked so that the files are executed during the various runlevels of a SysV system?
    A. `/etc/rc.S`
    B. `/etc/rc`
    C. `/etc/boot/rc`
    D. `/etc/rc.d`

148. As a systems administrator, you need to change options for automount. Which of the following files is the default configuration file for the `autofs` automounter?
    A. `/etc/autofs`
    B. `/etc/auto.master`
    C. `/etc/autofs.conf`
    D. `/etc/automounter.conf`

149. You have purchased new SSD hardware that uses the NVMe protocol, but you cannot find the disks in the normal `/dev/sd*` location where you have traditionally found such storage. In which location should you look for these drives?
    A. `/dev/nd*`
    B. `/dev/nvme*`
    C. `/dev/nv*`
    D. `/dev/nvme/*`

150. Which of the following directory hierarchies contains information such as the WWN for Fibre Channel?
    A. /sys/class/wwn
    B. /sys/class/fc_host
    C. /sys/class/fclist
    D. /sys/class/fc/wwn

151. Information about logical volumes can be found in which of the following directories?
    A. /dev/lvinfo
    B. /dev/map
    C. /dev/mapper
    D. /dev/lvmap

152. When configuring WiFi, which of the following commands displays information such as link status about the wireless device wlan0?
    A. iw dev wlan0 link
    B. wlan0 list
    C. iw wlan0 -l
    D. iw dev link

153. You are configuring a DHCP server. Which of the following commands will examine the system log for information regarding DHCP activity?
    A. grep -i dhcp /var/log/syslog
    B. grep -v dhcp /var/log/syslog
    C. grep -vi dhcp /var/log/kern.log
    D. dmesg | grep dhcp

154. Which option to dmesg clears the contents of the kernel ring buffer after they have been read once?
    A. -C
    B. -c
    C. -a
    D. -e

155. Which option to the rsync command provides archive mode?
    A. -r
    B. -o
    C. -a
    D. -f

156. When compiling software such as with the `gcc` compiler, which of the following is the recommended name for a file containing commands and relationships used with the `make` command?

   A. `Makefile`
   B. `makefile`
   C. `make.file`
   D. `Makefile.txt`

157. You have downloaded a source file with the extension `.gz`. Which of the following commands will uncompress the file?

   A. `unzip`
   B. `gunzip`
   C. `dezip`
   D. `uncomp`

158. Which target for `make`, typically included in the `makefile` for most projects, will place compiled files into their final destination and perform other operations such as making the appropriate files executable?

   A. `list`
   B. `distclean`
   C. `run`
   D. `install`

159. When creating a local package repository, which option within the `.repo` file in `/etc/yum.repos.d/` is used to set the URL for the repository?

   A. `url`
   B. `repourl`
   C. `httpurl`
   D. `baseurl`

160. When running the `lsblk` command, there is no separate partition listed for `/boot`. From which partition is the system likely booted?

   A. There is a `/boot` directory under the `/` partition.
   B. The `/boot` partition is hidden.
   C. The system has not yet built the `/boot` partition.
   D. The `/boot` partition does not show up with `lsblk`.

161. Which command can be used to search the contents of all files below your current location for files that contain the characters *DB*?

   A. `grep -r "DB" *`
   B. `grep -ri "DB" *`
   C. `cat * | less`
   D. `cat *.txt | grep DB`

162. You are working with a file server, and clients are reporting that the filesystems shared over NFS have become unreachable. Which option should be passed to umount in order to force the unmounting of the filesystem on the clients?

A. -nfs
B. --fake
C. -f
D. -n

163. Which character combination sets the body of the message to STDIN when using the mail command?

A. <
B. >
C. <<<
D. |

164. Which of the following commands displays a listing of who is logged in to the server along with the date and time that they logged in?

A. whois
B. who
C. loggedin
D. curusers

165. Which configuration file is used as the default configuration for a BIND server?

A. named.conf
B. named.cfg
C. bind.cfg
D. bind.conf

166. When creating a certificate authority server role, which of the following commands generates a private key for use with SSL and places it into the file /etc/ssl/example.com.private?

A. openssl genrsa -out /etc/ssl/example.com.private
B. openssl generate-private > /etc/ssl/example.com.private
C. openssl genpriv > /etc/ssl/example.com.private
D. openssh genkey -out /etc/ssl/example.com.private

167. When creating a Squid proxy configuration, you need to create an access control list for the local network. Which configuration option creates an access control list for Squid?

A. accesscontrol
B. acl
C. access-control
D. access-control-list

168. Which directive in a Squid configuration configures whether a given ACL can use the proxy?
   A. access_allow
   B. http_access
   C. proxy_access
   D. enable_access

169. Which of the Samba daemons is responsible for responding to NetBIOS name service requests?
   A. smbd
   B. nmbd
   C. winbindd
   D. samba

170. Which of the following options within an OpenSSH server configuration is used to determine whether the root user can log in directly with an SSH client?
   A. PermitRootLogin
   B. AllowRoot
   C. RootLogin
   D. PermitDirectRootLogin

171. Which option within an OpenVPN configuration lets a client know that it can reach the network 192.168.5.0/24?
   A. client-route 192.168.5.0
   B. push "route 192.168.5.0 255.255.255.0"
   C. send "route 192.168.5.0/24"
   D. client-route "192.168.5.0/24"

172. What is the name of the environment variable that is set if your display session is using Wayland?
   A. WAYLAND_DISPLAY
   B. WAYLANDORG
   C. WAYLAND_SESSION
   D. WAYLAND_DISP

173. Which command can be used to view device information such as interrupts?
   A. lsint
   B. ls -interrupts
   C. lsdev
   D. ls-int

174. When working with the udevadm command, you need to reload rules in order to add a new client device. Which option can be used to effect this change?
    A. `udevadm control -R`
    B. `udevadm --stop`
    C. `udevadm -stop-queue`
    D. `udevadm -R`

175. You will be deploying a large server solution with Linux as the base operating system. The server resources will be split into multiple, smaller virtual servers running Linux and Windows. Which of the following best describes the name for this type of server role and technology?
    A. Systemization
    B. MultiSys
    C. Containers
    D. UserDev

176. You need to restart an Apache server running on an older, non-`systemd` distribution of Linux. Which of the following commands can be used to restart the Apache server, assuming that it has a name of `apache2`?
    A. `apache2.service restart`
    B. `restart-daemon apache2`
    C. `service apache2 restart`
    D. `service restart apache2`

177. When using the NX or NoMachine display for access, which configuration option sets the display port?
    A. `DisplayPort`
    B. `DisplayBase`
    C. `ListenPort`
    D. `ListenXPort`

178. When choosing a login type, which of the following best describes the difference between the options titled Cinnamon and Cinnamon (Software Rendering)?
    A. The option described as Software Rendering is used for graphics production environments.
    B. The option described as Software Rendering uses 3D acceleration.
    C. The option described as Software Rendering is used to enhance the video driver.
    D. The option described as Software Rendering disables 3D acceleration.

179. When using a Raspberry Pi with Raspbmc Linux, you need to configure the system to turn on an LED. Which of the following is the interface typically used for this purpose?

  A. USB
  B. HBA
  C. GPIO
  D. SNP

180. Which of the following commands can be used to troubleshoot boot times of various services?

  A. `time`
  B. `bootmsg`
  C. `systemd-boot`
  D. `systemd-analyze blame`

181. You are troubleshooting an issue with HAProxy as a load balancer. Users are reporting that they have received a "400" response from the HAProxy server. What does a "400" response mean?

  A. The request was invalid or too large.
  B. The request was unauthorized.
  C. The request timed out.
  D. There is an out of memory condition.

182. In the MATE desktop environment, which of the following is the name of the file manager?

  A. Naut
  B. caja
  C. fm
  D. fileexp

183. Which option to SSH creates a port forwarding to which remote clients can also connect?

  A. `-L`
  B. `-R`
  C. `-P`
  D. `-E`

184. Which option to the `wget` command logs output?

  A. `-r`
  B. `-o`
  C. `-b`
  D. `-k`

185. When executed on a `systemd`-enabled server, the `service status` command is equivalent to which command?

   A. `systemd status`
   B. `journald status`
   C. `service-systemd status`
   D. `systemctl status`

186. You need to compare two files to determine if there are differences between them. Which command can be used for this purpose?

   A. dcat
   B. tar
   C. diff
   D. dtool

187. Which directive within an Apache configuration file facilitates serving websites for more than one domain using a single IP address?

   A. `<VirtualServer>`
   B. `<VirtualHost>`
   C. `<VirtContainer>`
   D. `<Virtualization>`

188. Which subcommand of `openssl` is used to create a Certificate Signing Request (CSR)?

   A. req
   B. csr
   C. gencsr
   D. newcsr

189. Which signal to the `kill` command can be used to signal that BIND should reload, including its configuration?

   A. -15
   B. -1
   C. -9
   D. -2

190. You are troubleshooting a daemon process and have started the daemon manually from the command line so that it does not fork into the background. Which key combination can be used to terminate the daemon?

   A. Ctrl+A
   B. Ctrl+B
   C. Ctrl+C
   D. Ctrl+D

191. You need to redirect output to a file, but rather than overwriting the existing file, the output should be appended instead. Which character combination is used to indicate that STDOUT should be appended?

A. <>
B. a>
C. >a
D. >>

192. Which service command is used to shut down a service?

A. shutdown
B. stop
C. norun
D. runstop

193. Which port is the default base port for use with VNC?

A. 59
B. 59000
C. 5900
D. 590

194. Which of the following directories is used with the automatic bug-reporting tool in CentOS 7?

A. /var/spool/abrt
B. /var/spool/autobug
C. /var/tmp/abrt
D. /var/tmp/autobug

195. Which of the following commands is used with udevadm to replay events?

A. replay
B. trigger
C. play
D. evplay

196. Which command with `hostnamectl` can be used to set the type of machine on which it is running?

A. set-machine
B. machine-type
C. set-type
D. set-chassis

197. As a system administrator, you have a custom service that needs to execute on boot. However, the service does not have the traditional service-management script. Within which file could you place the command so that it is executed on boot?

   A. /etc/rcd
   B. /etc/custom.service
   C. /etc/rc.local
   D. /etc/rc.d/rc.service

198. Which of the following commands is used to control a BIND name server?

   A. bind-config
   B. named-config
   C. rndc
   D. rdmc

199. You are tasked with configuring a cluster server role using Red Hat Enterprise Linux. Which of the following filesystems will most likely be used?

   A. ext2
   B. GFS
   C. CIFS
   D. FAT

200. Within which stanza would you add a video device when configuring Spice remote access?

   A. <display>
   B. <video>
   C. <videoDisplay>
   D. display=

201. You need to redirect STDIN until a certain character combination is encountered. Which of the following operators can be used for this purpose?

   A. >STDIN
   B. <<
   C. <&
   D. >

202. Which option to chkconfig enables you to set the runlevels for a given service?

   A. --level
   B. --runlevel
   C. -l
   D. -rl

203. Which option to the curl command sets the local filename to which the output will be saved?
  A. -f
  B. -o
  C. -O
  D. -l

204. Which of the following commands adds a group?
  A. groupadd
  B. addgrp
  C. grpadd
  D. creategroup

205. Which command enables you to determine the username associated with your current user ID?
  A. uid
  B. myid
  C. whoami
  D. w

206. Within which directory should scripts and other files to run at login be stored?
  A. /etc/login
  B. /etc/profile
  C. /etc/bash.defs
  D. /etc/profile.d

207. The Unity desktop is typically found on which distribution of Linux?
  A. Ubuntu
  B. Red Hat
  C. Slackware
  D. SuSE

208. Startup commands that are executed on boot for udev can be found in which directory on a Debian system?
  A. /etc/udev
  B. /etc/rcS.d
  C. /etc/rc5.d
  D. /etc/rc5/udev

209. You are attempting to stop a daemon on a system that previously used SysVinit but now uses `systemd`. Which is the correct command and order used to stop a service on this system?
   A. `systemctl <service> stop`
   B. `systemctl stop <service>`
   C. `systemd stop <service>`
   D. `systemd <service> stop`

210. When configuring a monitor for use with X11, within which section should details of the monitor be changed?
   A. `Video`
   B. `Display`
   C. `Monitor`
   D. `Disp`

211. You need to redirect output for a long-running process but do not need to see or capture the output. To which location can you redirect output so that it does not consume disk space?
   A. A regular file
   B. /dev/null
   C. /dev/random
   D. A network interface

212. Which option to the `paste` command is used to set the delimiter?
   A. `-f`
   B. `-d`
   C. `-o`
   D. `-m`

213. Which target for the `service` command will cause a daemon to re-read its configuration files without restarting the daemon itself?
   A. `read`
   B. `load`
   C. `start`
   D. `reload`

214. When configuring environment parameters for use with `systemd`, what is the name of the key used to create the variables?
   A. `ENV`
   B. `Environment`
   C. `Envvar`
   D. `ENVPARAM`

215. Which operator is used to redirect STDIN, such as when redirecting input from a file?
  A. >
  B. <
  C. ^
  D. *

216. While configuring a network adapter with udev so that it has a specific and consistent name, you edit the udev rules file. Which option within the rules file ensures that the device will always have a name of eth0?
  A. ATTR-NAME="eth0"
  B. NAME="eth0"
  C. DEV_NAME="eth0"
  D. NAME_DEV="eth0"

217. Within which directory would you typically find the Xorg configuration file xorg.conf?
  A. /etc/xorg
  B. /etc/x
  C. /etc/Xorg
  D. /etc/X11

218. Which command is used to view the mixer volumes when configuring audio with ALSA?
  A. alsaconfig
  B. alsacfg
  C. alsamixer
  D. amix

219. Which package provides an open source implementation of the Remote Desktop Protocol?
  A. ordp
  B. xrdp
  C. tdpx
  D. xr

220. You are configuring a database service and need to open the default port for MySQL. Which port is the default for MySQL?
  A. 6592
  B. 25
  C. 389
  D. 3306

221. You need to determine which video card is installed in a Linux system. Which command can be used to help with this purpose?
    A. dmesg | grep -i vga
    B. vgadetect
    C. lsvid
    D. lsvga

222. You have executed a daemon process manually from the command line and now need to suspend the process. Which key combination can be used for this purpose?
    A. Ctrl+S
    B. Ctrl+C
    C. Ctrl+Z
    D. Ctrl+B

223. When configuring Apache for a web server role, which of the following directives tells the server the location of the SSL private key?
    A. SSLKeyFile
    B. SSLCertificatePrivateKey
    C. SSLCertificateKeyFile
    D. SSLPrivateKey

224. Which command is used for setting parameters such as the essid, channel, and other related options for a wireless device?
    A. ifconfig
    B. iwconfig
    C. wlancfg
    D. iconf

225. Which command can be used to convert lowercase letters to uppercase letters across an entire file?
    A. du
    B. touc
    C. conv
    D. tr

226. You have been asked to recommend a simple command-line-based text editor for a beginning user. Which of the following should you recommend?
    A. Vi
    B. Nano
    C. nc
    D. ShellRedirect

227. You need to ensure that a service does not start on a `systemd` system. Which `systemctl` command should be used for this purpose?
   A. disable
   B. delete
   C. mask
   D. norun

228. Which of the following commands is a simple pager that is found on most Linux systems?
   A. more
   B. pg
   C. grep
   D. mr

229. Which of the following is an operator for redirecting STDOUT and STDERR?
   A. &>
   B. >
   C. ~
   D. !

230. Which device is used as the terminal for the current process?
   A. /dev/termcur
   B. /dev/tdev
   C. /dev/tty
   D. /dev/curproc

231. Which command can be used to print using a specially formatted string?
   A. printf
   B. echo
   C. print
   D. here

232. You need to remove a series of files programmatically through a script. Which command can be used to remove these files?
   A. remove
   B. rmfile
   C. unlink
   D. rem

233. You need to copy a file to a remote system, but that remote system does not have FTP or any other file-sharing services running. You have the ability to SSH into the server. Which of the following commands can be used for this purpose?

   A. scp
   B. ncftp
   C. go
   D. xfer

234. Which HTTP status code is returned when TraceEnable has been set to Off within Apache?

   A. 405
   B. 100
   C. 302
   D. 200

235. You are running a process in the background and need the process to continue after you log out. Which command should be used to ensure that the process continues even after logout?

   A. run
   B. cont
   C. nohup
   D. runproc

236. You have inserted a USB Bluetooth device into the computer. Which of the following commands is used to determine if the device was detected?

   A. bluetooth -d
   B. bludetect
   C. lsblue
   D. lsusb | grep -i bluetooth

Chapter 3

Security

THE FOLLOWING COMPTIA LINUX+ EXAM OBJECTIVES ARE COVERED IN THIS CHAPTER:

✓ **3.1 Given a scenario, apply or acquire the appropriate user and/or group permissions and ownership**

- File and directory permissions
  - Read, write, execute
  - User, group, other
  - SUID
  - Octal notation
  - umask
  - Sticky bit
  - GUID
  - Inheritance
  - Utilities
    - chmod
    - chown
    - chgrp
    - getfacl
    - setfacl
    - ls
    - ulimit
    - chage
- Context-based permissions
  - SELinux configurations
    - Disabled
    - Permissive

- Enforcing
- SELinux policy
  - Targeted
- SELinux tools
  - `setenforce`
  - `getenforce`
  - `sestatus`
  - `setsebool`
  - `getsebool`
  - `chcon`
  - `restorecon`
  - `ls -Z`
  - `ps -Z`
- AppArmor
  - `aa-disable`
  - `aa-complain`
  - `aa-unconfined`
  - `/etc/apparmor.d/`
  - `/etc/apparmor.d/tunables`
- Privilege escalation
  - `su`
  - `sudo`
  - `wheel`
  - `visudo`
  - `sudoedit`
- User types
  - Root
  - Standard
  - Service

✓ 3.2 Given a scenario, configure and implement appropriate access and authentication methods

- PAM:
  - Password policies
  - LDAP integration
  - User lockouts
  - Required, allowed, or sufficient
  - /etc/pam.d/
  - pam_tally2
  - faillock
- SSH:
  - ~/.ssh/
    - known_hosts
    - authorized_keys
    - config
    - id_rsa
    - id_rsa.pub
  - User-specific access
  - TCP wrappers
  - /etc/sshd/
    - ssh.conf
    - sshd.conf
  - ssh-copy-id
  - ssh-keygen
  - ssh-add
- TTYs:
  - /etc/securetty
  - /dev/tty#
- PTYs:
- PKI:
  - Self-signed
  - Private keys

- Public keys
- Hashing
- Digital signatures
- Message digest
- VPN as a client:
  - SSL/TLS
  - Transport mode
  - Tunnel mode
  - IPSec
  - DTLS

✓ 3.3 **Summarize security best practices in a Linux environment**

- Boot security
  - Bootloader password
  - UEFI/BIOS password
- Additional authentication methods
  - Multifactor authentication
    - Tokens
      - (i) Hardware
      - (ii) Software
    - OTP
    - Biometrics
  - RADIUS
  - TACACS+
  - LDAP
  - Kerberos
    - `kinit`
    - `klist`
- Importance of disabling root login via SSH
- Password-less login
  - Enforce use of PKI

- Chroot jail services
- No shared IDs
- Importance of denying hosts
- Separation of OS data from application data
  - Disk partition to maximize system availability
- Change default ports
- Importance of disabling or uninstalling unused and unsecure services
  - FTP
  - Telnet
  - Finger
  - Sendmail
  - Postfix
- Importance of enabling SSL/TLS
- Importance of enabling auditd
- CVE monitoring
- Discouraging use of USB devices
- Disk encryption
  - LUKS
- Restrict cron access
- Disable Ctrl+Alt+Del
- Add banner
- MOTD

✓ 3.4 **Given a scenario, implement logging services**

- Key file locations
  - /var/log/secure
  - /var/log/messages
  - /var/log/[application]
  - /var/log/kern.log
- Log management
  - Third-party agents
  - logrotate

- `/etc/rsyslog.conf`
- `journald`
  - `journalctl`
- `lastb`

✓ **3.5 Given a scenario, implement and configure Linux firewalls**

- Access control lists
  - Source
  - Destination
  - Ports
  - Protocol
  - Logging
  - Stateful vs. stateless
  - Accept
  - Reject
  - Drop
  - Log
- Technologies
  - `firewalld`
    - Zones
    - Runtime
  - `iptables`
    - Persistency
    - Chains
  - `ufw`
    - `/etc/default/ufw`
    - `/etc/ufw/`
  - Netfilter
- IP forwarding
  - `/proc/sys/net/ipv4/ip_forward`
  - `/proc/sys/net/ipv6/ip_forward`

- Dynamic rule sets
  - DenyHosts
  - Fail2ban
  - IPset
- Common application firewall configurations
  - `/etc/services`
  - Privileged ports

✓ **3.6 Given a scenario, backup, restore, and compress files**

- Archive and restore utilities
  - `tar`
  - `cpio`
  - `dd`
- Compression
  - `gzip`
  - `xz`
  - `bzip2`
  - `zip`
- Backup types
  - Incremental
  - Full
  - Snapshot clones
  - Differential
  - Image
- Off-site/Off-system storage
  - SFTP
  - SCP
  - `rsync`
- Integrity checks
  - MD5
  - SHA

1. Which command will create an image of the /dev/sda1 disk partition and place that image into a file called output.img?
   A. dd if=sda of=/dev/sda1
   B. dd if=output.img of=/dev/sda1
   C. dd if=/dev/sda1 of=output.img
   D. echo /dev/sda1 > output.img

2. Which command will watch the Apache log at /var/log/httpd/access.log and continually scroll as new log entries are created?
   A. watch /var/log/httpd/access.log
   B. tail /var/log/httpd/access.log
   C. tail -f /var/log/httpd/access.log
   D. mon /var/log/httpd/access.log

3. You receive a file with a .lzma extension. Which command can you use to decompress this file?
   A. xz
   B. lz
   C. gz
   D. bzip

4. Which of the following commands will correctly change the group ownership of the file called a.out to users?
   A. chgrp users a.out
   B. chgrp a.out users
   C. groupchg a.out users
   D. grpchg users a.out

5. Which option to umask will display the permissions to be used in a POSIX format?
   A. -P
   B. -p
   C. -S
   D. -v

6. According to the FHS, what is the correct location for site-specific data for a server?
   A. /etc
   B. /var
   C. /tmp
   D. /srv

7. Which of the following commands enables the sticky bit for a user on a file called homescript.sh?
   A. chmod +sticky homescript.sh
   B. chmod 755 homescript.sh
   C. chmod u+s homescript.sh
   D. chown u+sticky homescript.sh

8. The umask reports as 022. What is the permission that will be in effect for a newly non-executable created file?
   A. u+rw, g+r, w+r
   B. 755
   C. 022
   D. a+r

9. Which option to chown recursively changes the ownership?
   A. -f
   B. -R
   C. -a
   D. -m

10. Which option to chgrp will change group ownership of all files within a given directory?
    A. -directory
    B. -d
    C. -R
    D. -v

11. A command has the following listing obtained with ls -la:
    -rwsr-xr-x 1 suehring suehring 21 Nov 2 13:53 script.sh

    What does the s denote within the user permissions in the listing?
    A. The suid bit has been set for this program.
    B. This is a symlink.
    C. The file will not be executable.
    D. The file is a special system file.

12. When sourcing a file in bash, which chmod command would be necessary to provide the minimum privileges in order for the file to be sourced correctly, assuming that your current user owns the file?
    A. chmod 600
    B. chmod 755
    C. chmod 777
    D. chmod 400

13. Which of the following commands removes an expiration from an account?
    A. sudo chage -l username
    B. sudo chage -E -1 username
    C. sudo chage -E now username
    D. sudo chage --noexpire username

14. You need to determine whether LDAP integration is working correctly. In order to do so, you would like to obtain a list of users, as read by /etc/nsswitch.conf. Which command can be used for this purpose?
    A. getuser
    B. getent
    C. usermod
    D. userlist

15. Which file contains a list of users who are not allowed to create cron scheduled tasks?
    A. /etc/cron.users
    B. /etc/cron.deny
    C. /etc/cron.allow
    D. /etc/cron.userlist

16. Which system logging facility is used for messages from the kernel?
    A. syslog
    B. kernel
    C. kern
    D. system

17. Which of the following commands is used to examine the systemd journal or log file?
    A. journallist
    B. ctlj
    C. journalctl
    D. jctl

18. What is the name of the systemd service that provides logging facilities?
    A. systemd-journald
    B. systemd-loggingd
    C. systemd-syslog
    D. systemd-logger

19. Which configuration option in /etc/logrotate.conf will cause the log to be emailed to admin@example.com when the log rotation process runs for the selected log?
    A. mail admin@example.com
    B. sendmail admin@example.com
    C. maillog admin@example.com
    D. logmail admin@example.com

20. Assuming that the $ModLoad imudp configuration option has been set in the /etc/rsyslog.conf configuration file for rsyslogd, which of the following additional options is necessary to configure the port on which the server will listen?
    A. $Port 514
    B. $UDPServerRun 514
    C. $Listen 514
    D. $UDPListen 514

21. Which option in journald.conf controls the maximum file size for individual journal logs?
    A. SystemMaxFileSize
    B. MaxFile
    C. LogFileSize
    D. LogSize

22. You are deploying an Exim server and need to work with the firewall to ensure that the proper incoming ports are open. Which protocol and port should you allow inbound for normal SMTP traffic?
    A. TCP/23
    B. TCP/25
    C. TCP/110
    D. TCP/143

23. Which option within a logrotate configuration file disables compression of the log file?
    A. compressoff
    B. limitcompress
    C. nocompression
    D. nocompress

24. Which port(s) and protocol(s) should be opened in a firewall in order for the primary and secondary name servers to communicate for a given domain?
    A. udp/53
    B. Both tcp/53 and udp/53
    C. tcp/53
    D. udp/53 and tcp/503

25. When examining open ports on the server, you see that TCP port 3000 is listed with no corresponding protocol name, such as smtp, imaps, and so on. In which file would you find a list of port-to-protocol translations that could be customized to add this new port?
    A. /etc/ports
    B. /etc/p2p
    C. /etc/ppp
    D. /etc/services

26. On which port does ICMP operate?
    A. TCP/43
    B. UDP/111
    C. UDP/69
    D. ICMP does not use ports.

27. Which of the following protocols uses a three-way handshake?
    A. ICMP
    B. TCP
    C. UDP
    D. IP

28. Which of the following commands displays account information such as expiration date, last password change, and other related details?
    A. usermod -l
    B. userinfo -a
    C. chageuser -l
    D. chage -l

29. Which command is used to create a public/private key pair for use with SSH?
    A. ssh -k
    B. ssh-keygen
    C. ssh-genkey
    D. ssh -key

30. Within which file should you place public keys for servers from which you will accept key-based SSH authentication?
    A. ~/.ssh/authorized_keys
    B. ~/.ssh/keys
    C. ~/.ssh/keyauth
    D. ~/.sshd/authkeys

31. You need to execute a command as a specific user. Which of the following commands enables this to occur?
    A. sudo -u
    B. sudo -U
    C. sudo -s
    D. sudo -H

32. Which option in /etc/sudoers will cause the specified command to not prompt for a password?
    A. PASSWORD=NO
    B. NOPASSWD
    C. NOPASSWORD
    D. NOPROMPT

33. Which of the following commands will display the CPU time, memory, and other limits for the currently logged-in user?
    A. reslimit
    B. limitres -a
    C. ulimit -a
    D. proclimit -n

34. When working with TCP wrappers, which line within the /etc/hosts.deny file will prevent any host within the 192.168.1.0/24 network from accessing services that operate from xinetd?
    A. BLOCK: 192.168.1.0/24
    B. REJECT: 192.168.1.0
    C. ALL: 192.168.1.0/255.255.255.0
    D. NONE: 192.168.1/255.255.255.0

35. You are using an RSA-based key pair for SSH. By default, what is the name of the private key file in ~/.ssh?
    A. id_rsa
    B. id_rsa.priv
    C. id_rsa.key
    D. rsa_key.priv

36. Which option to the su command will execute a single command with a non-interactive session?
    A. -s
    B. -u
    C. -c
    D. -e

37. After specifying the key server, which option to gpg is used to specify the key to send to the key server?
    A. key-name
    B. keyname
    C. send-key
    D. sendkey

38. Which of the following commands should be used to edit the /etc/sudoers file?
    A. Any text editor such as Vi or emacs
    B. editsudo
    C. visudo
    D. visudoers

39. Which file can be used to store a server-wide cache of hosts whose keys are known for SSH?
    A. /etc/sshd_known_hosts
    B. /etc/ssh_known_hosts
    C. ~/.ssh/known_hosts
    D. /root/ssh_known_hosts

40. Which option must be enabled in /etc/sshd/sshd.conf (or /etc/ssh/sshd_config) on the destination server in order for X11 forwarding to work?
    A. XForward yes
    B. Xenable yes
    C. X11Forwarding yes
    D. Xconnection yes

41. Which of the following commands generates a GnuPG key pair?
    A. gpg --gen-key
    B. gpg --key
    C. gpg --send-key
    D. gpg --create-key

42. You need to disable a service found in /etc/inetd.conf. Which of the following is used as a comment character in that file?
    A. -
    B. #
    C. /
    D. %

43. Which file is used as the default storage for public keyrings for gpg?
    A. publickeys.gpg
    B. pubring.gpg
    C. public.gpg
    D. pubkeys.gpg

44. Which option to the su command is used to obtain the normal login environment?
    A. -u
    B. -U
    C. -
    D. -login

45. Which key-derivation function is used by LUKS?
    A. PBKDF2
    B. SSL
    C. RSA
    D. DSA

46. Which of the following commands is used to configure dm-crypt volumes?
    A. cryptsetup
    B. dm-cryptsetup
    C. dm-setup
    D. dm-crypts

47. Which wildcard can be used in /etc/hosts.allow to specify a match for a host whose name does not match its IP address?
    A. *
    B. ALL
    C. PARANOID
    D. NAMEMATCH

48. Which option to the tar command creates a tar file?
    A. -c
    B. -b
    C. -f
    D. -d

49. Which option to tar removes files after adding them to the archive?
    A. -r
    B. -d
    C. --remove-files
    D. -f

50. Which of the following files should be used to display a message to users prior to logging in locally?
    A. /etc/loginmesg
    B. /etc/logmessage.txt
    C. /etc/issue
    D. /etc/banner

51. Which option to the `rsync` command, when used in archive mode, will remove files that no longer exist on the host?
    A. --delete
    B. --remove
    C. -del
    D. -rem

52. When creating a `tar` archive, you need to exclude certain files from the archive. Which option facilitates this scenario?
    A. -x
    B. --exclude
    C. --ex
    D. --remove

53. Which file contains a message that is displayed after successful login?
    A. /etc/loginbanner
    B. /etc/issue
    C. /etc/motd
    D. /etc/message

54. Which of the following options to the `tar` command can be used to uncompress a file that has been compressed using `gzip`?
    A. -z
    B. -x
    C. -c
    D. -f

55. Which of the following files can be used to provide a message to users logging in remotely with a protocol such as telnet?
    A. /etc/telnet.msg
    B. /etc/issue.net
    C. /etc/login.msg
    D. /etc/telnet.login

56. Which option to the `rsync` command changes the resolution for determining file modifications?
   A. `--mod-time`
   B. `--modify-time`
   C. `--mod-res`
   D. `--modify-window`

57. Which of the following options to `bzip2` sends the output to STDOUT?
   A. `-s`
   B. `-c`
   C. `-d`
   D. `-f`

58. Which option to the `gzip` command will suppress all warning messages and might be useful in a situation where output is not appropriate?
   A. `-v`
   B. `-q`
   C. `-L`
   D. `-r`

59. Which option to `rsync` specifies that the remote shell or transport for the synchronization process should use SSH?
   A. `-t ssh`
   B. `--overssh`
   C. `-e ssh`
   D. `-F ssh`

60. When configuring BIND for a `chroot` jail scenario, within which of the following files should the home directory be set for the `chroot` user to use with bind?
   A. `/etc/bind.home`
   B. `/etc/bind.user`
   C. `/etc/passwd`
   D. `/etc/bindauth`

61. Which algorithm must be used for `rndc` authentication when generating a key with `dnssec-keygen`?
   A. `sha1`
   B. `sha256`
   C. `md5`
   D. `hmac-md5`

62. Which option enables SSL configuration for a given website or server?
  A. SSLEngine
  B. SSLDirect
  C. SSLEnable
  D. SSLConnect

63. On which port does Squid listen by default?
  A. 3000
  B. 3128
  C. 5150
  D. 10300

64. When using the net command in an Active Directory environment, which option enables authentication using Kerberos?
  A. -b
  B. -k
  C. -l
  D. -a

65. Within which directory are individual configuration files stored for the Pluggable Authentication Module mechanism?
  A. /etc/pamd
  B. /etc/pam
  C. /etc/pam.d
  D. /etc/pam.conf.d

66. On which port does the slapd LDAP daemon listen for connections?
  A. 389
  B. 3389
  C. 3306
  D. 110

67. Which PAM module prevents logins from accounts other than root when the file /etc/nologin exists?
  A. pam_login.so
  B. pam_preventlogin.so
  C. pam_nologin.so
  D. pam_logindef.so

68. Which PAM module is responsible for normal or standard password authentication?
    A. pam_auth.so
    B. pam_login.so
    C. pam_unix.so
    D. pam_standardlogin.so

69. Which PAM module provides a mechanism for checking and enforcing the strength of passwords in order to enforce a password policy?
    A. pam_passwdstr.so
    B. pam_cracklib.so
    C. pam_libpasswd.so
    D. pam_strpass.so

70. Which format should the certificate and key be in for a Postfix TLS configuration?
    A. PKCS
    B. PEM
    C. TLS
    D. SSL

71. Which iptables chain is used to create a port redirect?
    A. REDIRECT
    B. PREROUTING
    C. PORTREDIR
    D. ROUTING

72. Which of the following commands saves the current set of iptables rules into a file?
    A. save-iptables
    B. iptables-create
    C. iptables-save
    D. ipt-save

73. Which of the following commands lists the current iptables rules, while not attempting to resolve host or port names?
    A. iptables -L
    B. iptables -List -no-resolve
    C. iptables -a
    D. iptables -nL

74. Which of the following directories contains configuration files for the `fail2ban` system?
   A. /etc/fail2ban.cfg
   B. /etc/fail2ban.d
   C. /etc/f2b
   D. /etc/fail2ban

75. Within an OpenSSH configuration, which option disables the use of empty passwords?
   A. `DisableEmptyPass`
   B. `PermitEmptyPasswords`
   C. `EmptyPasswordAuth`
   D. `PermitPasswordLength`

76. Which of the following commands sets the default policy for the `INPUT` chain to discard packets that don't have a specific rule allowing them?
   A. `iptables INPUT DROP`
   B. `iptables chain INPUT policy DROP`
   C. `iptables -P INPUT DROP`
   D. `iptables POLICY=DROP CHAIN=INPUT`

77. On which port and protocol does OpenVPN listen?
   A. ICMP/1194
   B. UDP/1194
   C. TCP/1194
   D. VPN/1194

78. Which of the following best describes the difference between the `DROP` and `REJECT` targets in `iptables`?
   A. Both `DROP` and `REJECT` do the same thing.
   B. `DROP` silently discards packets, while `REJECT` sends back an ICMP acknowledgement.
   C. `REJECT` silently discards packets, while `DROP` sends back an ICMP acknowledgement.
   D. `DROP` sends back a direct message, and `REJECT` sends a redirect.

79. Which of the following partial `iptables` rules sets up a configuration that limits log entries to three per minute?
   A. `-m limit 3 -j LOG`
   B. `-m limit --limit 3/minute --limit-burst 3 -j LOG`
   C. `-m limit --limit 3`
   D. `-m limit --limit-minute 3 --burst 3 -j LOG`

80. Which of the following partial `iptables` rules allows incoming ICMP traffic?
    A. `-A INPUT -p ICMP -j ACCEPT`
    B. `-A IN -P ICMP`
    C. `-A INPUT -P ACCEPT-ICMP`
    D. `-A IN -P ICMP -j ACCEPT`

81. Which of the following partial `iptables` rules blocks all traffic from source IP 192.168.51.50?
    A. `-A INPUT -p ALL 192.168.51.50 -j ACCEPT`
    B. `-A INPUT -p ALL -s 192.168.51.50 -j DROP`
    C. `-A INPUT -p ALL -s 192.168.51.50 -j BLOCK`
    D. `-A INPUT -p ALL -f 192.168.51.50 -j DISCARD`

82. Which of the following partial `iptables` rules will allow all hosts to connect to TCP port 2222?
    A. `-A INPUT -p TCP -s 0/0 --destination-port 2222 -j ACCEPT`
    B. `-A TCP -s ALL -p 2222 -j ACCEPT`
    C. `-A INPUT -p TCP -s *.* --destination-port 2222 -j ALLOW`
    D. `-A INPUT --destination-port */* -j ACCEPT`

83. Which of the following commands enables forwarding such as would be used for NAT?
    A. `echo "1" > /proc/sys/net/ipv4/nat`
    B. `echo "1" > /proc/sys/net/ipv4/ip_forward`
    C. `iptables --enable-forwarding`
    D. `ip-forward --enable`

84. Within a jail configuration for `fail2ban`, which configuration option sets the name and location of the log file to monitor for failures?
    A. `logpath`
    B. `monitor`
    C. `logfile_mon`
    D. `monitor_log`

85. Which command sends a copy of the public key identity to another server for use with SSH?
    A. `ssh-key`
    B. `ssh-copy-key`
    C. `ssh-sendkey`
    D. `ssh-copy-id`

86. Which option in /etc/sudoers sets the destination address for administrative and security emails related to sudo?
   A. mail
   B. mailto
   C. secmail
   D. adminmail

87. Which port should be allowed through a firewall for NTP communication?
   A. Port 139
   B. Port 161
   C. Port 123
   D. Port 194

88. Which options are encompassed when the -a option to rsync is invoked?
   A. -rlpt
   B. -rlptgo
   C. -rpfsxl
   D. -rlptgoD

89. You are looking for files related to the SSL configuration on the server. After looking in /etc/ssl, within which other directory might the files reside?
   A. /etc/sslconfig
   B. /usr/share/ssl
   C. /etc/pki
   D. /etc/private

90. Which OpenSSH configuration directive is used to specify the users who will be allowed to log in using SSH?
   A. AllowUsers
   B. PermitUsers
   C. UsersAllowed
   D. AllowedUsers

91. Which option within a LOG target for iptables sets a string that will be prepended to log entries?
   A. --log-prefix
   B. --prepend
   C. --log-prepend
   D. --log-str

92. Within the SELinux configuration, which option controls whether the policy will be targeted or strict?
   A. SEPOLICY
   B. SELINUXTYPE
   C. SETARGET
   D. SELINUXPOLICY

93. Which of the following best describes the status of SELinux when the command getenforce returns Permissive?
   A. A Permissive return means SELinux is enabled, but rules are not enforced, although DAC rules are still in effect.
   B. A Permissive return means SELinux is not enabled.
   C. A Permissive return means SELinux is enabled, although rules are not enforced and DAC rules are not in effect.
   D. A Permissive return means SELinux is using an enforcing policy.

94. Which of the following describes the primary difference between the configuration files ssh.conf and sshd.conf (typically found in /etc/sshd/ or /etc/ssh)?
   A. sshd.conf is the configuration file for the system SSH, and ssh.conf is the options configuration file.
   B. sshd.conf is the configuration file for the system SSH daemon, and ssh.conf provides system-wide client SSH configuration.
   C. sshd.conf is used when SSH will be disabled, and ssh.conf is used when SSH is enabled.
   D. sshd.conf is the first configuration file read for a client connection, while ssh.conf is the first configuration read for a server configuration.

95. When working with PAM, a module that is marked as required has failed. Which of the following describes what happens to the other modules in that realm?
   A. Processing stops immediately when a failure of a required module occurs.
   B. Processing stops after all required modules are processed.
   C. Processing continues until another required module is encountered.
   D. Processing continues through other modules but ultimately fails.

96. What is the UID of the root account?
   A. 1000
   B. 0
   C. 100
   D. 65535

97. Using a system such as Google Authenticator to provide two-factor authentication is an example of which type of token?

A. Hardware

B. Software

C. Token-based

D. Usage-based

98. You need to disable the ability to reboot the Linux computer using the Ctrl+Alt+Del key combination. Within which file will you find the configuration for this key combination?

A. /etc/ctrlaltdel

B. /etc/shutdown

C. /etc/keymap

D. /etc/inittab

99. Within which directory are the predefined zones for firewalld?

A. /etc/firewalld/

B. /usr/lib/firewalld/zones/

C. /usr/firewalld/zones/

D. /etc/firewall/zones

100. You need to set a bootloader password for GRUB. To do so, which of the following configuration options should be set in /boot/grub/grub.conf?

A. login

B. prompt

C. boot-passwd

D. password

101. Assuming that the output from the sestatus command indicates that SELinux is in Permissive mode, which of the following commands is used to change the mode to Enforcing?

A. setenforce en

B. setenforce 1

C. setenforce on

D. setenforce --enable

102. Your organization uses ssh-agent for authentication assistance with SSH. Which command can be used to add a private key to ssh-agent?

A. ssh-privkey

B. ssh-agent-key

C. ssh-add

D. ssh-addkey

103. Which of the following commands is used to display information about the access control list for a given file?
    A. `getfacl`
    B. `getacl`
    C. `acldisp`
    D. `showacl`

104. Which of the following commands can be used to prevent the root user from logging in at the console?
    A. `echo > /etc/securetty`
    B. `echo "NoRootCon" > /etc/securetty`
    C. `rm /etc/securetty`
    D. `echo "RootCon=no" > /etc/securetty`

105. You need to provide a special username and other parameters related to a specific host to which you connect using SSH. To which file should you add this information?
    A. `~/.ssh/hosts`
    B. `~/.ssh/known_hosts`
    C. `~/.ssh/config`
    D. `~/.ssh/hostconfig`

106. You are using `chmod` in order to change several web-related files so that the web server/public can read them. Which option should you add to the `chmod` command in order for the permissions to inherit to other files?
    A. `-R`
    B. `-v`
    C. `-i`
    D. `-M`

107. Which of the following commands can be used to obtain more information about a GUID partition table?
    A. `guidinfo`
    B. `guid -info`
    C. `gdisk`
    D. `blkguid`

108. Which option to `setsebool` writes the current values to disk so that they will be applied at next reboot?
    A. `-A`
    B. `-P`
    C. `-D`
    D. `-M`

109. When working with AppArmor, within which directory are profiles located?
    A. /etc/apparmor/
    B. /etc/apparmor.d/
    C. /etc/appa.d/
    D. /etc/armor.d/

110. Which of the following protocols provides datagram security?
    A. DS
    B. DSSL
    C. DTLS
    D. DLS

111. Which of the following commands shows a list of failed login attempts?
    A. badlogin
    B. lastb
    C. lastf
    D. flogins

112. When using Kerberos authentication, which of the following commands shows the ticket cache?
    A. ktix
    B. ktel
    C. kinit
    D. klist

113. You suspect that a third-party logging agent is using a significant amount of system resources. Which of the following commands could help troubleshoot this issue?
    A. ps aux | grep <agent>
    B. uptime
    C. sysreport <agent>
    D. psrep

114. Which of the following options to the ls command displays ownership and permission information?
    A. -m
    B. -l
    C. -b
    D. -f

115. Which option to `getsebool` returns the entire list of SELinux booleans?
    A. -a
    B. -b
    C. -c
    D. -d

116. Which AppArmor command uses `netstat` to determine the network-related processes that do not have AppArmor profiles?
    A. aa-profiles
    B. aa-netstat
    C. aa-unconfined
    D. aa-netlist

117. Which group can be used to restrict access to execute the `su` command?
    A. super
    B. admins
    C. wheel
    D. runsu

118. You need to change the SELinux security context of a file. Which of the following commands should be used for this purpose?
    A. setcontext
    B. sesecon
    C. chcon
    D. setcon

119. Which of the following is an advantage of using an SSL-based VPN client?
    A. The transport may be able to get around firewalls that otherwise block VPN traffic.
    B. The use of SSL makes default configuration easier.
    C. The use of SSL means keys do not need to be configured.
    D. The use of SSL makes no difference.

120. When configuring PKI on a Red Hat system, which options are available as hashing algorithms when RSA is used as a key type?
    A. SHA256withRSA
    B. MD4
    C. SHA2048
    D. SHA1withEC

121. Which type of backup captures changes from the previous backup and only backs up those files that have changed?
   A. Full
   B. Snapshot clone
   C. Incremental
   D. Image

122. Two individuals within your organization share the same username and password for an administrative account. Which security best practice does this violate?
   A. Integrity
   B. Availability
   C. Shared IDs
   D. Password policy

123. Which of the following passwords can be used to secure a system such that it will not boot, even if the attacker has physical access to place a USB boot disk in the computer?
   A. GRUB password
   B. UEFI/BIOS password
   C. Root password
   D. SHA1 password

124. Which of the following can be used in Linux to provide biometric authentication?
   A. `finger`
   B. `fprint`
   C. `bio`
   D. `freader`

125. Which option to the `restorecon` utility can be used to view the current contexts without making changes?
   A. `-n`
   B. `-r`
   C. `-g`
   D. `-p`

126. You need to allow a user to edit a file that is owned by root. Which of the following commands should be used for this purpose, assuming the use of `sudo` to execute the command?
   A. `vim`
   B. `nano`
   C. `sudoedit`
   D. `visudo`

127. You need to view the SELinux contexts for various processes on the system. Which of the following commands will accomplish this task?
    A. showcon
    B. proccon
    C. lcon -Z
    D. ps -Z

128. Which PAM module can be used to lock accounts after failed login attempts?
    A. pam_lock
    B. pam_tally2
    C. pam_loginlock
    D. pam_watchlog

129. Which VPN mode is typically used for client-to-server VPN traffic?
    A. Tunnel
    B. Transport
    C. Site-to-Site
    D. Site-to-Server

130. What is the device-naming convention used to indicate a pseudo-terminal in Linux?
    A. /dev/ttyS0
    B. /dev/ttyP0
    C. /dev/pty
    D. /dev/tys

131. Which of the following commands places all AppArmor profiles into complain mode?
    A. aa-complain /etc/apparmor.d/*
    B. aa-enable -complain /etc/apparmor.d/*
    C. aa-enable -complain /etc/apparmor/*
    D. aa-complain /etc/apparmor/*

132. Which of the following logs is used to store information related to authentication and authorization?
    A. /var/log/sec.log
    B. /var/log/messages
    C. /var/log/kern.log
    D. /var/log/secure

133. Which option within the `sshd_config` file controls whether the root user can log in directly with SSH?

   A. `PermitRoot`
   B. `PermitRootLogin`
   C. `RootDirectLogin`
   D. `AllowRootLogin`

134. RADIUS provides AAA services for remote login. To what does AAA refer?

   A. Authentication, Authorization, Availability
   B. Authentication, Authorization, AppArmor
   C. Authentication, Authorization, Assistance
   D. Authentication, Authorization, Accounting

135. Which option to the `firewall-cmd` command sets the current runtime configuration to be available on next reboot of the computer?

   A. `--set-perm`
   B. `--make-perm`
   C. `--runtime-to-permanent`
   D. `--current-to-persistent`

136. One of your customers needs to transfer a large file and is asking for FTP to be enabled on the server. Thinking of security, what options can you offer that are more secure?

   A. USB
   B. Email (SMTP)
   C. SSL
   D. SFTP

137. Which site should you use to monitor for new security bulletins that have been reported using the CVE process?

   A. News sites
   B. `https://cve.mitre.org`
   C. `https://www.example.com`
   D. Vendor sites

138. When working with `ufw`, you need to allow SSH traffic. Which of the following commands facilitates this scenario?

   A. `ufw allow tcp/22`
   B. `ufw enable ssh`
   C. `ufw allow ssh`
   D. `ufw enable tcp/21-22`

139. Which daemon can be used to monitor the system for changes to system files?
    A. end
    B. alogd
    C. auditd
    D. mond

140. You need to provide authentication for various network components like routers and switches within the enterprise network. Which authentication service can be added to the Linux server to facilitate this scenario?
    A. SSH
    B. Kerberos
    C. TACACS+
    D. Telnet

141. Which of the following is the name for the firewall control software associated with Netfilter?
    A. iptables
    B. ipt
    C. netfw
    D. netfilterfw

142. You need to extract files from a backup created with an older version of HPUX. The tar command does not seem to work for these files. Which of the following may be able to extract from this backup?
    A. gzip
    B. bzip2
    C. cpio
    D. hpb

143. When copying files using scp, which port needs to be open in the firewall?
    A. TCP/21
    B. TCP/22
    C. TCP/20 and TCP/21
    D. UDP/53

144. You are viewing the contents of a directory with the ls command but do not see files that begin with a single dot (.). Which option to ls shows those files?
    A. -a
    B. -b
    C. -c
    D. -d

145. You believe that the system has been broken into and files may have been changed. After taking the system offline and unmounting one of the affected partitions, what could you do next?

   A. Use dd to make an image of the partition to preserve it.
   B. Create a backup using tar.
   C. Examine the partition with fdisk.
   D. Use mkfs to reformat the partition.

146. Which option to SSH specifies the private key to use for authentication?

   A. -m
   B. -i
   C. -k
   D. -a

147. Which utility can be used to create a checksum of a file in order to ensure its integrity?

   A. sha1sum
   B. mdsum
   C. shasum
   D. shacheck

148. Which option to the zip command causes the command to traverse directories?

   A. -g
   B. -m
   C. -r
   D. -a

149. You are working on a Debian system and need to set ownership on a file such that the user used to execute Apache can write to the file. What command can you use to determine which user Apache is running as?

   A. ps auwx | grep apache
   B. ls -a
   C. free | grep httpd
   D. monapache

150. You have found that the owner of the Apache process is www-data. What command will change the ownership of a file, given as <filename>, such that www-data can write to the file?

   A. chown www-data <filename>
   B. chown apache-www-data <filename>
   C. chmod www-data +w <filename>
   D. chmod www-data.apache <filename>

151. When using sudo in a scripted environment, which option can be used to specify a non-interactive mode?
    A. -f
    B. -m
    C. -n
    D. -l

152. On which port does telnet operate?
    A. TCP/22
    B. TCP/20
    C. TCP/100
    D. TCP/23

153. Which command is used to turn off AppArmor profiles?
    A. aa-disable
    B. aa-turnoff
    C. aa-enable -d
    D. aa-off

154. Which command and option are used to view the SELinux security context of a given file?
    A. ls -context
    B. file -Z
    C. ls -Z
    D. sel -context

155. Digital signatures can be provided in Linux through which of the following commands?
    A. gds
    B. gpg
    C. dmc
    D. gds2

156. You need to make a change to the global behavior of AppArmor. Rather than editing the profiles directly, which directory contains common settings that can be changed instead?
    A. /etc/apparmor.d/configs
    B. /etc/apparmor/globals
    C. /etc/apparmor/edits
    D. /etc/apparmor.d/tunables

157. Which of the following directories contains configuration for UFW?
- **A.** /etc/ufwd
- **B.** /etc/ufw.d
- **C.** /etc/ufw
- **D.** /etc/ufirewall

158. Which software can be used in connection with `iptables` in order to more effectively block traffic from entire network ranges?
- **A.** ipblock
- **B.** ipset
- **C.** iplist
- **D.** ipcoll

159. You have created a public key and private key for use with SSH. The contents of which key should be copied to a remote host in order to enable authentication?
- **A.** The public key
- **B.** The private key
- **C.** Both the public and private keys
- **D.** Neither the public nor the private key. It must be generated on the remote host.

160. What is the octal notation to specify that a directory should have read-write-execute permissions for the owner and read-execute permissions for the group and other?
- **A.** 711
- **B.** 644
- **C.** 755
- **D.** 777

161. When using `rsyslog` for logging, within which file can you look to determine what items are logged on the system?
- **A.** /etc/rsyslogd.conf
- **B.** /etc/rsys.conf
- **C.** /etc/rsyslog.conf
- **D.** /etc/rsys.cfg

162. Which option to `sestatus` shows the context of a file?
- **A.** -f
- **B.** -v
- **C.** -m
- **D.** -a

163. Which option to chage sets the maximum days that a password is valid?
   A. -v
   B. -m
   C. -M
   D. -d

164. Which option within an SSH server configuration enables authentication using Kerberos?
   A. UseKerberos
   B. KerberosAuthentication
   C. EnableKerberos
   D. KerberosEnable

165. You are working with iptables-save to examine the contents of tables in a scripted environment. Which option to iptables-save can be used to specify the table name rather than outputting information for all tables?
   A. -t
   B. -a
   C. -s
   D. -i

166. Ports below what number are considered to be the well-known ports?
   A. 256
   B. 512
   C. 1024
   D. 65535

167. Within which directory will you find configuration files for various logs that are to be rotated with logrotate?
   A. /etc/logrotate
   B. /etc/logs
   C. /etc/logrotate.d
   D. /var/spool/logrotate

168. Which option to the journalctl command will continuously update the display as new log entries are created?
   A. -tail
   B. -t
   C. -f
   D. -l

169. Which PAM module is responsible for enforcing limits such as the maximum number of logins and CPU time used?
    A. pam_enforce.so
    B. pam_limittest.so
    C. pam_max.so
    D. pam_limits.so

170. When using LDAP for authentication, what will be logged with the loglevel set to 0x10 in a slapd.conf configuration file?
    A. No debugging
    B. Trace debugging
    C. Stats logging
    D. Packets sent and received

171. On which port does LDAP over SSL listen for connections?
    A. 389
    B. 443
    C. 636
    D. 3128

172. Which of the following PAM modules can be used for authorization and authentication scenarios using external files?
    A. pam_fileauth.so
    B. pam_listfiles.so
    C. pam_filesauth.so
    D. pam_fileauth.so

173. Which option to ssh-keygen sets the type of key that will be created?
    A. -k
    B. -t
    C. -e
    D. -i

Chapter 4

Linux Troubleshooting and Diagnostics

THE FOLLOWING COMPTIA LINUX+ EXAM OBJECTIVES ARE COVERED IN THIS CHAPTER:

✓ **4.1 Given a scenario, analyze system properties and remediate accordingly**

- Network monitoring and configuration
  - Latency
    - Bandwidth
    - Throughput
  - Routing
  - Saturation
  - Packet drop
  - Timeouts
  - Name resolution
  - Localhostvs. Unix socket
  - Adapters
    - RDMA drivers
  - Interface configurations
  - Commands
    - nmap
    - netstat
    - iftop
    - route
    - iperf
    - tcpdump
    - ipset

- Wireshark
  - tshark
- netcat
- traceroute
- mtr
- arp
- nslookup
- dig
- host
- whois
- ping
- nmcli
- ip
- tracepath
- Storage monitoring and configuration
  - iostat
  - ioping
  - I/O scheduling
    - cfq
    - noop
    - deadline
  - du
  - df
  - LVM tools
  - fsck
  - partprobe
- CPU monitoring and configuration
  - /proc/cpuinfo
  - uptime
  - loadaverage
  - sar
  - sysctl

- Memory monitoring and configuration
  - `swapon`
  - `swapoff`
  - `mkswap`
  - `vmstat`
  - Out of memory killer
  - `free`
  - `/proc/meminfo`
  - Buffer cache output
- Lost root password
  - Single user mode

✓ **4.2 Given a scenario, analyze system processes in order to optimize performance**

- Process management
- Process states
  - Zombie
    - Uninterruptible sleep
    - Interruptible sleep
    - Running
- Priorities
- Kill signals
- Commands
  - `nice`
  - `renice`
  - `top`
  - `ps`
  - `lsof`
  - `pgrep`
  - `pkill`
- PIDs

- ✓ 4.3 **Given a scenario, analyze and troubleshoot user issues**
  - Permissions
    - File
    - Directory
  - Access
    - Local
    - Remote
  - Authentication
    - Local
    - External
    - Policy violations
  - File creation
  - Quotas
  - Storage
  - Inode exhaustion
  - Immutable files
  - Insufficient privileges for authorization
    - SELinux violations
  - Environment and shell issues

- ✓ 4.4 **Given a scenario, analyze and troubleshoot application and hardware issues**
  - SELinux context violations
  - Storage
    - Degraded storage
    - Missing devices
    - Missing volumes
    - Missing mount point
    - Performance issues
    - Resource exhaustion
    - Adapters
      - SCSI
      - RAID
      - SATA

- HBA
  - /sys/class/scsi_host/host#/scan
- Storage integrity
  - Bad blocks
- Firewall
  - Restrictive ACLs
  - Blocked ports
  - Blocked protocols
- Permission
  - Ownership
  - Executables
  - Inheritance
  - Service accounts
  - Group memberships
- Dependencies
  - Patching
  - Update issues
  - Versioning
  - Libraries
  - Environment variables
  - GCC compatibility
  - Repositories
- Troubleshooting additional hardware issues
  - Memory
  - Printers
  - Video
    - GPU drivers
  - Communication ports
  - USB
  - Keyboard mapping
  - Hardware or software compatibility issues
  - Commands
    - dmidecode
    - lshw

Chapter 4 ▪ Linux Troubleshooting and Diagnostics

1. You are troubleshooting a storage problem, and a Serial ATA (SATA) disk or mount point may be missing. Which of the following identifiers is used by SATA disks?
   A. /dev/hdX
   B. /dev/sataX
   C. /dev/sdX
   D. /disk/sataX

2. You are examining a problem report where a USB disk is no longer available. Which command is used to obtain a list of USB devices?
   A. usb-list
   B. lsusb
   C. ls-usb
   D. ls --usb

3. You have lost the password for a server and need to boot into single user mode. Which option given at boot time within the GRUB configuration will start the system in single user mode to enable password recovery and/or reset?
   A. single-user
   B. su
   C. single
   D. root

4. Which of the following is a good first troubleshooting step when a hard disk is not detected by the Linux kernel?
   A. Unplug the disk.
   B. Check the system BIOS.
   C. Restart the web server service.
   D. Run the disk-detect command.

5. The system that you're working with recently had a hard drive failure, resulting in degraded storage. A new hard drive has been installed and had Linux restored from backup to the drive. However, the system will not boot and instead shows a grub > prompt. Within the grub > prompt, which command will show the current partitions as seen by GRUB?
   A. ls
   B. showPart
   C. partitionlist
   D. ps

6. A legacy PATA disk is used to boot the system. You recently added an internal DVD drive to the computer, and now the system will no longer boot. What is the most likely cause?

   A. The BIOS has identified the DVD drive as the first disk, and therefore the system can no longer find the Linux partition(s).

   B. The hard drive became corrupt when the DVD drive was installed.

   C. The hot swap option has not been enabled in the BIOS.

   D. The DVD drive is not detected by the computer and needs to be enabled first in the BIOS and then in Linux prior to installation.

7. You have connected a USB disk to the system and need to find out its connection point within the system. Which of the following is the best method for accomplishing this task?

   A. Rebooting the system

   B. Viewing the contents of /var/log/usb.log

   C. Connecting the drive to a USB port that you know the number of

   D. Running dmesg and looking for the disk

8. How many SCSI devices are supported per bus?

   A. 7 to 15

   B. 2 to 4

   C. 12

   D. 4

9. Which command is used to update the links and cache for shared libraries on the system?

   A. ldcache

   B. cache-update

   C. link-update

   D. ldconfig

10. Which command and option are used to update a Debian system to the latest software?

   A. apt-update

   B. apt-get upgrade

   C. dpkg -U

   D. apt-cache clean

11. Which option given to a yum command will install a package?

   A. update

   B. configure

   C. install

   D. get

12. Which of the following commands adds /usr/local/lib to the LD_LIBRARY_PATH when using the bash shell?
    A. set PATH=/usr/local/lib
    B. export LD_LIBRARY_PATH=$LD_LIBRARY_PATH:/usr/local/lib
    C. LD_LIBRARY_PATH=/usr/local/lib
    D. connectpath LD_LIBRARY_PATH=/usr/local/lib

13. Within which directory will you find the repositories used by Yum?
    A. /etc/yum.conf
    B. /etc/repos
    C. /etc/yum.conf.d
    D. /etc/yum.repos.d

14. Which command is used to determine the libraries on which a given command depends?
    A. ldconfig
    B. librarylist
    C. listdeps
    D. ldd

15. Which of the following is true of Linux swap space?
    A. Swap is used to hold temporary database tables.
    B. Swap is used as additional memory when there is insufficient RAM.
    C. Swap is used by the mail server for security.
    D. Swap is used to scrub data from the network temporarily.

16. Which of the following is not typically used to store libraries?
    A. /lib
    B. /etc/lib
    C. /usr/lib
    D. /usr/local/lib

17. You are attempting to install a new package on a Debian system from a repository. The package does not seem to exist. Which of the following commands updates the package cache for a Debian system?
    A. apt-get cache-update
    B. apt-cache update
    C. apt-get update
    D. apt-get upgrade

18. Within which file are details of the current package repositories stored on a Debian system?
    A. /etc/apt.list
    B. /etc/sources.list
    C. /etc/apt/sources.list
    D. /etc/apt.d/sources.list

19. Which of the following commands initializes a physical disk partition for use with LVM?
    A. lvmcreate
    B. pvcreate
    C. fvcreate
    D. lvinit

20. Which command is used to create a logical volume with LVM?
    A. pvcreate
    B. lvmcreate
    C. lvcreate
    D. volcreate

21. What is the logical order for creation of an LVM logical volume?
    A. Physical volume creation, volume group creation, logical volume creation
    B. Physical volume creation, logical volume creation, volume group creation
    C. Logical volume creation, physical volume creation, volume group creation
    D. LVM creation, format, partition

22. Which option for yum performs a search of the package cache?
    A. seek
    B. query
    C. --search
    D. search

23. Which command option for rpm can be used to show the version of the kernel?
    A. rpm kernel
    B. rpm -q kernel
    C. rpm search kernel
    D. rpm --list kern

24. Which option in /etc/yum.conf is used to ensure that the kernel is not updated when the system is updated?
    A. exclude=kernel*
    B. exclude-kernel
    C. updatekernel=false
    D. include-except=kernel

25. Which partition type should be created for a Linux system, non-swap partition?
    A. 82
    B. 83
    C. 84
    D. L

26. Which command searches for and provides information on a given package on a Debian system, including whether the package is currently installed?
    A. `dpkg -i`
    B. `dpkg -s`
    C. `apt-cache`
    D. `apt-info`

27. Which command is used to search for physical volumes for use with LVM?
    A. `lvmcreate`
    B. `pvcreate`
    C. `lvmdiskscan`
    D. `lvmscan`

28. Which of the following installs a previously downloaded Debian package?
    A. `dpkg -i <package name>`
    B. `apt-install <package name>`
    C. `apt-slash <package name>`
    D. `dpkg -U <package name>`

29. You are troubleshooting an issue reported by a user and suspect it may be related to their environment variables. What command should the user run in order to view the current settings for their environment when using bash?
    A. `environment`
    B. `env`
    C. `listenv`
    D. `echoenv`

30. You need to write a script that gathers all the process IDs for all instances of Apache running on the system. Which of the following commands will accomplish this task?
    A. `ps auwx | grep apache`
    B. `pgrep apache`
    C. `processlist apache`
    D. `ls -p apache`

31. Users are reporting that various programs are crashing on the server. Examining logs, you see that certain processes are reporting out-of-memory conditions. Which command can you use to see the overall memory usage, including available swap space?
    A. tree
    B. pgrep
    C. uptime
    D. free

32. Which command can be used to determine the current load average along with information on the amount of time since the last boot of the system?
    A. uptime
    B. sysinfo
    C. bash
    D. ls -u

33. You need to start a long-running process that requires a terminal and foreground processing. However, you cannot leave your terminal window open due to security restrictions. Which command will enable you to start the process and return at a later time to continue the session?
    A. fg
    B. bg
    C. kill
    D. screen

34. Which command can be run to determine the default priority for processes spawned by the current user?
    A. prio
    B. nice
    C. renice
    D. defpriority

35. You have backgrounded several tasks using &. Which command can be used to view the current list of running tasks that have been backgrounded?
    A. procs
    B. plist
    C. jobs
    D. free

36. Which command can be used to kill any process by using its name?
    A. killproc
    B. killname
    C. killall
    D. kill -f

37. You are troubleshooting an issue with disk usage and suspect that the partition is out of inodes. Which of the following commands shows the usage of inodes across all filesystems?

    A. `df -i`

    B. `ls -i`

    C. `du -i`

    D. `dm -i`

38. When running an `fsck` on an ext3 filesystem, the process is taking longer than expected and requiring input from the administrator to fix issues. What option could be added to `fsck` next time so that the command will automatically attempt to fix errors without intervention?

    A. `-o`

    B. `-V`

    C. `-y`

    D. `-f`

39. You are using a storage area network (SAN) that keeps causing errors on your Linux system due to an improper kernel module created by the SAN vendor. When the SAN sends updates, it causes the filesystem to be mounted as read-only. Which command and option can you use to change the behavior of the filesystem to account for the SAN bug?

    A. `mount --continue`

    B. `tune2fs -e continue`

    C. `mkfs --no-remount`

    D. `mount -o remount`

40. Which command is used to format a swap partition?

    A. `fdisk`

    B. `mkswap`

    C. `formatswap`

    D. `format -s`

41. The system is running out of disk space within the home directory partition, and quotas have not been enabled. Which command can you use to determine the directories that might contain large files?

    A. `du`

    B. `df`

    C. `ls`

    D. `locate`

42. Which option is set on a filesystem in order to enable user-level quotas?
    A. quotaon
    B. enquota=user
    C. usrquota
    D. userquota

43. Which option to quotacheck is used to create the files for the first time?
    A. -f
    B. -u
    C. -m
    D. -c

44. In the context of an `if` conditional within a bash script, which of the following tests will determine whether a file exists and can be read by the user executing the test?
    A. -e
    B. -s
    C. -a
    D. -r

45. When configuring local user access, LightDM typically allows guest login by default. Which configuration option within SeatDefaults changes this to disallow guests?
    A. guest-login=false
    B. guest=false
    C. allowg=false
    D. allow-guest=false

46. Which of the following commands allows a host named cwa to connect to the X server?
    A. xconnect cwa
    B. xterm +cwa
    C. xhost +cwa
    D. xf cwa

47. To which shell can a user account be set if they are not allowed to log in interactively to the computer?
    A. /bin/bash
    B. /bin/tcsh
    C. /bin/zsh
    D. /bin/false

48. When troubleshooting disk usage, which of the following commands is used to determine the amount of disk space used by systemd journal logfiles?
    A. `journalctl --disk`
    B. `journalctl -du`
    C. `journalctl --disk-usage`
    D. `journalctl -ls`

49. You are having difficulty with an interface on the server, and it is currently down. Assuming that there is not a hardware failure on the device itself, which command and option can you use to display information about the interface?
    A. `ifconfig -a`
    B. `ifup`
    C. `netstat -n`
    D. `ifconfig`

50. Which of the following is not used as a private address for internal, non-Internet, use?
    A. 172.16.4.2
    B. 192.168.40.3
    C. 10.74.5.244
    D. 143.236.32.231

51. Which of the following commands adds a default gateway of 192.168.1.1 for interface eth0?
    A. `route add default gateway 192.168.1.1 eth0`
    B. `eth0 --dg 192.168.1.1`
    C. `route add default gw 192.168.1.1 eth0`
    D. `route define eth0 192.168.1.1`

52. Which option for the `host` command will query for the authoritative nameservers for a given domain?
    A. `-t ns`
    B. `-t all`
    C. `-ns`
    D. `-named`

53. Which option for the `ping` command enables you to choose the interface from which the ICMP packets will be generated?
    A. `-i`
    B. `-I`
    C. `-t`
    D. `-a`

54. Which of the following commands queries for the mail servers for the domain example.com?
    A. dig example.com mx
    B. dig example.com
    C. host -t smtp example.com
    D. dig example.com smtp

55. Which option to the traceroute command will use TCP SYN packets for the path trace?
    A. -T
    B. -t
    C. -s
    D. -i

56. Which command can be used to listen for netlink messages on a network?
    A. ip monitor
    B. netlink -a
    C. ip netlink
    D. route

57. Which of the following dig commands sends the query for example.com directly to the server at 192.168.2.5 rather than to a locally configured resolver?
    A. dig example.com @192.168.2.5
    B. dig -t 192.168.2.5 example.com
    C. dig -s 192.168.2.5 example.com
    D. dig server=192.168.2.5 example.com

58. Which of the following commands will enumerate the hosts database?
    A. getent hosts
    B. gethosts
    C. nslookup
    D. host

59. Which of the following configuration lines will set the DNS server to 192.168.1.4 using /etc/resolv.conf?
    A. dns 192.168.1.4
    B. dns-server 192.168.1.4
    C. nameserver 192.168.1.4
    D. name-server 192.168.1.4

60. Which of the following commands adds a route to the server for the network 192.168.51.0/24 through its gateway of 192.168.51.1?
  A. route add -net 192.168.51.0 netmask 255.255.255.0 gw 192.168.51.1
  B. route add -net 192.168.51/24 gw 192.168.1.51
  C. route -net 192.168.51.0/24 192.168.51.1
  D. route add 192.168.51.1 -n 192.168.51.0//255.255.255.0

61. Which of the following commands shows network services or sockets that are currently listening along with sockets that are not listening?
  A. netstat -a
  B. netlink -a
  C. sockets -f
  D. opensock -l

62. Which of the following represents a correct configuration line for /etc/hosts?
  A. 192.168.1.4 cwa.braingia.org cwa
  B. cwa.braingia.org cwa 192.168.1.4
  C. cwa.braingia.org 192.168.1.8 alias cwa
  D. alias cwa.braingia.org cwa 192.168.1.4

63. Which of the following commands configures the eth0 device with an IP address of 192.168.1.1 in a /24 network?
  A. ifconfig eth0 192.168.1.1/24
  B. ifconfig eth0 192.168.1.1/255.255.255.0
  C. ifconfig eth0 192.168.1.1 netmask 255.255.255.0
  D. ifconfig 192.168.1.1 netmask 255.255.255.0 eth0

64. Which of the following commands will change the default gateway to 192.168.1.1 using eth0?
  A. ip route default gw 192.168.1.1
  B. ip route change default via 192.168.1.1 dev eth0
  C. ip route default gw update 192.168.1.1
  D. ip route update default 192.168.1.1 eth0

65. When troubleshooting an issue where SSH connections are timing out, you think the firewall is blocking SSH connections. Which of the following ports is used for Secure Shell communication?
  A. TCP/23
  B. TCP/25
  C. TCP/22
  D. TCP/2200

66. Which options for netcat will create a server listening on port 8080?
    A. netcat -p 8080
    B. nc -l -p 8080
    C. nc -p 8080
    D. nc -s 8080

67. Which of the following commands displays the Start of Authority information for the domain example.com?
    A. dig example.com soa
    B. dig example.com authority
    C. dig example.com -auth
    D. dig -t auth example.com

68. Assume that you want to enable local client services to go to hosts on the network without needing to fully qualify the name by adding the domain for either example.com or example.org. Which option in /etc/resolv.conf will provide this functionality?
    A. search
    B. domain
    C. local-domain
    D. local-order

69. Which of the following commands prevents traffic from reaching the host 192.168.1.3?
    A. route add -host 192.168.1.3 reject
    B. route -nullroute 192.168.1.3
    C. route add -null 192.168.1.3
    D. route add -block 192.168.1.3

70. Which of the following describes a primary difference between traceroute and tracepath?
    A. The traceroute command requires root privileges.
    B. The tracepath command provides the MTU for each hop, whereas traceroute does not.
    C. The tracepath command cannot be used for tracing a path on an external network.
    D. The traceroute command is not compatible with IPv6.

71. Which of the following commands will emulate the ping command in Microsoft Windows, where the ping is sent for four packets and then the command exits?
    A. ping -n 4
    B. ping -t 4
    C. ping -p 4
    D. ping -c 4

72. You are troubleshooting a DNS problem using the `dig` command and receive a "status: NXDOMAIN" message. Which of the following best describes what NXDOMAIN means?

  A. NXDOMAIN means you have received a non-authoritative answer for the query.
  B. NXDOMAIN means the domain or host is not found.
  C. NXDOMAIN indicates a successful query.
  D. NXDOMAIN signifies that a new domain record has been added.

73. Which of the following commands should be executed after running `ip route change`?

  A. `ip route flush cache`
  B. `ip route reload`
  C. `ip route cache reload`
  D. `ip route restart`

74. Which option should be used to send a DNS query for an SPF record with `dig`?

  A. `-t txt`
  B. `-t spf`
  C. `-t mx`
  D. `-t mailspf`

75. When troubleshooting a connectivity issue, you have found that you can reach a server via the Web but cannot ping it. Which of the following best describes a possible cause for this scenario?

  A. TCP traffic has been blocked at the firewall.
  B. The DNS lookup is failing.
  C. ICMP traffic has been blocked.
  D. There is a reject route in place.

76. When viewing the available routes using the `route` command, one route contains the flags UG and the others contain U. What does the letter G signify in the route table?

  A. The G signifies that the route is good.
  B. The G signifies that the route is unavailable.
  C. The G signifies that this is a gateway.
  D. The G signifies that the route is an aggregate.

77. Which of the following commands requests a zone transfer of `example.org` from the server at 192.168.1.4?

  A. `dig example.org @192.168.1.4 axfr`
  B. `dig example.org @192.168.1.4`
  C. `dig example.org @192.168.1.4 xfer`
  D. `dig example.org #192.168.1.4 xfer`

78. You need to temporarily prevent users from logging in to the system using SSH or other means. Which of the following describes one method for accomplishing this task?
    A. touch /etc/nologin
    B. Disable sshd.
    C. Remove /etc/login.
    D. Add a shadow file.

79. Which of the following commands searches the entire filesystem for files with the setuid bit set?
    A. find ./ -perm suid
    B. find / -perm 4000
    C. find / -type suid
    D. find / -type f -perm setuid

80. Which of the following commands scans the IP address 192.168.1.154 for open ports?
    A. nmap 192.168.1.154
    B. lsof 192.168.1.154
    C. netstat 192.168.1.154
    D. netmap 192.168.1.154

81. Which of the following configuration options sets a hard limit of 25 processes for a user called suehring in /etc/security/limits.conf?
    A. suehring hard proc 25
    B. suehring hard nproc 25
    C. suehring proc 25 hard-limit
    D. proc 25 suehring hard

82. Which of the following commands displays the currently open ports and the process that is using the port?
    A. netstat -a
    B. lsof -i
    C. ps auwx
    D. netlist

83. You are using nmap to scan a host for open ports. However, the server is blocking ICMP echo requests. Which option to nmap can you set in order to continue the scan?
    A. -P0
    B. -no-ping
    C. -s0
    D. -ping-0

84. Which option within /etc/security/limits.conf is used to control the number of times a given account can log in simultaneously?
   A. nlogins
   B. loginmax
   C. maxlogins
   D. loginlimit

85. Which option to nmap sets the scan to use TCP SYN packets for finding open ports?
   A. -sS
   B. -sT
   C. -sY
   D. -type SYN

86. Which of the following commands searches a server for files with the setgid bit enabled?
   A. find / -perm 4000
   B. find ./ -perm setgid
   C. grep setgid *
   D. find / -perm 2000

87. When using iostat to assess performance, which option displays information on a per-partition basis for block devices?
   A. -a
   B. -c
   C. -d
   D. -p

88. Which of the following commands displays blocks in and blocks out as related to I/O?
   A. iorpt
   B. iptraf
   C. vmswap
   D. vmstat

89. Which of the following commands can be used to display a list of currently logged-in users along with the current load average and time since last reboot?
   A. uptime
   B. w
   C. swap
   D. sysinfo

90. Which of the following describes a method for changing the sort order when using the top command such that the highest memory utilizers will be shown at the top of the list?
    A. Within top, type **o** and then select mem.
    B. Within top, press Shift+F, scroll to %MEM, press S to select, and then press Q to quit.
    C. Within top, press S and then select %MEM.
    D. Within top, press Shift+S, select %MEM, then press Q to quit.

91. Which of the following monitoring tools can use SNMP and scripts to collect data for performance-related graphing such as throughput and bandwidth?
    A. ptop
    B. pstree
    C. Cacti
    D. Grafr

92. Which swapon option silently skips swap partitions that do not exist?
    A. -u
    B. -e
    C. -i
    D. -o

93. Which option to the `fsck` command causes it to run the check even if the filesystem is apparently marked as clean?
    A. -f
    B. -m
    C. -a
    D. -c

94. Which of the following commands deactivates swap space?
    A. swapoff
    B. swap -off
    C. unmountswap
    D. uswap

95. Which of the following swapon options displays information on the size of swap space along with its used space?
    A. --list
    B. -a
    C. --show
    D. -h

96. Which of the following commands displays information about a given physical volume in an LVM setup?
    A. pvdisp
    B. pvlist
    C. pvdisplay
    D. pvl

97. Which of the following commands looks for LVM physical volumes and volume groups involved in an LVM configuration?
    A. vgscan
    B. lvmscan
    C. lvlist
    D. pvlist

98. Which of the following commands is used to display a list of physical volumes involved in LVM?
    A. pvdisp
    B. pvlist
    C. pvscan
    D. pvmm

99. When using the `ip` command, which protocol family is used as the default if not otherwise specified?
    A. tcpip
    B. ip
    C. inet
    D. arp

100. You are using the `route` command to view routes. However, name resolution is taking a long time and causing delay in the response from the `route` command. Which option to `route` can be added to cause it to not perform name resolution?
    A. -d
    B. -e
    C. -f
    D. -n

101. You have replaced a device on the network but used the IP from another active device. Which command can be run to remove the MAC address entry from your computer so that it performs the address resolution again?
    A. arp -d
    B. netstat -rn
    C. hostname
    D. dig

102. When looking to parse the output of the `ip` command, which option can be set to remove newlines such that the output could be piped to the `grep` command?
    A. -n
    B. -o
    C. -l
    D. -f

103. Which option to the `arp` command creates a new entry for a given IP address to MAC address pair?
    A. -s
    B. -c
    C. -d
    D. --add

104. Which option to `tcpdump` displays a list of available interfaces on which `tcpdump` can operate?
    A. -a
    B. -d
    C. -D
    D. -i

105. Which option to `nmap` will cause it to always perform name resolution?
    A. -n
    B. -R
    C. -b
    D. -a

106. Which of the following commands provides a live `traceroute` of the route between two hosts, updating the information for each hop in near real-time?
    A. `traceroute --live`
    B. `mtr`
    C. `route -update`
    D. `liveroute`

107. You are using a local RAID array and investigating a performance issue. When using mdadm in monitor mode, which option sets the polling interval?
    A. --delay
    B. --internal
    C. --interval
    D. --poll

108. When viewing the results of a traceroute, you see !H. To what does !H refer?
    A. Network unreachable
    B. Host available
    C. Host unreachable
    D. High length

109. Assuming that policy routing has been enabled in the kernel, which option to the ping command can be used to mark the outgoing request appropriately in order to indicate that the packet should be processed according to a particular policy?
    A. -m
    B. -a
    C. -p
    D. -k

110. When troubleshooting a possible issue with bad blocks on a disk, which option to fsck will report statistics such as CPU time used on completion of the fsck operation?
    A. -s
    B. -r
    C. -l
    D. -f

111. Which of the following files provides information on memory utilization including free memory, buffers, cache usage, and several additional items?
    A. /proc/cpuinfo
    B. /proc/memtime
    C. /proc/memuse
    D. /proc/meminfo

112. Which scan mode for nmap provides an Xmas scan?
    A. -sT
    B. -sS
    C. -sP
    D. -sX

113. Which option to tcpdump sets the snapshot length of packets to capture?
    A. -s
    B. -l
    C. -d
    D. -c

114. On which port does the `ping` command operate for ICMP echo requests?
   A. 53
   B. 1337
   C. 33433
   D. No port is used for ICMP.

115. When running the `df` command, you need to change the scale such that the report shows terabytes instead of bytes. Which option will accomplish this task?
   A. -ST
   B. -BT
   C. -j
   D. -T

116. Which option to `mke2fs` is used to check for bad blocks during filesystem creation?
   A. -a
   B. -b
   C. -c
   D. -d

117. Which option to the `ping` command shows latency rather than round-trip time?
   A. -L
   B. -i
   C. -U
   D. -d

118. Which of the following commands is used to measure network throughput?
   A. tp
   B. iperf
   C. ith
   D. ithrough

119. You would like to monitor interrupt usage in real time on a Linux server in order to troubleshoot communication ports usage. Which of the following commands can be used for this purpose?
   A. int
   B. moni
   C. itop
   D. imon

120. You are configuring an RDMA interface. Which of the following commands displays information about InfiniBand devices?
    A. ibmon
    B. ibstat
    C. rdmon
    D. rdstat

121. You need to increase the performance of process ID 4382 by changing its priority. Which of the following commands will accomplish this task?
    A. renice -5 -p 4382
    B. renice 5 -p 4382
    C. renice 100 4382
    D. renice 4382 +5

122. Which option to netstat is used to disable DNS or hostname lookups?
    A. -b
    B. -h
    C. -q
    D. -n

123. You would like to find all of the process IDs associated with the sshd process on an Ubuntu system. Which of the following commands accomplishes this task?
    A. ps -sshd
    B. pidof sshd
    C. pids sshd
    D. ps --a=sshd

124. Which kill signal sends a hangup to a given process?
    A. 1
    B. 5
    C. 24
    D. 30

125. Which command is used to configure kernel parameters for a new GPU driver added to the system?
    A. gpuctl
    B. gpuload
    C. sysconfig
    D. sysctl

126. You would like to change the byte-to-inode ratio on a new filesystem in order to prevent inode exhaustion. Which option to `mke2fs` accomplishes this task?
    A. `-b`
    B. `-r`
    C. `-i`
    D. `-u`

127. Which directory contains information on FibreChannel HBA ports?
    A. `/sys/fc/ports`
    B. `/sys/class/hba`
    C. `/sys/class/fc_host`
    D. `/sys/class/fc/ports`

128. Which type of module interface for PAM is used to set a policy such as the time of day that a user can log in?
    A. `auth`
    B. `account`
    C. `password`
    D. `policy`

129. You need to create a restrictive access control list (ACL) on a server. Which policy should be the default for the `INPUT` chain within the firewall?
    A. `deny`
    B. `permit`
    C. `accept`
    D. `discard`

130. Which option to the `ls` command displays the ownership, including user and group owners of a given file or directory?
    A. `-o`
    B. `-a`
    C. `-l`
    D. `-d`

131. When creating a daemon process that will be used on the local server, which of the following communication methods should be used?
    A. Localhost/network
    B. Socket
    C. Message-passing
    D. RDP

132. When using the `free` command to determine memory usage, which column shows the memory used by the kernel for things like kernel buffers?
    A. used
    B. shared
    C. buffers
    D. cache

133. Which of the following commands provides a command-line interface into NetworkManager?
    A. nmc
    B. dmc
    C. nmcli
    D. netman

134. Which command displays network usage in a top-like interface?
    A. iftop
    B. iptop
    C. ptop
    D. netcap

135. You suspect saturation is affecting network performance with your Linux server. Which command can be used to help determine the amount of traffic being passed through a given interface?
    A. netp
    B. sat
    C. iptraf
    D. ipsat

136. You are looking to optimize the I/O scheduler for your Linux server. Which I/O scheduling algorithm is the default?
    A. deadline
    B. noop
    C. cfq
    D. iqueue

137. You would like to efficiently manage firewall rules such that you can define a group of IP addresses to which a single rule can be applied. Which command enables you to create a group of IP addresses?
    A. ipgroup
    B. iptables -group
    C. addrgroup
    D. ipset

138. You are receiving reports of timeouts from users attempting to SSH between servers. Which command should be used to help troubleshoot these reports?
    A. tcptraceroute
    B. ping
    C. telnet
    D. ps

139. Which command can be used to capture network traffic in pcap format for later analysis by a tool like Wireshark?
    A. tcpcap
    B. pdump
    C. tshark
    D. pcapr

140. You need to determine the owner of an IP address. You have attempted to use nslookup to determine the hostname, but there was no PTR record for the IP. Which command can be used to determine who owns the IP address?
    A. iplookup
    B. ipowner
    C. whois
    D. bg

141. Which command can be used to help diagnose latency issues with a disk?
    A. diskstat
    B. statd
    C. fdisk
    D. ioping

142. Which command can be used to trigger the kernel to update the partition table?
    A. ifdisk
    B. partup
    C. partprobe
    D. uppart

143. Which of the following commands can be used to display historical performance data across several different parameters?
    A. sar
    B. kernperf
    C. pkern
    D. perfshow

144. Which option to sysctl displays all of the available parameters?
    A. -a
    B. -b
    C. -c
    D. -d

145. When examining output from the state column of the ps command, there is a process with a state of D. What state is that process currently in?
    A. Debug
    B. Interruptible sleep
    C. Uninterruptible sleep
    D. Dead

146. Within which file is keyboard mapping set on a Debian or Ubuntu system?
    A. /etc/kbd.conf
    B. /etc/default/keyboard
    C. /etc/default/kbd.conf
    D. /etc/keymap

147. You are troubleshooting printer access on a Linux system. On which port does the CUPS printing daemon listen by default?
    A. 25
    B. 342
    C. 631
    D. 316

148. You need to change ownership of files within a directory to have that ownership inherit all subdirectories and files. Which option to the chown command accomplishes this task?
    A. -o
    B. -R
    C. -r
    D. -f

149. Which utility can be used to find SELinux context violations?
    A. sestat
    B. secv
    C. convio
    D. ausearch

150. You have added a new RAID adapter to the system. Which command can be used to ensure that the adapter was detected by the kernel?
  A. showraid
  B. lsadapt
  C. dmesg
  D. raidlist

151. Which option is used to send a signal to a process when using `pkill`?
  A. -<SIGNAL>
  B. -s
  C. -i
  D. -h

152. You are troubleshooting a directory permission issue. The directory and all subdirectories are owned by root. Within the top-level directory there is another directory that has 755 permissions on it. However, a non-root user cannot obtain a directory listing of that subdirectory. Which of the following might be the issue?
  A. Directory permissions inherit, so the top-level directory must be set to disallow execute for the "other" permission.
  B. Directory permissions need to be 777 on the subdirectory.
  C. The write permission is needed for the subdirectory.
  D. The other permission needs to be 7 for the subdirectory.

153. What is the default request size for `ioping`?
  A. 4 bytes
  B. 4 KB
  C. 512 KB
  D. 1024 KB

154. Within which file can you determine the current I/O scheduler algorithm?
  A. /sys/block/<device>/queue/scheduler
  B. /sys/block/<device>/iosch
  C. /etc/iostat.cfg
  D. /etc/default/ioscheduler

155. Which option to `iftop` prevents hostname lookups from occurring?
  A. -d
  B. -a
  C. -t
  D. -n

156. Which command can be used within the nslookup CLI to change the server to which the query will be sent?
   A. dest
   B. server
   C. srv
   D. auth

157. What are the minimum permissions needed for a user to write into a directory for which they are not the owner and are not in a group that owns the directory?
   A. Write
   B. Read/Write/Execute
   C. Read/Execute
   D. Write/Execute

158. Which of the following protocols provides a means for authentication to occur external to the Linux system?
   A. SSL
   B. SSH
   C. LDAP
   D. AD

159. When creating a file, a user is receiving an error. The file is very large. What command can the user execute in order to determine the file size limitation?
   A. limit
   B. ulimit
   C. filelimit
   D. flimit

160. What permissions are required for a bash script to be executable by everyone?
   A. 755
   B. 644
   C. 777
   D. 222

161. Which command can be used to set file attributes such as making a file immutable?
   A. chr
   B. fattr
   C. chattr
   D. fop

162. Which range of UIDs is typically used by service accounts?
    A. 1 to 999
    B. 1 to 100
    C. 32,768 to 65,535
    D. 1,000 to 1,999

163. Which of the following commands retrieves the current group membership list for a user?
    A. groupmem
    B. groups
    C. lsgr
    D. getgr

164. You have added a swap disk to a Linux server and have executed mkswap. However, on examination of the output from the free command, the swap space is not being used. Which command do you need to execute?
    A. swapon
    B. swap-en
    C. actswap
    D. swpact

165. Which option to ioping sets the size of the request?
    A. -m
    B. -n
    C. -f
    D. -s

166. Which message type(s) should be queried when looking for SELinux access denials or violations?
    A. AVC
    B. DEN
    C. AVC,USER_AVC
    D. STOP,VIOL

167. Which command can be used to obtain extended hardware information, including information about the motherboard?
    A. mbhw
    B. lsmb
    C. dmidecode
    D. lsallhw

168. You have found that a SATA disk within a RAID array has gone bad. Which option to mdadm removes the disk from the RAID array, placing it into a degraded state?

   A. rm
   B. fail
   C. rem
   D. del

169. Which option to whois suppresses the legal disclaimer information from certain registries?

   A. -L
   B. -q
   C. -H
   D. -s

170. Which option to iftop sets the interface on which iftop will listen?

   A. -m
   B. -i
   C. -l
   D. -a

171. To which file can you echo "- - -" in order to cause a scan of a SCSI host adapter for new disks?

   A. /sys/bus/scsi/hostscan
   B. /sys/class/scsi_host/hostN/scan
   C. /sys/class/<host>/scan
   D. /etc/scsiadm

172. When performing local authentication, which file provides encrypted password information?

   A. /etc/passwd
   B. /etc/shadow
   C. /etc/encrpass
   D. /etc/passen

173. Which option is used to display information about current file attributes?

   A. lsfile
   B. lsattr
   C. showfile
   D. exattr

174. The out-of-memory killer has been killing some processes on the system. Which columns within ps output are helpful for determining current memory usage for a given process?
   A. size and rss
   B. mem and swap
   C. free and cache
   D. phy and vir

175. Which signal number corresponds to SIGKILL?
   A. 1
   B. 5
   C. 9
   D. 12

176. Which of the following classes is the default class type queried by the host command?
   A. EX
   B. HS
   C. FO
   D. IN

177. Which option to the netstat command displays the current routing table?
   A. -r
   B. -t
   C. -a
   D. -l

178. Which option to the du command provides summary output?
   A. -o
   B. -h
   C. -s
   D. -u

179. Which of the following commands can be used to find zombie processes?
   A. ps -Z
   B. ps | grep Z
   C. ps | grep zombie
   D. ps -a -z

180. Which command can be used to list all of the detected hardware within a system?
   A. lshw
   B. showhw
   C. lspic
   D. slist

181. Which option to the ioping command sets the number of requests to send?
- **A.** -r
- **B.** -c
- **C.** -n
- **D.** -a

182. Which process state indicates that the process is currently running?
- **A.** C
- **B.** R
- **C.** T
- **D.** V

Chapter 5

Automation and Scripting

THE FOLLOWING COMPTIA LINUX+ EXAM OBJECTIVES ARE COVERED IN THIS CHAPTER:

✓ **5.1 Given a scenario, deploy and execute bash scripts**

- Shell environments and shell variables
  - PATH
  - Global
  - Local
  - export
  - env
  - set
  - printenv
  - echo
- #!/bin/bash
- Sourcing scripts
- Directory and file permissions
  - chmod
- Extensions
- Commenting
  - #
- File globbing
- Shell expansions
  - ${}
  - $()
  - ``

- Redirection and piping
- Exit codes
  - stderr
  - stdin
  - stdout
- Metacharacters
- Positional parameters
- Looping constructs
  - while
  - for
  - until
- Conditional statements
  - if
  - case
- Escaping characters

✓ **5.2 Given a scenario, carry out version control using Git**

- Arguments
  - clone
  - push
  - pull
  - commit
  - merge
  - branch
  - log
  - init
  - config
- Files:
  - .gitignore
  - .git/

✓ **5.3 Summarize orchestration processes and concepts**
- Agent
- Agentless
- Procedures
- Attributes
- Infrastructure automation
- Infrastructure as code
- Inventory
- Automated configuration management
- Build automation

1. You are writing a shell script using bash and need to print the contents of a variable. Which of the following commands can be used to do so?
   A. echo
   B. lf
   C. sp
   D. varpt

2. Which of the following packages provides orchestration for Linux in an agentless manner?
   A. Ansible
   B. Puppet
   C. Automat
   D. vid

3. Which of the following commands can be used to execute a command with a customized environment?
   A. set
   B. env
   C. run
   D. crun

4. Which of the following commands, when used with `git`, retrieves the latest objects from a repository and attempts to incorporate those changes into the local working copy of the repository?
   A. fetch
   B. pull
   C. retr
   D. get

5. Which of the following best describes the concept of infrastructure as code?
   A. The management of switches and routers using compiled programs
   B. The management of servers and other systems using scripting, source code management, and automation
   C. The deployment of hardware using Agile methodologies
   D. Planning for bugs in infrastructure code and allowing time to fix them

6. Which of the following commands changes a file called `script.sh` such that it can be executed by the owner of the file and no one else?
   A. chmod 700 script.sh
   B. chown +x script.sh
   C. chmod script.sh +x
   D. chmod 777 script.sh

7. Which command can be used to add functions and variables to the current shell?
   A. source
   B. echo
   C. en
   D. src

8. Which of the following is the correct method for invoking the bash shell for a script, typically found as the first line of the script?
   A. #!/BASH
   B. #!bash
   C. #!/bash
   D. #!/bin/bash

9. You need to send output from a command to a log file. Overwriting the contents of the log file is acceptable. Which of the following characters is used to redirect output in such a way as to fulfill this scenario?
   A. |
   B. <
   C. >
   D. &

10. You need to create a new empty git repository called repo. Which of the following sequences accomplishes this task?
    A. mkdir repo; cd repo; git init --bare
    B. mkdir repo; git init repo/
    C. git init repo -md
    D. git create repo/

11. Which of the following terms is used in orchestration and automation scenarios to refer to the collection of devices being managed?
    A. Device collection
    B. Inventory
    C. Machines
    D. UsableObjects

12. You need to print output from a bash script such that single quotes appear in the outputted string. Which character should be used as an escape sequence in order to get the single quotes into the output?
    A. /
    B. '
    C. "
    D. \

13. Which exit code indicates success for a bash script?
    A. 0
    B. 1
    C. 2
    D. EOF

14. Which of the following commands produces the output sit sat set?
    A. echo s{i,a,e}t
    B. echo s(i,a,e)t
    C. echo s[i,a,e]t
    D. echo s/i,a,e/t

15. Which of the following characters or character sequences begins a comment in a bash script?
    A. /*
    B. //
    C. #
    D. '

16. Which, if any, file extension is required in order for a bash script to execute?
    A. .sh
    B. .bash
    C. .bat
    D. No special extension is necessary.

17. After fetching changes for a previously cloned git repository, which git command is used to incorporate those changes into the local copy?
    A. put
    B. push
    C. merge
    D. inc

18. Which of the following best describes the role of an agent in software orchestration?
    A. An agent is software that listens for and executes commands from the server.
    B. An agent is used to migrate from one operating system to another.
    C. An agent is a hardware-based token used for authentication.
    D. An agent is not used in software orchestration.

19. Being able to deploy additional servers in response to high demand or load is an example of which type of automation?
   A. Build
   B. Compile
   C. Infrastructure
   D. Config

20. Which command can be used to indicate a local variable within a bash script?
   A. localvar
   B. ll
   C. local
   D. %local%

21. Which git command is used to retrieve a repository from a remote server?
   A. clone
   B. checkout
   C. co
   D. retr

22. You need to echo the name of the script back to the user for usage or help output. Which positional parameter can be used for this purpose?
   A. $me
   B. $1
   C. $myname
   D. $0

23. Which of the following commands can be used to print the contents of the current shell environment?
   A. echoenv
   B. printenv
   C. showenv
   D. envvar

24. You are writing a while loop in a bash script and need to compare two string values. Which operator is used for this purpose?
   A. -ne
   B. =
   C. equal
   D. eq

25. You need to create a bash script that will loop continually and perform some commands within the loop. Which of the following lines will accomplish this task?
    A. `if [ $exit -eq "exit" ]`
    B. `while true; do`
    C. `for ($i = 0, $i++)`
    D. `continue until ($exit)`

26. Which of the following commands changes the location to which HEAD is pointing with git?
    A. `git point`
    B. `git checkout`
    C. `git change`
    D. `git load`

27. You need to declare a variable as part of the environment prior to running a bash script. Which of the following commands accomplishes this?
    A. `dec`
    B. `create`
    C. `export`
    D. `get`

28. Which of the following commands displays the current path in bash?
    A. `echo PATH`
    B. `echo $PATH`
    C. `echo $CURPATH`
    D. `ext $PATH`

29. Which character sequence is used to execute a command within a subshell in a bash script?
    A. `$()`
    B. `subs()`
    C. `$%`
    D. `$(~`

30. You need to make a change to the configuration of the SSH daemon across your infrastructure. Being able to do so from a central server is an example of which type of automation?
    A. Security
    B. Automated configuration management
    C. Development configuration management
    D. Usability management

31. Which option is used with the env command in order to remove a variable from the environment?
    A. -r
    B. -u
    C. -n
    D. -d

32. Within a bash script, you need to run two commands, but only run the second command if the first succeeds. Which of the following metacharacters can be used to accomplish this task?
    A. <>
    B. &
    C. &&
    D. |

33. You need to redirect the output from a command and append that output to a file. Which of the following character sequences accomplishes this task?
    A. >
    B. >>
    C. |
    D. ^

34. You need to obtain a directory listing of all files and directories except those that begin with the letter *p*. Which of the following commands accomplishes this task?
    A. ls -l !p
    B. ls -l [!p]
    C. ls -l [^p]
    D. ls -l [^p]*

35. Which of the following files is used within a git repository in order to indicate files and file patterns that should not be versioned?
    A. novers
    B. .gitignore
    C. gitignore.txt
    D. gitnover

36. You need to iterate through a directory listing and perform an operation on certain files within it. To accomplish this task, you will be using a bash script and a looping construct. Which looping construct is most appropriate for this purpose?
    A. until
    B. do
    C. for
    D. foreach

37. You are debugging a bash script written by a different system administrator. Within the script, you see a command surrounded by backquotes, or `. What will be the result of surrounding the command with backquotes?

   A. The command will execute and send all output to the console.
   B. The command will not execute.
   C. The command will execute as if the $() command substitution was used.
   D. The command will execute and send all output to /dev/null.

38. Which git command displays a short history of commits along with the commit ID?

   A. showhist
   B. list
   C. log
   D. hist

39. You are committing code to a git repository and need to include a message on the command line. Which option enables this behavior?

   A. -m
   B. -h
   C. -f
   D. -l

40. Compiling software when a developer commits code to a certain branch in a repository is an example of which type of automation?

   A. Infrastructure
   B. Build
   C. Complex
   D. DevOps

41. You are working with a MySQL database and need to read in several SQL commands from a file and send them into the MySQL CLI for execution. You will be using STDIN redirection for this. Which of the following commands is correct, assuming a filename of customers.sql?

   A. mysql < customers.sql
   B. mysql | customers.sql
   C. mysql > customers.sql
   D. mysql >< customers.sql

42. You are collaborating on a coding project using git as the source code management tool. Teammates are saying that they cannot see your code, although you have been committing code regularly. Which of the following is most likely the problem?

   A. You have not added commit messages.
   B. You need to send the commit IDs to the teammates.
   C. You have not executed git push to send the code to the server.
   D. You are committing using the -h flag.

43. Which option to the chmod command performs a recursive change?
    A. -re
    B. -R
    C. -c
    D. -v

44. Which character sequence is used to indicate the default case within a case statement in a bash script?
    A. ()
    B. *.*
    C. **
    D. *)

45. Which character sequence indicates the end of an if conditional in a bash script?
    A. }
    B. fi
    C. end
    D. endif

46. What is the name of the default branch in a git repository?
    A. source
    B. main
    C. primary
    D. master

47. You need to use the output from a command as input for another command. Which character facilitates this scenario?
    A. >
    B. |
    C. !
    D. `

48. Which git command shows the current state of the working copy of a repository?
    A. git list
    B. git status
    C. git state
    D. git view

49. Which option to the echo command suppresses the ending newline character that is normally included?
    A. -a
    B. -n
    C. -d
    D. -y

50. Determining the version of software installed on each client node is an example of collecting information for which collection in an automated infrastructure?
    A. Inventory
    B. Group
    C. Procedure
    D. Build

51. You need to redirect STDERR from a command into a file to capture the errors. Which character sequence can be used for this purpose?
    A. >
    B. %2>
    C. 2>
    D. %%>

52. You need to make a change to your git environment because your email address has changed. Which of the following commands ensures that your new email address will be used for all subsequent commits?
    A. git config user.email
    B. git change email
    C. git config email.addr
    D. git config email.address

53. Which shell built-in command is used to display a list of read-only variables?
    A. ro
    B. readonly
    C. env-ro
    D. ro-env

54. Assume that you're using the bash shell and want to prevent output redirects from accidentally overwriting existing files. Which command and option can be used to invoke this behavior?
    A. setoutput -f
    B. overwrite=no
    C. overwrite -n
    D. set -C

55. You have received a file that does not have a file extension. Which command can you run to help determine what type of file it might be?
    A. grep
    B. telnet
    C. file
    D. export

56. Which of the following commands will display the last 50 lines of your command history when using bash, including commands from the current session?
    A. `bashhist 50`
    B. `history 50`
    C. `cat .bash_history`
    D. `tail -f .bash_history`

57. When using bash, how would you execute the last command starting with a certain string, even if that command was not the last one that you typed?
    A. Precede the command with ! and then the string to search for.
    B. Search for the command in history.
    C. Precede the command with a ? and then the string to search for.
    D. This is not possible with bash.

58. Which shell built-in command can be used to determine the location from which a given command will be run?
    A. `type`
    B. `when`
    C. `find`
    D. `help`

59. Which command is used to read and execute commands from a file in the bash shell?
    A. `run`
    B. `execute`
    C. `source`
    D. `func`

60. You need a command to be executed on logout for all users. Within which file should this be placed (assuming all users are using bash)?
    A. `~/.bash_logout`
    B. `/etc/bash.bash_logout`
    C. `/home/.bash_logout`
    D. `/etc/bash_logout`

61. Which of the following commands removes an environment variable that has been set?
    A. `profile --unset`
    B. `env -u`
    C. `set -u`
    D. `import`

62. When setting the shebang line of a shell script, which of the following commands will help to determine the location of the interpreter automatically?
    A. `#!/usr/bin/env bash`
    B. `#!/bin/bash`
    C. `#!env`
    D. `/bin/int bash`

63. Which of the following best describes the PS1 environment variable?
    A. PS1 is used to set the location of the `PostScript` command.
    B. PS1 is used to define the default shell prompt for bash.
    C. PS1 is used as a per-system variable.
    D. PS1 is user-defined and does not have a default value or setting.

64. Which variable within a bash script is used to access the first command-line parameter?
    A. `$ARG`
    B. `$0`
    C. `$1`
    D. `$ARG0`

65. Which of the following commands will print a list of six numbers beginning at 0?
    A. `list 0-5`
    B. `seq 0 1 5`
    C. `echo 0-5`
    D. `seq 0 1 6`

66. Which of the following commands will execute a script and then exit the shell?
    A. `run`
    B. `source`
    C. `./`
    D. `exec`

67. Which command within a shell script awaits user input and places that input into a variable?
    A. `exec`
    B. `get`
    C. `read`
    D. `prompt`

68. What characters are used to mark a sequence of commands as a function within a shell script?
  A. Parentheses to declare the function (optional), and curly braces to contain the commands
  B. Curly braces to declare the function, and parentheses to contain the commands
  C. Square brackets to declare the function, and curly braces to contain the commands
  D. Run quotes to denote the function

69. Which character sequence is used to terminate a `case` statement in a bash script?
  A. end
  B. done
  C. esac
  D. caseend

70. Which option to `declare` displays output in a way that could then be used as input to another command?
  A. -o
  B. -n
  C. -p
  D. -m

71. Which characters are used to denote the beginning and end of the test portion of a `while` loop in a shell script?
  A. Parentheses ( )
  B. Curly braces { }
  C. Square brackets [ ]
  D. Double quotes " "

72. When using the `test` built-in with one argument, what will be the return if its argument is not `null`?
  A. false
  B. true
  C. unknown
  D. -1

73. Which environment variable is used when changing directory with the tilde character, such as cd ~ ?
  A. HOMEDIR
  B. HOMEPATH
  C. HOME
  D. MAILPATH

74. You would like to examine the entries for a single file through the `git commit` history. Which command should be used for this purpose, assuming a filename of nhl_scores.php?

   A. `git log --history nhl_scores.php`
   B. `git log --follow nhl_scores.php`
   C. `git history nhl_scores.php`
   D. `git commit-history nhl_scores.php`

75. Which of the following best describes attributes of an inventory within an automated infrastructure?

   A. Parameters such as the client IP address and software versions
   B. The number of client nodes
   C. The software used on the server for the orchestration
   D. The architectural pattern for deployment

76. Which operator should be used when comparing integers to determine if one is equal to another in a bash script?

   A. `-ro`
   B. `===`
   C. `-eq`
   D. `-fe`

77. You would like to run several commands in succession but not have the output sent into the next command. Which of the following metacharacters will accomplish this task?

   A. `&`
   B. `>`
   C. `;`
   D. `|`

78. Which escape sequence is used to denote the alert or bell?

   A. `\a`
   B. `\b`
   C. `\c`
   D. `\d`

79. Which of the following is a valid variable declaration in a bash script, setting the variable NUM equal to 1?

   A. `NUM = 1`
   B. `$NUM = 1`
   C. `NUM= 1`
   D. `NUM=1`

80. Which of the following commands will obtain the date in seconds since the epoch and place it into a variable called DATE within a shell script?
    A. DATE="$(date +%s)"
    B. DATE="date"
    C. DATE="$(date)";
    D. DATE="$date %s"

81. Which sequence is used to mark the beginning and end of the commands to execute within a for loop in a shell script?
    A. Curly braces { }
    B. The keywords do and done
    C. Semicolons ;
    D. Tabs

82. Which option to the declare command will create a variable that is read-only?
    A. -r
    B. -ro
    C. -p
    D. -x

83. Which environment variable controls the format of dates and times, such as a 12-hour or 24-hour formatted clock?
    A. LOCALE_DATE
    B. DATE_FORMAT
    C. LC_TIME
    D. LC_DATE

84. Which option to netstat displays interface information in a table-like format that might be suitable for use with scripting?
    A. -i
    B. -r
    C. -t
    D. -l

85. You are running a shell script from within your SSH session. Which key combination can be used to terminate the script?
    A. Ctrl+X
    B. Ctrl+-
    C. Ctrl+C
    D. Ctrl+Esc

86. Which of the following conditionals in a bash script will test if the variable DAY is equal to SUNDAY?
    A. if ($DAY == "SUNDAY")
    B. if ($DAY -eq "SUNDAY")
    C. if [[$DAY == "SUNDAY"]]
    D. if [DAY = "SUNDAY"]

87. Which of the following commands adds ~/code/bin to the path?
    A. PATH=~/code/bin:$PATH
    B. PATH=/code/bin:$PATH
    C. PATH=/home/code/bin:$PATH
    D. PATH=PATH:~/code/bin

88. Which option to git merge can be used to attempt to roll back a merge that has conflicts?
    A. --rollback
    B. --abort
    C. --rewind
    D. --restart

89. Which environment variable can be used to change the default path for a new git repository created with git init?
    A. GIT_DIR
    B. GIT_HOME
    C. GIT_DEST
    D. GIT_LOC

90. Which character sequence is used to add a horizontal tab using echo with a bash script?
    A. \h
    B. \t
    C. \a
    D. \f

91. You need to exclude a build file, called build.o, from being tracked by git. Which character sequence can be used in the .gitignore file to exclude or ignore that file in all directories?
    A. build.o
    B. /build.o
    C. **/build.o
    D. build.*

92. Which file-globbing sequence will match all files that begin with an uppercase *A* or an uppercase *F*?
    A. [AF]*
    B. [af]*
    C. *AF*
    D. AF*

93. Assuming a remote name of origin, which git command can be used to obtain additional information about the remote?
    A. git show origin
    B. git remote show origin
    C. git show remotes
    D. git remote list

94. Which character sequence displays the number of command-line arguments that were passed to a bash script?
    A. $NUM
    B. $CLA
    C. $+
    D. $#

95. Which environment variable can be set if you wish to automatically log users out of their shell after a certain period of inactivity?
    A. TIMEOUT
    B. TMOUT
    C. TO
    D. IDLETIME

96. You are debugging a bash script and notice a line that contains: echo $NUM   #sending $NUM to output. What will be the result of this line when executed?
    A. It will not output anything, because it is commented out.
    B. It will cause a syntax error, because it is invalid syntax.
    C. It will output the contents of the NUM variable.
    D. It will output the sequence "$NUM".

97. When cloning a repository with git clone, you need to change the name of the remote so that it is not called origin. Which option can be added to git clone to accomplish this task?
    A. --origin
    B. --remote
    C. --name
    D. --remote-name

98. When working in a virtual server environment, which column within `iostat` output shows the amount (percentage) of time spent in an involuntary wait scenario due to the hypervisor?
    A. proc
    B. wait
    C. user
    D. steal

99. If you need to temporarily reconfigure all locale variables and settings for a given session, which environment variable can be used?
    A. LC_LIST
    B. LC_GLOBAL
    C. LC_ALL
    D. ALL_LOCALE

100. A set of commands to execute on a client node is an example of which type of infrastructure automation?
    A. Procedure
    B. Subset
    C. Agent
    D. Collection

101. Which character sequence is used to indicate the end of an individual clause within a case statement in a bash script?
    A. //
    B. 'eol
    C. ;;
    D. <

102. Which of the following commands removes a currently defined aliased command?
    A. remove
    B. rm
    C. unalias
    D. delete

103. Which of the following tests will determine if a file exists in the context of a shell script?
    A. -a
    B. -e
    C. -m
    D. -i

104. Which of the following values for the LANG environment variable will configure the system to bypass locale translations where possible?
- **A.** LANG=COMPAT
- **B.** LANG=NONE
- **C.** LANG=C
- **D.** LANG=END

105. Which option to the `git config` command shows all of the configuration parameters that have been set?
- **A.** --list
- **B.** --show
- **C.** -u
- **D.** --display

106. Which character sequence should be used if you need to redirect STDERR to a file and append to the file?
- **A.** 2>
- **B.** 2>>
- **C.** &>>
- **D.** 1>>

107. When working with infrastructure as code, you have received a file with a .yml extension. What is the likely format for the contents of this file?
- **A.** YAML
- **B.** XML
- **C.** Tab-delimited
- **D.** Text

108. Which of the following best describes the result of the command `cat /etc/passwd | cut -d: -f1 > users.txt`?
- **A.** The first field will be extracted from the passwd file and placed into a file called users.txt.
- **B.** The second field will be extracted from the passwd file and placed into a file called users.txt.
- **C.** The passwd file will be separated based on a colon and output placed into users.txt.
- **D.** The passwd file will be sent to the terminal where only fields beginning with a colon will be shown and placed into a file called users.txt.

109. Which shell built-in can be used to move positional parameters down, where $2 becomes $1, $3 becomes $2, and so on?

  A. move
  B. rev
  C. shift
  D. dec

110. You are using `git pull` to obtain changes to a shared repository. Which option should you add to `git pull` in order to prevent autocommit so that you can look at the results of the merge first?

  A. --pre-merge
  B. --no-auto
  C. --nc
  D. --no-commit

111. Which of the following pairs indicates the beginning and end of an `until` loop in a bash script?

  A. do; done
  B. start; stop
  C. beg; end
  D. until; litnu

112. Which exit code is used to indicate a general error within a bash script?

  A. 0
  B. 1
  C. 255
  D. -1

113. When scripting for build automation, you need to run a configure script prior to running the make command. Which of the following will execute the configure script, assuming that it's in the same directory as the script invoking it?

  A. configure
  B. ./configure
  C. ../configure
  D. /configure

114. Assuming that a file has been previously added and committed to git, which option to the `git commit` command can be used to automatically add and commit the file?

  A. -a
  B. -b
  C. -c
  D. -d

115. Which locale-related environment variable is used for currency-related localization?
    A. LC_MONE
    B. LC_CURRENCY
    C. LC_MONETARY
    D. LC_CURR

116. Which of the following lines added to .profile in a user's home directory will set their time zone to Central time?
    A. TZ=/Central ; export TZ
    B. TIMEZONE='America/Chicago' ; export TIMEZONE
    C. set TZ=/Central
    D. TZ='America/Chicago'; export TZ

117. Which of the following creates an array in a bash script?
    A. ARRAY=(val1 val2)
    B. ARRAY = "val1 val2"
    C. ARRAY_PUSH($ARRAY,"val1","val2");
    D. ARRAY{0} = "val1"

118. Which test within a shell script while loop will examine one value to see if it is less than another?
    A. -less
    B. -lessThan
    C. -lt
    D. -lthan

119. Assuming that a space-separated list of values has been defined as LIST="one two three four", which of the following for loop constructs will iterate through the elements in the list?
    A. for LIST
    B. for VAR in LIST
    C. for VAR in $LIST
    D. for $LIST -> $VAR

120. Which keyword(s) is/are used to begin an alternate condition within a bash script?
    A. if
    B. else if
    C. elif
    D. elsif

121. Within which directory does git store a local copy of the repository metadata?
    A. .gitmeta
    B. gitlocalmeta
    C. .git
    D. git

122. You need to redirect both STDERR and STDOUT to a file. Which of the following character sequences accomplishes this task?
    A. 2>
    B. 2>&1
    C. 2+1
    D. +2+1

123. Within a bash script, you need to run two commands, but only run the second command if the first fails. Which of the following metacharacters can be used to accomplish this task?
    A. <>
    B. &
    C. &&
    D. ||

124. Which of the following commands creates a new branch called `project1` and points the HEAD toward that branch?
    A. `git branch project1`
    B. `git checkout project1`
    C. `git checkout -b project1`
    D. `git create project1 -H`

125. Which of the following best describes the difference between a `while` and an `until` loop in a bash script?
    A. A `while` loop always executes once; an `until` loop does not.
    B. An `until` loop always executes once; a `while` loop does not.
    C. A `while` loop executes as long as a condition is true; an `until` loop executes until the condition is false.
    D. An `until` loop executes until a condition is true; a `while` loop executes until a condition is false.

126. Which statement can be used in a bash script to determine if variable $num1 is greater than $num2, assuming both variables contain integers?
    A. `if [ "$num1" -gt "$num2" ]`
    B. `if [ "$num1" > "$num2" ]`
    C. `if ($num1 -gta $num2)`
    D. `if [ $num1 gt $num2 ]`

127. Which of the following protocols is typically used for agentless infrastructure orchestration?
- **A.** SMTP
- **B.** ICMP
- **C.** SSH
- **D.** FTP

128. Which of the following character sequences expands or interpolates a variable called VAR within a bash script?
- **A.** VAR
- **B.** $(VAR}
- **C.** ${VAR}
- **D.** *VAR*

Chapter 6

Practice Exam

1. Which command enables you to view the current IRQ assignments?
   A. view /proc/irq
   B. cat /proc/interrupts
   C. cat /dev/irq
   D. less /dev/irq

2. Configuration of udev devices is done by working with files in which directory?
   A. /udev/devices
   B. /devices/
   C. /udev/config
   D. /etc/udev

3. Which command is used to automatically load a module and its dependencies?
   A. modprobe
   B. lsmod
   C. insmod
   D. rmmod

4. During boot of a system with GRUB, which key can be pressed to display the GRUB menu?
   A. Shift
   B. E
   C. V
   D. H

5. Which command can be used to view the kernel ring buffer in order to troubleshoot the boot process?
   A. lsboot
   B. boot-log
   C. krblog
   D. dmesg

6. Which statement best describes the following, displayed using the ls -la command?
   lrwxrwxrwx. 1 root root 35 Jul 8 2014 .fetchmailrc -> .configs/fetchmail/.fetchmailrc
   A. It is a file called .fetchmailrc that is linked using a symbolic link.
   B. It is a file called .configs/fetchmail/.fetchmailrc that is owned by lrwxrwxrwx.
   C. It is a directory called .fetchmailrc that is owned by user Jul.
   D. It is a local directory called .configs/fetchmail/.fetchmailrc.

7. Which command is used with systemd in order to list the available service units?
   A. systemd list-units
   B. systemctl list-units
   C. systemd unit-list
   D. systemctl show-units

8. Which option to lspci is used to display both numeric codes and device names?
   A. -numdev
   B. -n
   C. -nn
   D. -devnum

9. Which command and option can be used to determine whether a given service is currently loaded?
   A. systemctl --ls
   B. telinit
   C. systemctl status
   D. sysctl -a

10. When partitioning a disk for a mail server running postfix, which partition/mounted directory should be the largest in order to allow for mail storage?
    A. /etc
    B. /usr/bin
    C. /mail
    D. /var

11. Which YUM option displays the dependencies for the package specified?
    A. list
    B. deplist
    C. dependencies
    D. listdeps

12. Which options for an rpm command will display verbose output for an installation along with progress of the installation?
    A. -ivh
    B. -wvh
    C. --avh
    D. --ins-verbose

13. Which command will search for a package named zsh on a Debian system?
    A. apt-cache search zsh
    B. apt-get search zsh
    C. apt-cache locate zsh
    D. apt-search zsh

14. Which rpm option can be used to verify that no files have been altered since installation?
    A. -V
    B. -v
    C. --verbose
    D. --filesum

15. Which of the following command lines would monitor a single process called nagios in a continuous manner?
    A. top -n 1
    B. top -p 23
    C. ps -nagios
    D. top -p `pidof nagios`

16. Which option to xfs_metadump displays a progress indicator?
    A. -g
    B. -p
    C. -f
    D. -v

17. The SAN has crashed again, and one of the filesystems in a Linux server has become significantly corrupt as a result. Which command and option can be used to attempt to examine the contents of the drive without causing more damage?
    A. fdisk -f
    B. mke2fs -c
    C. debugfs -c
    D. ls -a

18. Which of the following commands helps you to determine information about a given window within an X session, including information on the window size and its position?
    A. xkbinfo
    B. xdspy
    C. xwininfo
    D. xver

19. Which file is used to indicate the local time zone on a Linux server?
    A. /etc/timez
    B. /etc/timezoneconfig
    C. /etc/localtime
    D. /etc/localtz

20. Within which directory will you find files related to the time zone for various regions?
    A. /etc/timezoneinfo
    B. /etc/zoneinfo
    C. /var/zoneinfo
    D. /usr/share/zoneinfo

21. Within which directory should you place files in order for the files to be copied to a user's home directory when the user is created?
    A. /etc/skel
    B. /etc/homedir
    C. /home/usertemplate
    D. /etc/template

22. Which command displays a list of jobs currently scheduled with at?
    A. atlist
    B. atq
    C. atl
    D. at --jobs

23. Which of the following encodings provides a multibyte representation of characters?
    A. ISO-8859
    B. UTF-8
    C. ISO-L
    D. UFTMulti

24. On which port does LDAP over SSL operate?
    A. Port 53
    B. Port 389
    C. Port 636
    D. Port 443

25. Which of the following commands will set an account to expire based on the number of days elapsed since January 1, 1970?
    A. `passwd -e`
    B. `chage -E`
    C. `usermod -l`
    D. `chguser`

26. Which option to SSH enables the use of a key for authentication?
    A. `-i`
    B. `-k`
    C. `-f`
    D. `--key`

27. In a scripting scenario, you need to prevent `sudo` from prompting for credentials or for any other reason. Which option to `sudo` is used to indicate this?
    A. `-n`
    B. `--noprompt`
    C. `-i`
    D. `-q`

28. Which runlevel is typically used for single user mode, as indicated in `/etc/inittab`?
    A. 1
    B. 2
    C. 5
    D. 6

29. Which of the following commands provides an overview of the current memory usage along with swap space and its current utilization?
    A. `mem`
    B. `free`
    C. `pstat`
    D. `swap`

30. Which of the following commands can be used to display the current disk utilization, including free space?
    A. `df`
    B. `du`
    C. `diskutil`
    D. `diskuse`

31. Which of the following commands displays CPU-related performance information a total of 10 times gathered every two seconds?
    A. `sar -u 2 10`
    B. `sar -u 10 2`
    C. `sar -u 2`
    D. `uptime -t`

32. Which option to `iostat` causes the display to output in megabytes?
    A. `-k`
    B. `-l`
    C. `-m`
    D. `-o m`

33. You are working with a legacy CentOS 5 system and need to re-create the initial RAM disk. Which of the following commands is used for this purpose?
    A. `mkinitrd`
    B. `mkramdisk`
    C. `mkdisk --init`
    D. `mkfs.init`

34. Which compression method is used for creation of a bzImage?
    A. zip
    B. bzip3
    C. gzip
    D. Cannot be determined

35. Which options to the `fsck` command will find and automatically assume that it should repair errors that it finds?
    A. `-ry`
    B. `-vy`
    C. `-my`
    D. `-xy`

36. What is the name of the unit to which a `systemd` system is booted in order to start other levels?
    A. `default.target`
    B. `init.target`
    C. `initial.target`
    D. `load.target`

37. Which command is used to format a swap partition?
   A. `mkfs -swap`
   B. `mkswap`
   C. `format -swap`
   D. `mksw`

38. You see the word `defaults` within `/etc/fstab`. Which options are encompassed within the defaults?
   A. ro, exec, auto
   B. rw, suid, dev, exec, auto, nouser, async
   C. rw, exec, auto, nouser, async
   D. rw, exec, nouser, async, noauto, suid

39. Which command is used to remove unused filesystem blocks from thinly provisioned storage?
   A. `thintrim`
   B. `thtrim`
   C. `fstrim`
   D. `fsclean`

40. Which option to `mdadm` is used to create a new array?
   A. `--create`
   B. `--start`
   C. `--begin`
   D. `--construct`

41. Which of the following commands creates a logical volume with LVM?
   A. `lvc`
   B. `lvcreate`
   C. `lvlist`
   D. `lvmake`

42. Which of the following commands shows network sockets and their allocated memory?
   A. `ss -m`
   B. `mpas`
   C. `mem`
   D. `free`

43. When troubleshooting a potential hardware problem, you need to determine which physical interface is being used for a certain address. One way to accomplish this is with the `ping` command in order to monitor the activity lights on the device. Which of the following options to `ping` will flood the interface with ECHO_REQUEST packets?
    A. -e
    B. -a
    C. -c
    D. -f

44. Which of the following dd commands reads and writes bytes one megabyte at a time?
    A. `dd bsl=1024M`
    B. `dd size=1M`
    C. `dd bs=1M`
    D. `dd rw=1M`

45. Which option to the `rsync` command examines only the file size as a means of determining whether the file should be synchronized?
    A. `--filesize`
    B. `--size-only`
    C. `--list-size`
    D. `--file-size`

46. When creating MX records for a zone, which of the following is the highest-priority mail exchanger?
    A. 0
    B. 10
    C. 20
    D. 100

47. On which protocol and port are zone transfer requests sent?
    A. UDP/53
    B. ICMP/53
    C. TCP/143
    D. TCP/53

48. Which type can be used with the `dig` command to test a zone transfer?
    A. xfr
    B. transfer
    C. zxfr
    D. axfr

49. Which of the following files is used to define the filesystems shared by NFS?
    A. /etc/nfs.cfg
    B. /etc/nfs.conf
    C. /etc/export.nfs
    D. /etc/exports

50. Which option in dhcpd.conf specifies the maximum amount of time that a client is allowed to have a DHCP lease?
    A. max-time
    B. max-lease-time
    C. lease-max
    D. maximum-lease-duration

51. You are troubleshooting an authentication issue for a user. You believe the system uses local files and LDAP for authentication. Which of the following lines in /etc/nsswitch.conf shows those authentication mechanisms?
    A. passwd: files ldap
    B. passwd [files ldap]
    C. auth: local ldap
    D. auth: localfiles ldap

52. Which of the following commands can be used to generate a private and public key pair for authentication with SSH?
    A. ssh-createkey
    B. sshkey
    C. ssh-key
    D. ssh-keygen

53. Which file contains a list of keys that will be accepted for authentication for a given user?
    A. ~/ssh/keys
    B. ~/.ssh/pubkeys
    C. ~/.ssh/keyauth
    D. ~/.ssh/authorized_keys

54. A newly added SATA disk is not showing up during the boot process. Where can you check to begin troubleshooting this issue?
    A. Using system logging
    B. Using debugfs
    C. Within the fdisk utility
    D. Within the computer BIOS or firmware

55. Which of the following commands will set the environment variable JAVA_PATH equal to /home/user/java2 when using the bash shell?

   A. `invoke JAVA_PATH=/home/user/java2`
   B. `export JAVA_PATH=/home/user/java2`
   C. `envvar JAVA_PATH=/home/user/java2`
   D. `echo JAVA_PATH=/home/user/java2`

56. Which option in `.bashrc` sets the number of commands to keep in the `.bash_history` file?

   A. HISTLIMIT
   B. HISTORYFILE
   C. HISTFILESIZE
   D. HISTNUM

57. You are creating a bash script of user information. Which of the following commands prints the username and real name of all users in /etc/passwd in a tab-separated format?

   A. `cut -d: -f 1,6 /etc/passwd`
   B. `sed 's/://' /etc/passwd`
   C. `awk -F: '{print $1,$5}' OFS="\t" /etc/passwd`
   D. `cat -o "\t" /etc/passwd`

58. Which `git clone` command will clone a repository called `portalutils` into a directory called `utils`?

   A. `git clone ssh://sourcehost/portalutils -d utils`
   B. `git clone ssh://sourcehost:/portalutils utils`
   C. `git clone ssh://sourcehost/:portalutils utils`
   D. `git clone ssh://sourcehost::portalutils -d utils`

59. Which of the following commands is necessary for making a variable defined in your current shell available to child processes?

   A. export
   B. source
   C. let
   D. def

60. You are watching another administrator perform some work on a server. As part of that work, the admin uses the following command: `. variables.sh`

   Which of the following is the equivalent of `. variables.sh`?

   A. `let variables.sh`
   B. `set variables.sh`
   C. `source variables.sh`
   D. `var variables.sh`

61. Which of the following shows a valid bash function called sayHello?
    A. function sayHello() { echo "hello"; }
    B. function sayHello{}
    C. function sayHello() { echo Hello }
    D. function sayHello() { echo Hello } ;

62. Which option to useradd sets the number of days between password expiration and when the account is disabled?
    A. -n
    B. -f
    C. -e
    D. -g

63. Which command option can be used to remove all cron jobs for a given user using the crontab command?
    A. -d
    B. -e
    C. -r
    D. -l

64. Which command is used to parse log-file entries on a systemd-based system?
    A. logger
    B. journalentry
    C. jrnctl
    D. journalctl

65. Which of the following syslog facilities captures messages from the lp printing facility?
    A. auth
    B. messages
    C. lpr
    D. root

66. Which port needs to be allowed through the firewall for standard LDAP traffic to be received by the server?
    A. TCP port 25
    B. TCP port 443
    C. TCP port 143
    D. TCP port 389

67. Which of the following is the correct syntax to connect to host.example.com using SSH on port 2200?
   A. ssh -l 2200 host.example.com
   B. ssh host;example.com
   C. ssh host.example.com:2200
   D. ssh host:2200 -d example.com

68. Which option to the tar command preserves permissions?
   A. -x
   B. -v
   C. -z
   D. -p

69. When working with a patch file, which option can be used to have the patching process ignore whitespace?
   A. -w
   B. -i
   C. -e
   D. -p

70. When using the dm-crypt command, which type of encryption is used by default?
   A. plain
   B. SHA-256
   C. LUKS
   D. loop

71. Which option to journalctl displays the output in reverse, with newest entries first?
   A. -n
   B. -r
   C. -f
   D. -b

72. Which systemd target can be used as an alternative to rescue mode when recovery is not possible in rescue mode?
   A. emerg
   B. recover
   C. control-recover
   D. emergency

73. When performing an `rsync` across devices, you receive errors that file ownership cannot be preserved, likely due to missing users or groups on the destination system. Which option should be removed from the `rsync` options in order to not preserve user and group ownership?
   A. -go
   B. -o
   C. -no-ownership
   D. -remove-owners

74. Which option to `ping` enables the bypass of the routing tables?
   A. -q
   B. -r
   C. -b
   D. -A

75. Which option to the `patch` command makes a backup of files?
   A. -d
   B. -b
   C. -s
   D. -c

76. A piece of software on client machines that listens for connections and executes commands on behalf of the server in an orchestration is commonly known as which of the following?
   A. Executor
   B. Runner
   C. Agent
   D. Host

77. Which escape characters represent a carriage return and newline in bash?
   A. \enter
   B. \r\n
   C. \n
   D. \c\n

78. Which file test within a bash script checks to see if the file exists?
   A. -f
   B. -o
   C. -l
   D. -p

79. Which of the following will execute a bash script called `test.sh` even if the execute bit is not set?
    A. `./test.sh`
    B. `test.sh --execute`
    C. `bash test.sh`
    D. `run test.sh`

80. When testing an exclude pattern for a `.gitignore` file, which `git` command and option can be used to see the results of what will be ignored?
    A. `git ls-files -i --exclude-standard`
    B. `git ls-files --ignored`
    C. `git show-ignored`
    D. `git -ls ignored`

81. Which of the following characters is used to redirect `STDIN`, sending the contents of a file called `file.txt` into a script called `script.sh`?
    A. `script.sh < file.txt`
    B. `script.sh | file.txt`
    C. `file.txt | script.sh`
    D. `./script.sh > file.txt`

82. Which option to the `tune2fs` command sets the maximum mount count before the system will automatically run `fsck` on the partition on boot?
    A. `-b`
    B. `-c`
    C. `-C`
    D. `-a`

83. Which option to the `mount` command can be used to simulate the mount process without actually mounting the filesystem?
    A. `-q`
    B. `-v`
    C. `-l`
    D. `-f`

84. Which of the following commands shows the current default route without performing DNS lookups on the IP address(es) involved?
    A. `netstat -rn`
    B. `netstat -n`
    C. `netstat -r`
    D. `netstat -f`

85. Which tool can be used to measure the memory usage of individual processes in order to aid in capacity planning?
    A. ps
    B. iotop
    C. iostat
    D. ifconfig

86. When viewing statistics with vmstat, which statistic represents the time that the CPU spent waiting for I/O?
    A. sy
    B. us
    C. wa
    D. io

87. What time intervals are represented by the three numbers in the load-average output obtained with the uptime command?
    A. 1, 5, and 15 minutes
    B. 5, 10, and 15 minutes
    C. 10, 30, and 60 seconds
    D. 1, 3, and 5 minutes

88. Which option to sysctl displays all values and their current settings?
    A. -a
    B. -b
    C. -d
    D. -c

89. When using systemctl to kill a process, what is the default signal sent to a process?
    A. SIGKILL
    B. SIGTERM
    C. SIGINT
    D. SIGCALL

90. You are having difficulty with shared libraries on the system. Which of the following commands will print the current directories and libraries in the cache?
    A. ldconfig -C
    B. ldd -f
    C. ldconfig -p
    D. ldd -b

Appendix

Answers and Explanations

Chapter 1: Hardware and System Configuration

1. A. The `modprobe` command loads the module and its dependencies, if applicable. The `lsmod` command is used to list currently loaded modules, making answer B incorrect. The `insmod` command will load a given module but not its dependencies. Answer D, `rmmod`, is used to remove a module from memory.

2. C. The keyword `single` given on the Linux kernel command line will boot the system into single-user mode. The other options are not valid.

3. A. The Shift key, if pressed when control has first been handed to GRUB, will cause the GRUB menu to be displayed.

4. D. The `dmesg` command displays the contents of the kernel ring buffer. On many Linux distributions, this log is also saved to `/var/log/dmesg`. The other options shown for this question are not valid commands.

5. D. The `lsmod` command is used to list currently loaded kernel modules, thereby making answer D correct for this question. The `insmod` command (answer A) is used to load modules. Answer C is a valid command but not a valid option for that command, and answer B does not exist.

6. D. The ESP is typically mounted at `/boot/efi`. Files with an `efi` extension, like `linux.efi`, might be found in dual-boot scenarios, but the `.efi` extension is not technically required.

7. A. The `mount` command is used to mount drives in Linux. The source and destination mount point are expected as arguments. Drive partitions begin at number 1, making the first partition number 1.

8. D. If a working device does not appear in `lsmod`, it typically means the kernel has a driver already loaded by virtue of being compiled into the kernel itself rather than loaded through a module. The use of `systemd` (answer A) or `initramfs` (answer B) would have no effect.

9. C. The -w option causes the module to wait until it's no longer needed prior to unloading. The other options are not valid for `rmmod`.

10. A. The `update-grub` command sends its output to `STDOUT`. Therefore, you must redirect using > and send that output to the correct file. The other options are not valid for this purpose. Answers C and D are not valid commands, while answer B contains invalid options and an invalid location for the destination file.

11. B. MBR-based disks can be partitioned with up to four primary partitions, one of which can be further partitioned or extended into logical partitions.

12. B. 0x82 is Linux swap, while 0x83 is Linux. NTFS is 0x07, and FAT is 0.0c.

13. A. The /etc/default/grub file can be used for this purpose. You may also edit /boot/grub/grub.cfg, but this was not an option given for this question.

14. C. The -o option can be used to specify a destination file to which output will be sent instead of STDOUT. The other options listed in this question do not exist.

15. A. The /boot partition will typically be much less than 500 MB but should not be undersized. The used space within /boot will increase as more kernels are added, such as during an upgrade process.

16. B. The pvcreate command initializes a physical partition for future use as a logical volume with LVM.

17. D. The grub2-install command is used to install GRUB onto a disk. The second SATA disk would be /dev/sdb, therefore making answer D the correct option.

18. C. The lvcreate command is used to create logical volumes with LVM. The pvcreate command initializes physical volumes prior to creating logical volumes. The commands in the other two options for this question do not exist.

19. A. Physical volumes are initialized first, followed by volume group creation, and then logical volume creation.

20. B. The grub-mkconfig command should be run after making a change to the /etc/default/grub file so that a new configuration file can be created with the changed option(s).

21. C. The lvmdiskscan command looks for physical volumes that have been initialized for use with LVM.

22. D. GRUB Legacy begins counting at 0 and separates the disk letter and partition with a comma, therefore making 0,0 the first partition on the first disk. Answers A and C are not the first disk on the system, and answer B contains a nonexistent partition.

23. B. The command to install GRUB is grub-install, and the first SATA drive is /dev/sda. A device listed as hda is typically a PATA drive, thereby making those options incorrect.

24. C. The -y option will attempt to repair automatically, essentially answering 'y' or yes instead of prompting. Of the other options, only -V is valid and will produce verbose output.

25. D. The first step is to use fdisk to create one or more partitions. Then format the partitions, and then mount the partitions for use. Various filesystem types can be created with mkfs and its subcommands. These filesystem types include ext3, ext4, xfs, and ntfs.

26. B. The tune2fs command can be used for this purpose but should be used with care because it can result in data corruption.

27. B. The addition of journaling in ext3 increased filesystem reliability and performance.

Appendix • Answers and Explanations

28. D. The /srv hierarchy is used for data for server programs. The /etc hierarchy is configuration information, while /var is also data files but variable files such as mail files. The /tmp directory is for temporary files. Because each path begins with a /, it is considered an absolute path.

29. C. The -a option mounts all filesystems in /etc/fstab that are currently available. Of the other options listed, only the -f option is available, and it is a shortcut to the "fake" option, which does not do anything except perform a dry run of the mount.

30. A. The tune2fs command displays a lot of information about filesystems including the number of times the filesystem has been mounted.

31. A. The -g option displays progress of the dump. The other options listed do not exist.

32. A. The du command will report on disk usage in a recursive manner, unlike the other commands shown here.

33. C. The /etc/fstab file is used to store information about the filesystems to mount within the system.

34. D. The /media mount point is used for removable media. See https://refspecs.linuxfoundation.org/FHS_3.0/fhs/index.html for more information on the FHS.

35. A. The /etc/mtab file contains currently mounted filesystems. Note that /etc/fstab contains filesystem information but not about which filesystems are currently mounted.

36. B. The -r option causes umount to attempt to remount in read-only mode. The -v option is verbose mode, and the -f option forces the operation. The -o option does not exist.

37. D. The proper order is the device (UUID or partition) followed by the directory to mount that device, followed by its type and options, and then the dump and fsck settings.

38. A. The blkid command will show partition UUIDs. You can also get this information with the lsblk -no UUID <partition> command. The other commands shown in this question do not accomplish the required task.

39. D. The xfs_info command is equivalent to xfs_growfs -n.

40. B. The mkfs.btrfs command is used to create btrfs filesystems and does not require the drive to be partitioned.

41. A. The tune2fs command is used for this purpose, and the -c option sets the mount count for the specified partition. The dumpe2fs command is used to print the superblock and block group information.

42. B. The parted command can be used to resize partitions in such a way. The mkfs command is not used for this purpose, and the other two options do not exist.

43. C. The VFAT filesystem is known as vfat to the mount command, and the other elements of the mount command are standard.

44. D. The c option in gdisk is used to change the partition name. The n option creates a new partition, the v option verifies the disk, and the b option creates a backup of GPT data to a file.

45. C. The -b option prints known bad blocks. The -f option is used to force the display of information, and the other options don't exist.

46. B. The -A option checks all filesystems in /etc/fstab, while the -M option excludes the root filesystem.

47. C. The fsck option, which is represented as a number in the /etc/fstab file, sets the order that the device is checked at boot time.

48. C. The file /etc/timezone is used to indicate the local time zone. The other files listed as options do not exist.

49. D. Within the /usr/share/zoneinfo hierarchy, you will find information on the various regions and time zones available. The files within this hierarchy can be symlinked to /etc/localtime.

50. B. The dominfo command within virsh displays information regarding the domain. The other commands are not valid.

51. C. The LC_TIME environment variable is used to control the display and behavior of the date and time and can be changed to a different locale in order to achieve the desired display and behavior of date and time formatting. The other options shown for this question do not exist.

52. B. UTF-8 provides multibyte character encoding and is generally accepted as the standard for encoding moving forward. ISO-8859 is single-byte encoded. The other answers are not valid.

53. C. The timedatectl command includes a list-timezones subcommand to show known time zones. The tzsel command does not exist; but there is a similar command called tzselect that will, by default, display a step-by-step menu to select a time zone. The eventual output will include a region/time-zone line, such as America/Chicago, as output.

54. D. The TZ environment variable is used for this purpose and the general format is as shown, thus making option D the correct answer.

55. C. Setting LANG=C is an alias for POSIX compatibility and will cause programs to bypass locale translations. The other options shown for LANG are not valid.

56. C. The LC_ALL variable can be used to set environment variables such as the locale and will override others. This can be used when there is a need for a temporary change. The other variables listed here are not used for this purpose and are not created by default.

57. A. The ln command is used for this purpose, and the -s option creates a symbolic link, while -f forces or overwrites the destination. The other options and order of commands are not valid.

58. C. The `LC_MONETARY` variable is used by certain programs to determine the localization for currency.

59. D. The `hwclock` command is used to both query and set the hardware clock, such as the one maintained by the system firmware or BIOS. The `ntpdate` command is used to set the local system time but is not related to the hardware clock. The other commands are not valid.

60. D. The `-s` option sets the date and time as specified within the command. If there is another means to automatically set the date, it may override the change. For example, if `ntpd` is running, that process may alter the date even after it has been set with `date -s`.

61. A. The `-w` option sets the hardware clock to the current system time. The `-s` option does the opposite, setting the system time to the hardware clock. There is no `-a` or `-m` function for `hwclock`.

62. A. `--systohc` will set the hardware clock according to the current system time. The use of `--utc` is required in order to ensure that the time is set to UTC. If `--utc` is omitted, the time will default to whatever was used last time the command was run, which could be UTC but might be local time instead. Therefore, the best option is A.

63. A. The `netstat` command can be used for this purpose, and the `-r` option displays the current routes. The addition of `-n` prevents DNS lookups, which can help with performance.

64. D. Private IP addresses are found within the 10.0.0.0/8, 172.16.0.0/12, and 192.168.0.0/16 ranges, thus making an address in the 143 range a public IP.

65. C. The `route` command is used for this purpose, and adding a route is done with the add option. The default gateway is added using the `default gw` keywords followed by the IP of the gateway and the adapter.

66. A. The `host` command enables changing of the query type with the `-t` option. Using `ns` as the type will query for the name servers for a given domain. There is no `all` type, and the other options are also invalid.

67. B. The `-I` option enables the choice of interface. A lowercase `-i` option sets the interval, while `-a` indicates an audible ping. Finally, `-t` enables a TTL-based ping only.

68. A. The `host` or `dig` command can be used for this purpose by setting the type to mx. The mx type will query for the mail exchanger for the given domain. There is no `smtp` type.

69. B. The localhost address for IPv6 can be written as `::1`. Addresses shown like 127 represent the IPv4 localhost range but are not written properly for IPv4 or IPv6.

70. A. The `ip` command with the `monitor` option/subcommand will display netlink messages as they arrive. There is no `netlink` subcommand for `ip`, and the `route` command will not work for this purpose.

71. A. The syntax is `database: databasename` with additional database names separated by spaces, as shown in the correct option for this question.

Chapter 1: Hardware and System Configuration 207

72. A. The @ symbol is used to indicate a server to which the query will be sent directly. This can be quite useful for troubleshooting resolution problems by sending the query directly to an authoritative name server for the domain. Of the other options, -t sets the type, and the other options are not valid.

73. A. The getent command is used for working with NSS databases, and getent hosts will display the available hosts using the databases configured in /etc/nsswitch.conf.

74. C. The configuration option is nameserver, and the value for the option is the IP address of the desired name server. Several options affect how name resolution is performed, such as the number of attempts and timeout. See resolv.conf(5) for more information.

75. A. The route command can be used for this purpose, and the syntax includes the network range, denoted with the -net option, followed by the word netmask and the masked bits, followed by the letters gw and the IP of the gateway. The other options shown are invalid for a variety of reasons including missing keywords and options and order.

76. A. The netstat command is used for this purpose, and the -a option displays all sockets, listening and non-listening. Note that it's frequently helpful to add the -n option, or combine options as in netstat -an, in order to prevent name lookup. Doing so can significantly improve performance of the command.

77. A. The correct format is IP address followed by canonical hostname followed by any aliases for the host. You can use entries in /etc/hosts to override DNS lookups, which can be useful to prevent those names from resolving or to provide a different resolution.

78. B. The ip route command can be used for this purpose, and its syntax uses a change command and the via keyword. The same operation could be completed with the route command but would require deleting the existing gateway first and then re-adding a new default gateway.

79. A. The soa type is used to query for Start of Authority records for a domain. Note that in many cases, dig will attempt to look up the domain within a given command and may not appear to have had an error. For example, when running option D (dig -t auth example.com), you will receive information about example.com, and there will be a line in the output saying that dig has ignored the invalid type of auth.

80. A. The search option is used for this purpose and can be provided with multiple domain names, each separated by a space or tab. The domain option is valid within /etc/resolv.conf but does not allow for multiple domain names.

81. A. The route command can be used for this purpose, and in the scenario described, a reject destination is used for the route. The other options shown are invalid because they use invalid options to the route command.

82. D. The -c option provides the count of the number of pings to send. The -n option specifies numeric output only, while -p specifies the pattern to use for the packet content. Finally, the -t option sets the TTL.

83. D. The best option for this question is to add an entry for the host in /etc/hosts. Doing so will always cause DNS queries to resolve to 127.0.0.1. The other options are not as robust because they rely on www.example.com always having the same IP address, or the solutions require additional maintenance to constantly add new IP addresses if www.example.com's IP address changes.

84. A. The ip route flush cache command should be executed after changing the routes. The other commands shown for this question are not valid.

85. A. SPF records are stored in the txt record type in DNS, thereby making -t txt the correct option for this. Of the other answers, only -t mx is valid; it returns the mail exchangers for the given domain.

86. C. The G signifies a gateway within the route table.

87. A. The axfr type is a zone transfer, and the @ symbol signifies the server to which the query will be sent. There is no xfer type, and option B is just a normal query for the domain sent to the specified server.

88. D. The -p option to iostat displays information on devices and partitions. The -c option shows CPU utilization, and -d shows device utilization. There is no -a option.

89. A. The df command displays information on disk usage and can help with planning disk utilization over time. For example, if you note that disk utilization is increasing significantly, preparations can be made to bring more disks online or even to change the log rotation schedule such that logs are rotated faster, thereby freeing up space.

90. A. The mkinitrd command is used on older systems to create the initial RAM disk. The initial RAM disk is used to load (some might say preload) essential modules for things like disks and other vital components needed for booting.

91. B. The lsmod command is used to display currently loaded modules. This is useful for scenarios where you are migrating from the stock or distribution-provided kernel to a custom kernel and need to know which modules to compile into the new kernel.

92. B. The depmod command is used to create a list of modules. The list is kept in a file called modules.dep, the location of which is dependent on the distribution of Linux in use.

93. A. The -a option displays all values and their current settings for sysctl. The -b option is binary and displays values without any newlines. The -d option is an alias for -h, which is help display. There is no -c option. The sysctl options can also be found in /etc/sysctl.conf.

94. B. The modprobe command examines dependencies for a given module and loads both the dependencies and the requested module.

95. A. The modinfo command provides information on a given kernel module. You can use modinfo to find out the parameters needed for a given module and the modules on which it depends, among other information. The modprobe command is used to load a module. There is no tracemod or modlist command.

96. C. The `insmod` command inserts a module into the running kernel. It does not, however, attempt to resolve dependencies but rather outputs an error if there are dependent modules or kernel symbols that are not available.

97. B. The `-r` option removes the named kernel modules and attempts to remove any modules on which the named module depends, where possible. The `-d` option sets the root directory for modules, while `-v` is verbose and `-f` forces the module to load.

98. B. The `/etc/modprobe.d` directory is used for storing configuration information related to modules such as that used for blacklisting purposes, and also for other configuration information such as `udev` and module options.

99. B. The `dracut` command is used to create the initial RAM disk for newer systems and has replaced the legacy `mkinitrd` command used for the same purpose.

100. B. Variables and values placed in `/etc/sysctl.conf` will take effect on boot. The other files listed are not valid.

101. B. The `--show-depends` option displays the dependencies for a given module. The other options are not valid for the `modprobe` command.

102. C. The format for the `mount` command is `[partition] [target]`, thereby making option C correct. The other options are not valid because the arguments are in the wrong order.

103. D. The `-n` option changes the boot order for the next boot only and boots from the specified partition. The `-b` along with `-B` modifies and then deletes the option. The `-o` option sets the boot order. The `-c` option creates a boot number.

104. A. ISOLINUX provides a means by which CD-ROMs formatted as ISO 9660 can be booted. It's very common to have live CDs or rescue/recovery CDs that use ISOLINUX for boot. The other bootloaders are not valid for this purpose or don't exist.

105. B. Due to the decidedly insecure decisions made with the design of Microsoft's UEFI, a shim is often needed to enable Linux to boot on a system with UEFI. The file `shim.efi` can be used as an initial bootloader for this purpose.

106. B. The `bcfg` command within the UEFI shell is used to configure bootloaders on a UEFI-based system. The command can accept various parameters to configure how the bootloader and kernel will load on boot. Of the other commands shown, `grub-install` is valid but not within the UEFI shell.

107. B. The Master Boot Record, or MBR, is the first sector on a disk and contains information about the structure of the disk. If the MBR becomes corrupt, all data on the disk may be lost. The other options shown for this question are not valid.

108. D. The file `pxelinux.0` must exist within `/tftpboot` on the TFTP server in order for a system to use PXELINUX for booting. The other files are not valid or necessary for PXELINUX. Once booted, PXE boot can boot using an NFS-mounted filesystem where the filesystem is physically hosted on a different computer.

109. D. The `--boot-directory` option enables you to specify an alternate location for GRUB images rather than the default /boot. The other options shown for this question are not valid.

110. C. The `shim.efi` bootloader loads another bootloader, which is `grubx64.efi` by default. The other options are not valid filenames for the purpose described.

111. C. The `-t` option sets the filesystem type as ext2, ext3, or ext4. The `mke2fs` command is typically symlinked from /sbin/mkfs.ext2, /sbin/mkfs.ext3, and /sbin/mkfs.ext4. The `-f` option forces `mke2fs` to create a filesystem. The `-a` and `-e` options do not exist.

112. B. The /etc/crypttab file contains the filesystems and devices that are encrypted. The other file locations do not exist by default and are not related to this question.

113. C. Bad blocks are shown with the `-b` option. The `-f` option forces `dumpe2fs` to perform the requested operation, and the other command options do not exist.

114. C. The `-f` option specifies that `xfs_check` should check the contents of the named file for consistency. The `-v` option sets verbosity, and there are no `-d` or `-a` options.

115. A. The block size for import or restore must match the block size used on export or dump. Block size is specified with the `-b` option, thus making option A correct. The other options are not valid for `xfsrestore`.

116. B. A filesystem with the word `defaults` for its mount options will be mounted read-write (`rw`), `suid`, with the ability to have executables (`exec`). The filesystem will be auto-mounted (`auto`), but users will not be able to mount it (`nouser`). Character and block special devices will be interpreted (`dev`), and operations on the disk will be performed in an asynchronous manner (`async`).

117. C. The `-z` option sets the maximum size for files to be included in the dump. The `-b` option sets the block size but is not related to what is being asked for in this scenario. The `-s` option sets the path for inclusion in the dump, and `-p` sets the interval for progress indicators.

118. D. A partition type of 0xFD is used for software RAID arrays. This can be set or viewed using a tool such as `fdisk`. The other options shown are not valid partition types.

119. C. The /dev/disk/by-id directory contains symbolic links to /dev/sd, such as /dev/sda. Because WWIDs can be used to identify a device across systems, they are often used within the context of SANs. The other directories listed as options do not exist.

120. C. The `pvdisplay` command shows information about a given physical volume. You can use `pvdisplay` to view the device on which the PV is built along with the extent size of the PV. The other commands shown are not valid.

121. B. Logical Unit Numbers (LUNs) that contain the characters `fc` are those found through Fibre Channel. Therein lies the difference between options B and C, where option C contains the letters `scsi`, which would usually represent a local disk. The other options are not valid.

122. C. The `multipath` command is used for administration of devices such as LUNs and can be used for finding the path to LUNs for a server, such as in a SAN configuration. The other commands are not valid, with the exception of `ls`: it is valid, but the option shown is related not to LUNs but rather is a combination of various flags to the `ls` command.

123. C. The `fstrim` command is used to remove blocks that are not in use. The `fstrim` command is frequently used in a SAN configuration to give back unused storage to the SAN. The `fstrim` command can also be used with solid-state drives for the same purpose. The other commands shown are not valid.

124. B. The `-E` option signals that an extended option follows, such as `stripe_width`. The `-f` option forces an operation but should not be necessary for this solution, and the `-e` option sets the behavior on error. There is no `-extend` option.

125. A. The `--create` option enables creation of a RAID array that will use md. The typical argument is the `/dev/mdN` device. The other options listed are not valid for `mdadm`.

126. C. The `/dev/mapper` directory contains information about multipath devices such as logical volumes. The other directories are not valid.

127. C. The `--monitor` option is used to actively watch an array for issues such as disk failure. The monitoring can be done as a daemon and run in the background, thereby alerting when there is an issue.

128. B. The `MAILADDR` option sets the destination address for mail about RAID events that are noted by `mdadm` when in monitor mode.

129. C. The `ip` command defaults to the `inet` family if not otherwise specified with the `-f` option. The command will attempt to guess the correct family and fall back to `inet`. The other families listed as options for this command are not valid for use with the `ip` command.

130. B. The `iwconfig` command, which is similar to the `ifconfig` command, works with an individual wireless interface to set and display parameters. Of the other commands, the `ifconfig` command is valid but not used for wireless. The other commands are not valid.

131. A. The `ss` command provides many of the same functions as `netstat` but can show some extended information, such as memory allocation for a given socket. The `free` command shows memory usage but not by socket, and the other two commands do not exist.

132. C. The `-p` option shows the process IDs associated with a given socket within the `ss` output. The `-a` option is all sockets, while `-l` is listening sockets. The `-f` option is used to specify the protocol family.

133. D. The `/etc/network` directory contains information on network interfaces and contains directories that then further contain scripts to be executed when interfaces are brought up or down. The other directories listed do not exist.

134. B. Only alphanumerics, a minus sign (or dash), and dot are valid for hosts in `/etc/hosts`.

135. B. Options within /etc/resolv.conf are preceded with the options keyword followed by one or more options such as debug.

136. C. The -f option will force the umount to occur. The --fake option is essentially a dry run in that it won't actually unmount a filesystem. The other two options do not exist.

137. A. The --output option configures the location for output of the command instead of STDOUT.

138. A. The file lpxelinux.0 contains the necessary code to support booting from HTTP and FTP.

139. B. The file /etc/grub2.cfg is usually a symbolic link to /boot/grub2/grub.cfg.

140. C. The vmlinuz file has been compressed and therefore consumes less disk space than vmlinux. Both contain the Linux kernel in binary format.

141. C. Modules are stored in /usr/lib/modules/{kernel-version}.

142. C. The file /var/log/kern.log contains kernel messages and can be used to troubleshoot a kernel panic.

143. B. JSON-formatted files are JavaScript Object Notation. These files, along with YAML files, are frequently used to provide templates and configuration information because both formats are lightweight and descriptive. When working with a VM template or automation, you may encounter these formats.

144. D. A persistent volume keeps data between deployments of the virtualized environment. A container image is used for the original boot.

145. B. A dual-homed networking configuration is one that has two network interfaces. Bridged networking refers to using the host adapter in a virtualization scenario. An overlay network is one that is built on top of another network. Forwarding is not related to this solution.

146. C. The localectl command is used to view and configure settings such as the keyboard layout for a given locale. The other commands listed do not exist.

147. D. The directory /etc/sysconfig/network-scripts contains files related to network configuration. It is not preferable to edit these files directly any longer but rather to use commands such as nmcli and nmtui through the Network Manager. The other paths do not exist by default.

148. A. The e2label command changes the filesystem label. The other commands do not exist.

149. B. OVF is formatted in XML. There is a file extension frequently seen as YML that typically contains YAML-formatted data, but that is not related to this question. HTML is a valid document standard but not for OVF files. There is no OVFMeta document standard.

150. A. Network Address Translation (NAT) effectively hides the virtual machine behind the host IP address. Bridging enables the virtual machine to get its own IP and thus have external clients access it as well.

151. B. The file /etc/modprobe.conf, which is a legacy file and may be removed in a later version of Linux, contains information on the configuration of modules on the system. The other files do not exist.

152. C. The mode active-backup is used for creating an active-passive configuration where if one adapter goes down, the other takes over. The other options are not valid.

153. D. The kernel-install command uses the files found in the /usr/lib/kernel directory to install a kernel and related files into /boot. The other commands listed here are not valid.

154. C. A relative path begins with something other than a / whereas an absolute path always begins with a /, indicating the root of the filesystem. The other options, virtual and symbolic, are not valid names used to describe paths.

155. C. A raw device is one that has not been partitioned. Raw devices are sometimes used for virtualization and also database scenarios, where the higher-layer software manages the disk. The other options shown are not relevant to this answer. Highly available would only typically refer to a redundant disk or network scenario.

156. A. The value of 1 enables debug logging. The value 2 is info, 3 is warn, and 4 is error.

157. B. Anaconda is the name for the installer for Red Hat and CentOS systems. Kickstart can be used to script and automate the installation process.

158. A. The time command includes timing information such as sys time, user time, and real time. The other commands are not valid.

159. D. Blob, or Binary Large Object, is a storage format frequently associated with cloud environments. Blob storage enables a single object to be stored as an individual object. The other formats are valid, but none of the other options is the most appropriate mechanism for this scenario.

160. A. The virtual filesystem (VFS) provides a layer of abstraction between the real filesystem and upper-layer applications. The other answers are not relevant to this question.

161. C. The ext3 and ext4 filesystems can be resized using resize2fs. Both NFS and CIFS are network filesystems and therefore are not relevant to this question.

162. D. The connect subcommand connects to the hypervisor. The other options are not valid subcommands for virsh.

163. C. The --list option shows the available character sets on the system. Character sets such as ASCII, UTF-8, and UNICODE are displayed if they are supported on the system. The other options given for this question do not exist.

164. A. The /dev/ filesystem is used to store information about connected devices. The /etc/ filesystem is used for configuration files, and there are no proscribed directories for development or kernel device lists.

165. B. The /proc/mounts file shows the currently mounted filesystems. The file /etc/fstab is used for mounting filesystems but is not kept up to date with filesystem mounts as they change. The other files listed do not exist.

166. B. CIFS is the Common Internet File System and is now considered a legacy filesystem, having been superseded by SMB3. CIFS is an implementation of SMB typically used by older versions of Microsoft Windows.

167. B. The YAML format is used for configuration files that will be used with cloud-init. XML and the other formats listed are not used for cloud-init.

168. C. The -g option clears the cache to remove devices that do not exist. The -p option bypasses the cache. There are no -a or -m options for blkid.

169. D. The /dev/disk/by-uuid file shows the UUID of the disks on a system. The other locations do not exist.

170. C. The /etc/sysconfig/network file is created by default but is no longer populated on systems like RHEL7. It can be used in place of Network Manager for environments that rely on this location. The other options given for this question do not exist.

171. B. The switch should support LACP for aggregation to work correctly. The 802.11 protocol is for wireless, and there is no LinkAG or 802.3ag protocol specification.

172. A. The virt-install command is used to create a virtual machine. The other answers given do not exist.

173. C. The -R option skips the root filesystem when the -A option is used. The -M option does not check mounted filesystems. There is no -S option.

174. A. A Type 1 hypervisor is also known as a bare-metal hypervisor and can be installed without a host operating system. A hosted hypervisor is sometimes called a Type 2. The other options listed are neither Type 1 or Type 2.

175. D. The /proc/partitions file contains a list of partitions on the system along with their major and minor numbers and the number of blocks. The /dev/disk/ option is a directory and not a file and so is not correct for this question. The other options shown do not exist.

176. C. The file /sys/block/sda/stat contains information about the sda device. The /sys/block hierarchy contains information about block devices on the system.

177. A. The OVA file is an appliance file, meaning it contains information and an image that can be executed as an appliance, needing little or no configuration by the end user. The other options given for this question are not used or do not describe the OVA file.

178. B. Files in /etc/netplan, which are used for network configuration on newer Ubuntu systems, should be formatted with YAML and named with a .yaml extension.

179. D. The -s option summarizes the output by directory, while the -h option presents the output in a more human-friendly manner.

180. B. The WWID, or Worldwide Identifier, is globally unique. UUID and GUID are not valid acronyms for multipath devices. UUID is typically found for plain block devices, and GUID is a term sometimes used in applications. There is no DISKID name relevant as a potential answer for this question.

181. D. SFTP cannot be used with kickstart. The other options, as well as FTP and local drive (not listed), are valid for use with kickstart.

182. C. The balance-rr mode is used to provide round-robin load balancing. The other options given are not valid modes.

183. B. The -D option tells dmesg to stop displaying messages to the console. The -F option is valid but is used to read from a file, so it is not relevant for this question. There are no -o or -Q options.

184. A. The -f option forces unload of the module. The other options are not valid for rmmod.

185. A. The -A option examines modules.dep for newer modules rather than regenerating the file automatically if there are no changes. The -C option changes the configuration file location. The other options are not valid for depmod.

186. B. The lsblk command shows device information in a treelike structure and shows the other information specified along with major and minor information and whether the partition is read-only. Of the other options given, fsck is the only command, and it is not used for the purpose described.

187. C. The -m option displays output in a machine-readable format. The -v option prints the version of parted. There is no -p or -S option.

188. B. The brctl command is used to create ethernet bridges and is also used to manage bridges once created. The other options shown are not valid.

189. A. The file /etc/dhcpd.conf is used for configuration of DHCP. It is worth noting that the location of this file varies between distributions and can sometimes be found at /etc/dhcp/dhcpd.conf as well. The other options given for this question are not valid file locations.

190. C. The ethtool command will be used for this purpose, and the -i option displays the driver in use. The other commands are not valid for this purpose.

191. B. The server command changes the destination for queries sent from nslookup during that session. The other options shown are not valid.

Chapter 2: System Operations and Maintenance

1. B. Current interrupt (IRQ) assignments are contained in the file /proc/interrupts. Therefore, viewing the contents of the file with a command such as cat will work. There is no view command, thus making answer A incorrect. Likewise, there is no /dev/irq file, thereby making answers C and D incorrect.

2. D. Configuration files for udev are found in /etc/udev and the related /etc/udev/rules.d, which makes answer D correct. The other options do not exist.

3. B. The lsusb command is used to obtain a basic list of USB devices on a system. The other commands are not valid. In the case of answer D, the ls command is valid, but there is no --usb option.

4. C. Runlevel 1, sometimes displayed as runlevel s or S, is single-user mode, in which many services are not started. Runlevels 5 and 6 are used for other purposes, and runlevel SU is not a valid option.

5. D. Scripts are stored in /etc/init.d on a system using SysVinit. You may sometimes find these linked from /etc/rc.d/init.d as well. The other options are not valid for this question.

6. A. The init command can be used to access different runlevels. Runlevel 6 is used for rebooting the system. Answer B will shut down the system entirely, not reboot it. Answer C will place the system into single-user mode. Answer D is not a valid option.

7. B. The --list option will show all services on a system along with their status for each runlevel. The on and off options enable and disable a service, respectively.

8. C. USB devices are generally considered to be hotplug devices. Hotplug devices can be inserted and removed while the system is "hot" or powered on, whereas coldplug devices are those that must be inserted and removed when the system is powered off.

9. C. The ExecStart option indicates the command to be executed on startup of a systemd service.

10. D. The systemctl get-default command will show the default target. The other commands and options are not valid.

11. A. The enable option configures the service to start on boot. The start option, answer D, is used to start a service immediately. The other options are not valid for this command.

12. C. The /proc filesystem contains information about currently running processes and additional information about the kernel and current boot of the system.

13. D. The `ldconfig` command updates the current shared library cache and list. `ldconfig` reads `/etc/ld.so.conf` and incorporates any changes found within it. The other commands listed as options for this question do not exist.

14. B. The `upgrade` option for `apt-get` will upgrade the system to the latest version of software for packages already installed. The `apt-update` command does not exist, nor does the `-U` option to `dpkg`. The `apt-cache` command is used to work with the package cache.

15. C. The `yum install` command will install a given package. The `update` option will update a package. The other options listed do not exist.

16. A. `rpm2cpio` sends its output to `STDOUT` by default, and therefore that output needs to be redirected to a file in most cases.

17. D. The `ldd` command will list the libraries on which the command's argument depends.

18. C. The `-t` option to `lsusb` will print output in a treelike format so that you can see which devices are connected to which bus. The other arguments to `lsusb` are not valid, and the `usblist` command is not real.

19. A. SCSI supports 7 to 15 devices per bus, depending on the type of SCSI.

20. C. Out of the options given, the `systemctl status` command and option are the most appropriate. The `telinit` and `sysctl` commands are not used for this purpose. Likewise, the `--ls` option is not valid for `systemctl`.

21. B. The `isolate` option is used to move the system into the target specified, thereby making option B the correct one. The other options do not exist.

22. C. The `telinit` command can be used to refresh the system after changes have been made to `/etc/inittab`. Notably, answer B will reboot the system, but that was not an option given the question asked. Answers A and D are not valid commands.

23. D. The `runlevel` command displays the current runlevel for a system. Answer B is not a valid option to the `init` command, while adding `sudo` in front of the `init` command makes no difference. Answer A is not a valid command.

24. C. Unit configuration files are stored in `/lib/systemd/system`. The other directory options for this question are not relevant or do not exist by default.

25. A. The listing shows a symbolic linked file created with the `ln` command located in the current directory, linked to `.configs/fetchmail/.fetchmailrc`. The file is owned by the root user and root group and was created on July, 8, 2014.

26. B. The `systemctl` command is used to work with services and targets. The `list-units` command is used to list targets. The other commands are not used for this purpose or do not exist with the required option.

27. C. The `-nn` option displays both numbers and device names, thus making answer C correct. The `-n` option (answer B) displays only numbers. The other two options do not exist.

28. D. The /proc/bus/usb directory contains information about USB devices. The other directories are not valid for this purpose. With udev-based kernels, /proc/bus/usb may not exist by default. The path is part of the legacy usbfs.

29. C. SATA disks are addressed as /dev/sdX, just like a SCSI disk. /dev/hdX is a traditional ATA disk. The other options do not exist.

30. D. The partition containing /var should be the largest for a mail server because mail spools are stored within this hierarchy. The /etc/ hierarchy is usually small, as is /usr/bin. The /mail directory does not exist by default.

31. B. The deplist option displays the dependencies for the given package. The list option displays information about a specific package, while the other two options are not valid.

32. A. The -ivh options will install a file using rpm, displaying both verbose output and hash marks for progress. The other options presented do not exist or do not accomplish the specified task.

33. A. The apt-cache command is used to work with the package cache, and the search option is used to search the cache for the supplied argument, in this case zsh. The apt-get command is used to work with packages themselves, while the apt-search command does not exist.

34. D. Configuration files related to the repositories for yum are located in /etc/yum.repos.d. Of the other options, /etc/yum.conf is a file and not a directory, and the other directories do not exist.

35. A. The -V or --verify option will check the files in a given package against versions (or checksums) in the package database. If no files have been altered, then no output is produced. Note that output may be produced for files that are changed during installation or for other reasons. Note also the use of an uppercase V for this option, as opposed to the lowercase v for *verbose*.

36. B. The /etc/lib directory is not typically associated with library files and does not typically exist on a Linux system unless manually created. The other options either contain system libraries or can be used for that purpose.

37. C. The apt-get update command will cause the package cache to be updated by retrieving the latest package list from the package sources. There is no cache-update option or update option to apt-cache. The upgrade option is used to update the system's packages, not the cache.

38. C. The file sources.list located in /etc/apt contains the list of repositories for Debian packages. The other file locations do not exist by default.

39. A. The dpkg-reconfigure program will cause an already-installed package to be reconfigured or changed. The -r option for dpkg removes a package, thus making answer B incorrect. There is no reconf option for dpkg or reinstall option for apt-get.

40. D. The search option performs a search of various fields such as the package name and description.

41. B. The `rpm -q kernel` command will show the kernel version. You can also use `uname -r` for the same purpose.

42. A. The `exclude` option can be used to exclude certain packages. The argument accepts wildcards, and therefore excluding all `kernel*` updates will create the desired behavior.

43. B. The `-s` option to dpkg searches for the given package and provides information about its current status on the system. The `apt-cache` command is not used for this purpose, and the `-i` option for dpkg installs a package. The `apt-info` command does not exist.

44. A. The `-i` option to dpkg will install a previously downloaded `.deb` Debian package. The other commands don't exist, and the `-U` option for dpkg does not exist.

45. C. A `.tgz` file typically indicates a zipped (compressed) tar file. The `-z` option is used to indicate that the file should be decompressed, and `-x` that the file should be unarchived. The `-v` option is not required but provides verbose output. Finally, the `-f` option indicates the file to use. If the file is not zipped, likely noted by having a `.tar` file extension, then the `-z` option can be omitted.

46. C. The `info` option displays information about a given package on a system that uses the zypper tool.

47. A. The `search` option looks for packages by the name given on the command line. The other options are not valid for the `dnf` command.

48. A. The g option, also known as `global` or `greedy`, will apply the matched operation to the entire line rather than just the first instance of the match. The other options apply as they would for a Perl-Compatible Regular Expression.

49. C. The `-l` option provides the number of lines given as input. For example, `wc -l /etc/passwd` would print the number of lines in the `/etc/passwd` file. The other options given in this question are not valid for the `wc` command.

50. C. Both head and `tail` print 10 lines of output by default.

51. B. The `-rf` options to `rm` will recursively remove contents of a directory, including other directories. The `-f` option alone will not work in this case because of the additional directories. The other options given for `rmdir` do not exist.

52. D. The `-type` option causes `find` to limit its search to directories only, while the `-name` option limits the names of returned elements. Note the use of the wildcard due to the phrasing of the question. Also note the use of `./` to denote beginning the search in the current directory.

53. A. The `cat` command will display the contents of the file `/etc/passwd` and then pipe that output to the `awk` command. The `awk` command then parses its input, splitting along the specified separator for `/etc/passwd`, which is a colon (`:`). The output is then printed and piped to the `sort` command. The `sort` command in option B will not work because the `cut` command requires an argument. Likewise, the `echo` command in option C will only echo `/etc/passwd` to STDOUT.

54. C. The -l option for ls produces long or listed output, and -t sorts by timestamp. The -r option reverses the order, and -a is needed to include hidden (dot) files, thus making answer C correct.

55. A. The timestamp of the file will change when touch is run on a file that already exists.

56. D. The -i option will cause both cp and mv to be interactive; that is, prompt before overwriting. The -f option will force the command to run, while -r is recursive.

57. C. The tee command will send output to both STDOUT and to the specified file, thus making answer C correct. Option A will redirect output to the correct file but not to STDOUT simultaneously. The other answers will not work for this question.

58. A. The -p option will cause mkdir to create additional levels of directories without error. Running mkdir without options will not work in this case. The -r and -f options to mkdir do not exist.

59. B. The -R option will copy directories recursively. Note that if the -i option is not enabled, the recursive copy will overwrite files in the destination. The -v option adds verbosity but does not cause any recursion, while the -Z option does not exist.

60. B. The cut command uses Tab as its default delimiter. This can be changed with the -d option.

61. D. The fg command will bring a command to the foreground if it has been backgrounded with either & or the bg command.

62. A. You need to write the changes to the file, so you'll need :w. The addition of q will also quit. Note that you could use ZZ to write and quit as well. The dd command in Vi deletes a line, while x deletes a single character.

63. D. The -n option changes the number of lines of output for both head and tail to the number specified. The other options listed in this question are not valid for head, and the -f option follows a file with tail as the file grows.

64. C. The -9 option invokes SIGKILL, which will force the process to end. The 15 signal is the default. The -f and -stop options do not exist.

65. C. Within bash, the number 1 represents STDOUT and 2 represents STDERR. Redirecting both means combining them in the manner shown in option C.

66. D. Within a regular expression, * represents 0 or more characters, and in this case the problem doesn't care whether a person is using /bin/bash or /usr/bin/zsh. Likewise, . matches a single character. But in the case of bash and zsh, you need to look at both the first and optionally a second character: thus the ?, which makes the second . optional. Finally, $ anchors the pattern at the end of the string and is key for this regular expression.

67. C. The o command opens a new line below the current cursor location. The a command begins an insert-mode session at the character after the cursor, not the line. The i command begins an insert-mode session at the current cursor location.

68. A. Sending -HUP as part of the `kill` command will restart a process. Of the other answers, -9 will kill the process completely. The other two answers do not exist as valid means to kill a process.

69. B. The `find` command beginning with the path and then the -name argument will locate all files called `.bash_history`. The output from the `find` command should be piped to `xargs`, which can then build further commands from standard input. Note that this question and solution assume that all users use the bash shell and are keeping history.

70. A. Adding -type f to the `find` command will limit the search to only files, and the -mtime option will limit to modification time in day format.

71. C. The `mv` command is used to move files, and `*.txt` will look for all files with a `.txt` extension. Note the fully qualified destination with a / preceding the name `tmp`.

72. A. The file needs to first be sorted to group common zip codes together. After that, piping the output to `uniq` will display the unique zip codes, and the -c option provides a count.

73. C. The ? will search backward in a file within `less`. The / is used for searching forward. The H key displays help, and there is no function mapped to the X key.

74. A. The `which` command returns the full path to the given command and is useful for determining both whether a given command is available and the location from which the command will run.

75. C. The file is almost certainly a hard link to the original script. While `ls` won't show this information, the `stat` command will show that it is a link and also show the inode to which the file is linked.

76. C. The -i option to `ls` shows the inode index number of files in the directory. The other options do not exist.

77. B. The -s option to `ln` creates a symbolic link or symlink.

78. C. The `whereis` command displays pertinent information about the command given as its argument. For example, entering `whereis apache2` on a Debian system will show the binary location, configuration file location, and other relevant details.

79. D. The quotacheck command is used to update the quota file for the given filesystem. The `quota -u` command will display the current quota for a given user. The other commands do not exist.

80. B. The l within the listing indicates a symlink. There is no way to tell if a file or directory is temporary. A directory will display a d instead of an l.

81. B. The `repquota` command is used for this purpose, and the -a option will display information for all filesystems. If the command is given a -g option, group quota information is shown.

82. C. The `updatedb` command will update the database used by the `locate` command.

83. A. The best option among these choices is to change the group to `www-data` and change the permissions such that the group can write into the directory. Option B should never be used because it enables world-writing to the directory. The other options will not allow the web server group to write into the directory.

84. D. The `-inum` option searches for files by their inode number. This can be useful when searching for the files involved in hard links.

85. B. User-based configuration files are located in the order `.bash_profile`, `.bash_login`, and `.profile`. Only the first file found is executed; the others are ignored. The file `/etc/profile` is a system-wide bash profile.

86. C. The `/etc/skel` directory contains files to be copied to the user's home directory. The other directories listed for this question do not exist by default.

87. C. The `--norc` option causes bash to execute without reading the `/etc/bash.bashrc` (Debian derivatives) or `/etc/bashrc` (Red Hat derivatives) file or the local `~/.bashrc` file. The other options listed do not exist as options for bash.

88. A. The `.bash_profile` file, if it exists in your home directory, will be executed on login. Note that placing the function in `/etc/profile` would technically work, but then the function would be available to all users, which is not what the question asked for.

89. B. The `Screen` section of `xorg.conf` is used to logically bind a given graphics card and monitor each of which would be defined in its own respective section in the configuration file. The other options shown for this question do not exist.

90. A. The `DISPLAY` variable can be used to remotely send the windows of an X session to another computer when using protocols like SSH. There is no `XTERMINAL` or `XDISP` environment variable, and `XTERM` is typically a terminal window and not an environment variable.

91. D. The `Welcome` option sets the message to be displayed to users within the display manager when they log in. For users that are remote, the `RemoteWelcome` message can be used for the same purpose.

92. C. The Shift key can be used to enable and disable sticky keys within Gnome and other graphical interfaces for accessibility purposes.

93. A. The Orca project provides assistive screen-reading capabilities within Gnome. Of the other options given, the `screen` command is valid but is not used for this purpose.

94. D. The `kmag` program magnifies items on a desktop and is used as an assistive technology. In general, `kmag` can be used with other window managers as well.

95. B. The `X11Forwarding` option must be enabled in order for X connections or windows generated from the X server to be sent over an SSH connection.

96. C. The `/etc/passwd` file contains various information about users on a system such as username and real name, along with user id (UID) and login shell. The file is world-readable.

97. B. The format for cron is [minute hour day-of-month month-of-year day-of-week], thereby making option B the correct option for this question.

98. B. The /etc/cron.allow file is a list of users who have permission to create and remove their own cron jobs. The /etc/crontab file is used to store cron jobs. The other files do not exist.

99. B. The at command is used to run a series of commands that you enter. Unlike cron, you can schedule commands from the command line to be executed in the same order entered rather than having to create a specific script for the commands. The syntax shown in option B sets the time to be one hour from now.

100. B. The userdel command is used for this purpose, and the -r option (lowercase) deletes both the home directory and mail spool files. The -R (uppercase) option informs the userdel command to use a chroot directory.

101. A. The groupmod command is used for this purpose, and the -n option is used to change the group name. The other commands listed do not exist.

102. A. The /var/spool/cron/crontabs directory contains a file for each user that currently has one or more cron jobs or entries. Note that the other files listed here are not valid for this purpose.

103. C. The atrm command removes jobs given their ID. The ID can be obtained with the atq command. The atq and at -l commands shown will list jobs but not delete them. The rmat command is not valid.

104. C. The /etc/crontab file is a plain-text file that is treated as a system-wide cron file. As such, the file is generally not associated with any single user, and it's not necessary to run a special command after editing this file.

105. A. The /etc/cron.daily directory contains files such as scripts that are executed daily. There are corresponding cron.hourly, cron.weekly, and cron.monthly directories that run on their respective schedules as indicated by the name of the directory.

106. B. The -m option causes the user's home directory to be created. By default, if this option isn't specified and CREATE_HOME has not been set, the home directory won't be created. The -h option displays help text, and the other options shown are not valid.

107. A. The usermod -L command locks an account by placing an ! in the encrypted password. If the user has another means to log in, such as with an SSH key, using usermod -L will not prevent their login.

108. A. The format when adding a username places the username between the schedule and the command to run, thereby making option A correct. The other options shown for this question are invalid. In the case of option B, there is no schedule. In the case of options C and D, the schedule is incorrectly formatted.

109. C. The passwd command will be used for this purpose. The -a option displays all users but requires the use of -S to indicate status. The -S option alone will not produce a report for all users, and the --all option is an alias for -a.

110. B. The /etc/shadow file contains usernames, UIDs, and encrypted passwords and is not readable by any non-root user on the system due to the sensitive nature of the encrypted passwords. The /etc/passwd file contains usernames and UIDs but not encrypted passwords. The other two files listed for this question do not exist.

111. D. There is no direct relationship between the UIDs and GIDs on a system. UIDs represent users, while GIDs represent group IDs. On some systems, the UID and GID numbers will match for regular users, but this is not a requirement and is more of a coincidence.

112. A. The usermod command is used for this purpose. The -d option changes the home directory, while -m moves the contents. The other commands shown for this question are not valid.

113. D. The -G option is a list of supplemental groups to which the user will be added. A lowercase -g option provides the primary GID. The -l option causes the user to not be added to the lastlog and faillog databases. There is no -x option.

114. D. The chage command is used for this purpose. The -d option sets the days since the last password change and is measured in days since January 1, 1970. The -W option is the days of warning for changing a password, and the -l option displays a list of the various settings related to the account.

115. A. The crontab command can be used for this purpose, and the -l option is used to list the crontab entries. The -u option is needed to specify a user other than the current user.

116. A. The -r option creates a system user, which will typically entail no expiration, no home directory, and a UID below 1000. The -s option defines the shell and is not typically used for this purpose. The -a and -S options do not exist.

117. B. The /etc/gshadow file contains secure information such as an encrypted password for groups, where applicable. The /etc/group file contains general information on groups. The other two files listed as options do not exist.

118. B. The groupdel command cannot delete groups unless there are no users who have the given group as their primary GID. Therefore, option B best fits the scenario. There is no -f or -r option, making options A and D incorrect.

119. A. The id command shows the username, UID, primary group and GID, along with supplemental groups. The passwd and chage commands are not used for this purpose. There is no getid command.

120. D. The -c option changes the comment field in /etc/passwd. The comment field is typically associated with the real name of the account. The -R option indicates a chroot directory, while -d indicates a change of home directory. There is no -n option.

121. D. The find command will be used for this purpose. The correct syntax is shown in option D. The group command will merely look in the specified files for the number 1501; and the -u option to grep includes byte offsets, which is not applicable for this question.

122. A. Setting your address to `127.0.0.1` will use the localhost interface. Other local NTP clients would contact this server by its normal IP address.

123. B. The `newaliases` command re-creates the aliases database on servers running Postfix, Sendmail, and qmail. There is no need to restart the mail server after running `newaliases`. The `alias` command shown in option C will create an alias for the command shell but is not related to Postfix.

124. D. Configuration files for CUPS are found in `/etc/cups`. However, it is also common to manage CUPS through its web interface. The other directories listed are not valid.

125. B. Qmail directories are contained within `/var/qmail` by default. The queue directory is `/var/qmail/queue`. The other directories are not valid on a default configuration of Qmail.

126. D. The `info` severity level provides information messages for a given facility. Of the options given, `emerg` is used for emergency messages and not normally used by applications, while `debug` is the highest or most verbose level of logging available through `syslog`.

127. C. The `ntpq` command provides an interactive, menu-like interface into the NTP server. You can use `ntpq` to check statistics on peers, for example. The `ntpdate` command shown as option B is used as a command-line means to set the time. The `ntpd` command shown as option A would execute the NTP daemon itself.

128. A. The `lpr` command places a file (or standard input) into the print queue for `lpd` to work with. The `lpq` command prints the current queue. There is no `lpx` command.

129. D. TCP port 631 is used as the administrative interface into CUPS. Visiting an active CUPS server on that port will show the administration website for working with print queues and other configuration items related to CUPS.

130. A. The URL shown will display the jobs area of the local CUPS server with a query string name of `which_jobs` and a value of `completed`. The other URLs shown are not valid.

131. A. The `postqueue -f` command is used to flush the queue. The command will process all emails that are awaiting delivery. The other commands are not valid for this purpose.

132. C. The application could theoretically use any of the logging facilities, depending on the type of application being developed. However, the requirement to log to a custom log file means the logs will have a different name and possibly a different location than the standard logs. Therefore, logging to any of the standard or system-level facilities is not appropriate for this scenario, so one of the local (`local0` through `local7`) facilities is appropriate.

133. B. The `usermod` command with the `-aG` option is used to append a group onto the user's list of groups. In this case, the user needs to be a member of the `lpadmin` group.

134. B. The `mailstats` command is used for the purpose described. Of the other options, the `mailq` command will display the current mail queue but not statistics on mail that has been processed. The other two options are not valid commands.

135. A. The `systemctl` command is used for controlling services. In this case, `restart` should be sent to the CUPS service as denoted by the name `cups.service`.

136. D. SNMP traffic takes place on ports 161 and 162. Although the traffic is usually on UDP, the TCP ports are also reserved for SNMP. Ports 110 and 143 are used for POP3 and IMAP, respectively, while 23 and 25 are telnet and SMTP. Finally, ports 80 and 443 are HTTP and HTTPS.

137. D. Loading of alternate files is accomplished using the `-f` option. Doing so facilitates exactly the scenario described: being able to examine logins from old log files. The `-a` option controls the location of the display for the host, while `-t` controls the display to show the logins as of the specified date and time. There is no `-e` option.

138. D. The `w` command shows currently logged-in users along with information such as uptime and load average. The `fuser` command is used to show open files, and the `-u` option to `ls` controls the display for file listings. There is no `listuser` command.

139. A. The correct format is YYYY-MM-DD for the `usermod` command.

140. A. The `systemctl` command will be used for this purpose, and the subcommand is `disable`. There is a `stop` subcommand, but it will only stop the given service rather than prevent it from starting on boot. The other options are invalid for various reasons, including that they use `systemd` as the command name rather than `systemctl`.

141. C. The date of the last password change, as measured in days since January 1, 1970, is contained in the third field of a `shadow` entry. The expiration date would be the eighth field, as separated by colons.

142. D. Nagios provides advanced monitoring capabilities appropriate for the scenario described. Nagios works using various plugins that monitor numerous aspects of devices and systems. Ntop and mrtg both provide graphical statistics but do not have the alerting capabilities specified.

143. B. The `make oldconfig` command will integrate the existing configuration file into the new configuration for the kernel. Care still needs to be taken for items that have moved or changed within the new kernel, to ensure that the configuration is correct.

144. D. The udevadm command is used to work with the udev interface into the kernel, and the `monitor` subcommand displays kernel uevents and other udev events in real-time.

145. C. The `systemctl` command will be used for this purpose, with the `daemon-reload` subcommand. The `reboot` option would work to reload the `systemd` configuration but is not correct because it requires the entire server to reboot, which is not what was asked for in this question.

146. B. The /etc/inittab file contains the various runlevels and what to run at the given runlevel. For example, runlevel 1 is single user, runlevel 6 is reboot, and so on. The other files listed do not exist.

147. D. The /etc/rc.d hierarchy contains symbolic links to files found within /etc/init.d. These symlinks are then used for executing the scripts at the appropriate runlevel. For example, on boot, the system will execute the scripts found in the runlevel directory for each runlevel executed at boot time.

148. B. The file /etc/auto.master contains the configuration for autofs. The other files listed as options are not valid for this scenario.

149. B. NVMe-capable drives are named as /dev/nvme*. No special drivers are needed other than those found in the native kernel on a modern system. The other answers do not exist as paths by default.

150. B. The directory /sys/class/fc_host contains other directories based on the Fibre Channel connections available. Within those host directories will be found the WWN (World Wide Name) in a file called port_name. The other directory hierarchies are not valid.

151. C. The /dev/mapper directory contains information about multipath devices such as logical volumes. The other directories are not valid.

152. A. The iw command will be used for this purpose. When using iw with a specific device, the dev keyword appears next, followed by the device name, followed by the command to execute on that device. In this case, the link command is used.

153. A. The grep command should be used, and the -i option should be used in order to make the grep case insensitive. When used with -v, grep will exclude the argument, thus doing the opposite of what's needed here. The kernel ring buffer probably will not contain information about DHCP, therefore making dmesg not the correct option.

154. B. The -c option clears the kernel ring buffer after first read. The -C option clears it immediately. The -e option displays relative time and local time. There is no -a option.

155. C. The -a option provides archive mode, which is a substitute for several other options. The -r option is recursive, the -o option indicates that ownership should be preserved, and the -f option enables a filter.

156. A. According to the man(1) page for the make command, the name Makefile, with an uppercase M, is the recommended name for the file. The name makefile is valid as a default but is not the recommended option. The other files are not valid as default names.

157. B. The gunzip command is used to uncompress files that have been compressed using gzip compression.

158. D. The install target installs the final compiled files in their appropriate location and makes them executable, if applicable. Of the other options, distclean is sometimes included as a target to return source files to their pristine state. The other targets listed are not valid.

159. D. The baseurl option is used to set the URL and must be fully qualified, meaning it must include the protocol such as http:// or file://.

160. A. The /boot directory almost certainly exists but has not been partitioned into its own space. The /boot partition would not be hidden from lsblk if it was indeed a separate partition.

161. A. The grep command will be used for this purpose. Note the difference between grep -r and grep -ri. The question did not ask for case insensitivity, and therefore the use of -i in option B makes it incorrect.

162. C. The -f option will force the unmount to occur. The --fake option is essentially a dry run in that it won't actually unmount a filesystem. The other two options do not exist.

163. C. The <<< character combination reads input from STDIN or Standard Input and uses it as the body of the message for the mail command.

164. B. The who command displays who is currently logged in and the date and time they logged in. The whois command displays information about domains. The other commands are not valid.

165. A. The file named.conf, located in /etc/ or /etc/bind/, is the default configuration file for the BIND server. The file typically loads or includes other configuration files for specific configurations.

166. A. The openssl command will be used for this purpose, with the genrsa option. An output file is specified with -out. The other commands containing openssl all contain an invalid option. The final command is openssh and is not used for this scenario.

167. B. The acl configuration directive creates an access control list. Access control lists are powerful features of a Squid proxy setup and can include networks, MAC addresses, ports, browsers, and much more.

168. B. The http_access directive is combined with ACL directives to define access to use the Squid proxy. The other directives are not valid for use in Squid.

169. B. The nmbd daemon is responsible for NetBIOS name service request handling. The smbd daemon is responsible for file and print sharing, and winbindd provides user and group information. There is no daemon called samba.

170. A. The PermitRootLogin directive, set to yes or no, determines whether the root user can log in directly. The other options shown are not valid.

171. B. The push directive is used to send a route to clients on connection. In this case, the network and netmask are sent, with 255.255.255.0 being appropriate for a /24. The other options are not valid.

172. A. The WAYLAND_DISPLAY environment variable is set if you are using Wayland. You can see it by running echo $WAYLAND_DISPLAY. If there is output, then you are using Wayland.

173. C. The lsdev command can be used to view information such as interrupts and DMA addresses. In the case of option B, there is no -interrupts option to the ls command. The other commands shown are not valid.

174. A. The `control` subcommand is used for this purpose. When given the uppercase `-R` option, it will cause `udev` to reload the rules.

175. C. Containers, expressed through several types of underlying technologies, describes the virtualization used in Linux. For example, Docker operates with the concept of containers, and Red Hat also deploys a technology simply called Linux Containers.

176. C. The `service` command will be used for this purpose and requires the name of the service, which was given as part of the question, and the operation to perform. In this case, a restart of the service was required by the scenario.

177. B. The `DisplayBase` configuration option is used to configure the local port on which NX will listen. This option is added to 11000. For example, the default value is 1001, making the port 11000 + 1001 = 12001.

178. D. Software Rendering disables 3D acceleration and can be used if there are problems with the video driver.

179. C. GPIO (General Purpose Input/Output) is the interface used on a Raspberry Pi for working with external electronics such as LEDs. While it might be possible to use a USB interface for this purpose, it would not normally be used in this scenario. An HBA is a Host Bus Adapter and is used for disk communication. There is no SNP interface.

180. D. The `systemd-analyze blame` command can be used to troubleshoot boot times. The output from the command shows the time that it took various service units to start. Of the other options, only the `time` command is valid, but it is not used for this purpose.

181. A. A 400 response means something was wrong with the request, such as an invalid format or the request was too large. An unauthorized request will also typically receive a response in the 400-level, but not a 400.

182. B. The name of the file manager or file explorer tool in MATE is caja. The other answers do not exist as file managers.

183. B. The `-R` option creates a port forward and enables remote clients to connect. The `-L` option also creates a port forward but does not allow remote clients to connect. The `-P` and `-E` options are not valid for this scenario.

184. B. The `-o` option logs output to the file specified. The `-k` option converts links, and the `-r` option indicates recursive. There is no `-b` option.

185. D. The `service status` command is equivalent to `systemctl status` on systemd-enabled computers. The other commands do not exist with the specified option.

186. C. The `diff` command is used to compare two (or more) files. Of the other options shown, only `tar` is a valid command, and it is not used for this purpose.

187. B. The `<VirtualHost>` directive begins a stanza that facilitates serving websites using virtual servers. The other directives are not valid for Apache.

188. A. The `req` option begins the CSR generation process, typically also requiring `-new` as an additional option. The other subcommands are not valid.

189. B. The -1 or -HUP signal reloads the given process. The -15 signal is the default terminate signal, while -2 is an interrupt signal. The -9 signal is kill and is considered bad practice except in emergencies when the process doesn't respond to normal signals.

190. C. The Ctrl+C key combination terminates or kills a process in a scenario such as the one described here.

191. D. The >> character combination is used to append output to a file. Because it is being appended, the output will not overwrite an existing file. The other character combinations shown are not valid for this purpose.

192. B. The stop command, when used with the service command, causes a given service to shut down. The service can be started again with the service start command. The other options shown are not valid commands to use with the service command.

193. C. Port 5900 is the default port number for VNC. The port is added to the display such that the first display is accessed at port 5901, the second at 5902, and so on. The other ports are not used with VNC.

194. C. The automatic bug-reporting tool, abrt, uses /var/tmp/abrt on CentOS 7. In CentOS 6, /var/spool/abrt was used.

195. B. The trigger command is used to replay or trigger events. The other options shown are not valid for use with udevadm.

196. D. The set-chassis command configures the type of machine on which the hostnamectl command is running. This can be useful for certain types of applications. The other commands shown are not valid.

197. C. The file /etc/rc.local can be used for this purpose. Commands within /etc/rc.local will be executed after the computer has gone into multiuser mode. The other options shown are not valid files for this purpose.

198. C. The rndc command is used to control a BIND server, including over a remote connection. The other commands shown are not valid.

199. B. Global FileSystem (GFS), specifically GFS2, will likely be used as the clustered or shared filesystem in this scenario. The ext2 filesystem would not be used for this purpose. It may be possible to use CIFS for this purpose, but GFS2 is the Red Hat clustered filesystem of choice. The FAT filesystem would not be used for this purpose.

200. B. The <video> stanza is used to add a video device when configuring Spice. The other options shown are not valid for use with Spice.

201. B. The << operator is used for this purpose and will read from STDIN until the specified character or characters are encountered. This is sometimes called a Here Document or HEREDOC. Among the other options for this, only > is valid and causes STDOUT to be redirected.

202. A. The --level option enables the setting of specific runlevels. The other options given are not valid for use with chkconfig.

203. B. The `-o` option sets the local filename. The `-O` option preserves the remote filename. The `-f` option causes `curl` to fail silently, and the `-l` option is used with FTP to cause a name-only listing.

204. A. The groupadd command is used to add a group to the system. The other options shown are not valid.

205. C. The `whoami` command shows the username of your current effective user ID. Of the other commands shown, only the `w` command is valid, and it shows who is logged in but not a user-ID-to-username association.

206. D. The `/etc/profile.d` directory can be used to store files and scripts that are then executed on login. Of the other answers, `/etc/profile` does exist, but it is a file and not a directory. The other answers are not valid directories.

207. A. The Unity desktop is most closely associated with Ubuntu. The other distributions use different desktop managers.

208. B. The `/etc/rcS.d` directory contains a script to configure udev at boot on Debian. The other directories are not used for the scenario described.

209. B. The correct command and order is `systemctl stop <service>`. This is different from the `service` command, which would be `service <service> stop`. The other commands are not valid for the scenario described.

210. C. The `Monitor` section is where configuration for a specific monitor goes within an X11 configuration. The other options shown are not valid for this scenario.

211. B. The `/dev/null` location will accept input and not consume additional disk space when output is redirected to it. The `/dev/random` device exists but is not valid for this scenario. Likewise, redirecting to a network interface or regular file does not meet the criteria for this scenario.

212. B. The `-d` option sets the delimiter for use with `paste`. The other options shown are not valid for the `paste` command.

213. D. The `reload` target or command, used as part of a `service` command, causes the daemon to reload or re-read its configuration files.

214. B. The `Environment` key is used to configure environment parameters or variables for use with a `systemd` unit file.

215. B. The `<` operator redirects input from a file into a command in order for that command to read from a file. The `>` operator redirects `STDOUT`, and the other operators are not valid for this scenario.

216. B. The `NAME` parameter sets the name for the device. The other options shown are not valid udev parameters.

217. D. The `/etc/X11` directory is typically used for configuration of the X Window system including the main configuration file for Xorg, `xorg.conf`. The other paths are not valid.

218. C. The `alsamixer` command shows an ncurses-based interface that looks like a mixer in order to set volumes for various audio devices. None of the other options are valid for this purpose.

219. B. The `xrdp` package is an open source implementation of the Remote Desktop Protocol (RDP). The other options shown for this question are not valid packages for the scenario.

220. D. Port 3306 is the default port for MySQL. Of the other options, 25 is SMTP, and 389 is typically used with LDAP.

221. A. The `dmesg` command will view kernel messages such as those for video card detection. When piped to `grep` with `-i` (case insensitive), you can easily search for a detected VGA card.

222. C. The Ctrl+Z key combination will suspend a process. The other options are not valid for this purpose. The Ctrl+C key combination kills the process.

223. C. The `SSLCertificateKeyFile` directive points to the location of the private key for an SSL configuration. The other options shown are not valid directives.

224. B. The `iwconfig` command, which is similar to the `ifconfig` command, works with an individual wireless interface to set and display parameters. Of the other commands, the `ifconfig` command is valid but not used for wireless. The other commands are not valid.

225. D. The `tr` command can be used for the purpose described. The `tr` command is quite powerful for text conversion. The other commands shown do not exist.

226. B. The Nano editor is appropriate for this scenario. While Vi is indeed a text editor, beginners typically struggle with it. The `nc` command is not used for text editing, and there is no ShellRedirect text editor.

227. C. The `mask` command links the unit file to `/dev/null`, thereby ensuring that the service cannot run. The `disable` command deletes the symlink between `/etc/systemd` and `/lib/systemd`, but the service could still run. The other options shown are not valid.

228. A. The `more` command provides simple paging capabilities. Unlike the `less` command, which needs to be installed on many systems, `more` is usually available even on base installs. The `grep` command is not a pager, and the other commands are not valid.

229. A. The `&>` operator is used to redirect STDOUT and STDERR. The `>` operator redirects STDOUT, and the other options shown are not valid for this scenario.

230. C. The `/dev/tty` device is a special file on a Linux system and is the terminal for the current process. The other locations are not valid.

231. A. The `printf` command can be used to add special formatting to strings for printing. The `echo` command can be used somewhat for this purpose but is not as powerful at special-formatting capabilities as the `printf` command is. The other commands are not valid for this purpose.

232. C. The `unlink` command can be used to remove files and is sometimes faster than `rm` for simple uses. The other options are not valid.

233. A. The `scp` command copies or transfers a file over SSH. The `ncftp` command cannot be used for this purpose. The other commands are not valid.

234. A. A "405, Method not allowed" response will be sent when TraceEnable is off. A 100 code is continue, while 302 is redirect and 200 is OK.

235. C. The `nohup` command causes the `SIGHUP` signal to be ignored, thereby enacting the scenario required for this question. The other commands are not valid.

236. D. The `lsusb` command shows USB devices. When combined with `grep -i` (case insensitive), you can search for Bluetooth devices. The other options shown are not valid.

Chapter 3: Security

1. C. The `dd` command is used to create disk images, among other things. In this case, the input file is `/dev/sda1` and the output file is `output.img`. It's also common to add the `blocksize` option by using the `bs` argument, such as `bs=1M`.

2. C. The `tail` command provides the end portion of the file given as an argument. Adding the `-f` option will cause the output to update as new lines are added to the file being tailed.

3. A. The `xz` command can compress and decompress files in a variety of formats, one of which is LZMA.

4. A. The `chgrp` command can be used to change group ownership of a file. The order is `chgrp <groupname> <target>`.

5. C. The `-S` option displays output in a format such as `u=rwx,g=rx,o=rx`. The other options listed do not exist.

6. D. The `/srv` hierarchy is used for data for server programs. The `/etc` hierarchy is configuration information, while `/var` is also data files but variable files such as mail spool files. The `/tmp` directory is for temporary files. Keeping data on a separate partition can be helpful to maximize system availability in the event of a problem with an operating system partition.

7. C. The `chmod` command is used for this purpose, and the `u+s` option sets the sticky bit for the user on the specified target.

8. C. The 022 umask will translate into 644 permissions on a new non-executable file.

9. C. The `-R` option will perform the change ownership in a recursive manner.

10. C. The `-R` option sets the recursive option, which means `chgrp` will traverse the given directory and perform the group ownership change operation throughout the specified hierarchy.

11. A. The suid bit enables the program to run as the user who owns the file, regardless of who executes the program. Using SUID typically is not recommended for security reasons. The other permissions allow read (r) and write (w) for the owner of the file. The group and "other" permissions include read (r) and execute (x) but not write.

12. D. You minimally need to be able to read the file being sourced, therefore chmod 400 will correctly set the permissions. Any chmod that gives additional permissions is not necessary. When permissions are granted using octal notation, the number 4 is read, 2 is write, and 1 is execute. There are three permissions: user (owner), group, and other or world. Therefore, chmod 400 grants "read" privileges to the owner and no permissions to group and other/world.

13. B. The chage command will be used for this purpose, specifically with the -E option. When provided with a date, chage will expire the account on that date. When provided with -1, the expiration will be removed, thus removing the user lockout.

14. B. The getent command is used to display entries based on the /etc/nsswitch.conf file. One use case for getent is when integrating with Microsoft Active Directory or another LDAP service, to check whether the connection can be made to the LDAP server. The usermod command is valid but is not used for this purpose, and the other commands shown for this question are not valid.

15. B. The /etc/cron.deny file contains a list of users that cannot create cron scheduled tasks. The file /etc/cron.allow is used to provide a list of users who are allowed to create cron jobs. The other two files do not exist by default.

16. C. The kern facility receives messages from the kernel for logging purposes. Of the other options, syslog is used for logging messages about syslog itself. The other two options shown are not valid syslog facilities. Kernel messages are sometimes placed in a separate log called /var/log/kern.log.

17. C. The journalctl command is used to work with the systemd journal. On systemd-based systems, journalctl is a central command for debugging and troubleshooting.

18. A. The service used for logging on a computer managed by systemd is called systemd-journald. You use journalctl to view logged entries rather than the standard Linux toolset.

19. A. The mail option will send the log to the specified email address on completion of the logrotate process. The other options shown do not exist as options in /etc/logrotate.conf.

20. B. The $UDPServerRun option is used for the purpose described. The port on which the server should listen is then provided as the value for this option. The other options shown are not valid configuration items for rsyslogd.

21. A. The SystemMaxFileSize option controls the size of the journal log file to ensure that a log does not cause problems related to disk usage. The SystemMaxUse option controls overall size of journal files, and the default for SystemMaxFileSize is one-eighth of the SystemMaxUse setting to allow for rotation of files.

22. B. SMTP operates on TCP port 25, and if other servers are contacting your SMTP server, you'll need to listen on this port and allow traffic to it as well. Port 23 is used for telnet, port 110 is POP3, and port 143 is IMAP, none of which are necessary for SMTP traffic.

23. D. The nocompress option is used to prevent the log file from being compressed or zipped as part of the rotation process. This might be needed on systems where compression negatively affects performance or where additional processing is necessary.

24. B. Traditionally, udp/53 is used for DNS queries, but with a primary and secondary server, it is assumed that zone transfers may occur. DNS zone transfers typically take place over tcp/53.

25. D. The /etc/services file contains standard port-to-protocol information based on the well-known and assigned ports from IANA. If you'd like to provide a custom name for the service, you can do so by editing this file. There is no /etc/ports or /etc/p2p file by default, and /etc/ppp is usually a directory for the point-to-point protocol daemon and related services.

26. D. ICMP is a layer 3 protocol, meaning it does not use ports for communication. TCP/43 is used for whois, while port 111 is used for sunrpc. UDP/69 is used for the TFTP protocol.

27. B. TCP is a connection-oriented protocol that uses a three-way handshake to establish a connection and provides a stateful protocol. ICMP does not use ports for communication, while UDP is connectionless or stateless. IP is the core Internet Protocol and does not use a handshake.

28. D. The chage command is used for working with account aging information such as expiration date, password change, days between password changes, and so on. The -l command lists information for the given account. The usermod command is used to make changes to an account, and the other two commands are not valid.

29. B. The ssh-keygen command is used to create a key pair for use with SSH instead of a password. Of the other options, the ssh command does exist, but the -k option is used to disable GSSAPI credential forwarding and not for the purpose described.

30. A. The file authorized_keys, stored in the .ssh directory in your home directory, contains public keys that are authorized to login to the server using their corresponding private key.

31. A. The -u option is correct for this purpose. An uppercase -U option sets the user context for listing privileges. The -s option sets the shell, and the -H option sets the home directory.

32. B. The NOPASSWD option causes sudo to not prompt for a password for a given sudo command. This is useful for scripted scenarios where a password prompt would cause problems.

33. C. The `ulimit` command shows such limits, and the `-a` option shows all limits for the currently logged-in user. The other commands are not valid.

34. C. The syntax to block access to every service uses the `ALL` keyword followed by the address or network to which the policy will apply. This is important because you may notice attacks coming from certain IP blocks, and blocking with TCP wrappers provides a fast method for effective blocking.

35. A. The file is named `id_rsa` by default, and the public key is named `id_rsa.pub`. For DSA keys, the names are `id_dsa` and `id_dsa.pub`.

36. C. The `-c` option executes a single command but does so without an interactive session. The `-s` option specifies the shell to be used. There is no `-u` or `-e` option for the `su` command.

37. C. The `send-key` option followed by the name of the key sends the key to the key server specified by the `keyserver` option. This is a typical scenario for sending a locally generated public key to a public server for others to use. The other options shown as potential answers do not exist.

38. C. While any text editor can be used, it is highly recommended to use the `visudo` command to edit /etc/sudoers. Using `visudo` enables syntax checking, which will help prevent issues with an invalid configuration causing problems for those who rely on sudo.

39. B. The file `ssh_known_hosts`, usually kept in either /etc/ or /etc/ssh/, is used for the purpose described. Note that on some systems, this file and other SSH-related configurations may be found in /etc/sshd/. The answers that indicated ~ or within /root are incorrect because the question specified a server-wide list. A `known_hosts` file found within ~/.ssh would indicate the user's home directory.

40. C. The option is called `X11Forwarding` and must be set to yes in order for the destination server to forward X-based windows to the local client computer. The other options shown are not valid. Note that on some distributions, the configuration files are found in /etc/sshd/, while on other distributions, the configuration files are found in /etc/ssh/.

41. A. The `--gen-key` subcommand is used for the purpose described and will generate a self-signed private and public key pair in a PKI scenario. The other options shown do not exist.

42. B. Lines can be commented out of /etc/inetd.conf with a pound sign or hash mark (#). After making changes to /etc/inetd.conf, the service should be restarted.

43. B. The file `pubring.gpg`, found in ~/.gnupg, contains the public keyring.

44. C. The `-` option is the typical option passed to `su` for login. There is no `-u` or `-U` option, and the `-login` option does not exist. There is a `--login` option with two dashes, but that is not what's shown.

45. A. Password-Based Key Derivation Function 2 (PBKDF2) is used for key derivation for the password-based cryptography used with LUKS. SSL is Secure Sockets Layer, and it is typically used for encryption of HTTP traffic. Both RSA and DSA are encryption algorithms but not related to this question.

46. A. The `cryptsetup` command is used to set up and help configure `dm-crypt` volumes. The other commands shown for this question are not valid.

47. C. The `PARANOID` wildcard specifies that the hostname and IP must match. The `ALL` keyword is also a valid wildcard in TCP wrappers for use in both `/etc/hosts.allow` and `/etc/hosts.deny`.

48. A. The `-c` option indicates the creation of a `tar` file. The `-d` option is used for diffing between two `tar` files, the `-b` option provides the block size, and `-f` specifies the file for use with `tar`.

49. C. The `--remove-files` option removes files from the filesystem after adding them to the archive. The `-r` option appends files to the end of an archive. The `-d` option provides a diff between the filesystem and an archive, and the `-f` option specifies the file.

50. C. The `/etc/issue` file is used to provide a message to users, such as a login banner, prior to local login. The other files shown are not valid for the purpose described.

51. A. The `--delete` option removes files that no longer exist on the host system when syncing with archive mode in `rsync`. The other options shown are not valid for `rsync`.

52. B. The `--exclude` option excludes files matching a pattern from the archive. This option can greatly reduce the size of an archive by excluding unnecessary files from the archive. The `-x` option is the only other valid option that extracts files from an archive.

53. C. The contents of the file `motd`, an abbreviation for Message of the Day, are displayed when a user logs in successfully. Among the other options, the contents of `/etc/issue` are displayed prior to local login. The other filenames are not valid for this purpose.

54. A. The `-z` option will uncompress a `tar` file that has been compressed with `gzip`. The `-x` option extracts, while `-c` creates a `tar` file. Finally, `-f` specifies the `tar` file to work with.

55. B. The file `/etc/issue.net` is used to provide a message for remote logins such as telnet. The other files listed are not valid for the purpose described. It is worth noting that insecure protocols like telnet are typically disabled, or should be, in favor of secure protocols like SSH.

56. D. The `--modify-window` option modifies the behavior of how file synchronization is determined. The default behavior is to match to the nearest second. This option is useful for synchronizing between filesystem types, such as Microsoft FAT, which don't have the precision of Linux-based filesystems.

57. B. The `-c` option sends output to `STDOUT`. The `-d` option decompresses, while `-f` forces an operation. Finally, `-s` reduces the memory footprint for `bzip2`.

58. B. The `-q` option suppresses all warnings. The `-v` option is verbose, while `-L` displays the license. The `-r` option is recursive.

59. C. The -e option, also available as --rsh=ssh, uses SSH as the means for transport, thereby ensuring an encrypted tunnel over which the synchronization process will occur. The other options shown are not valid.

60. C. The home directory should be set in /etc/passwd and should be set to the chroot directory. The other files listed are not valid.

61. D. The only available algorithm for rndc is hmac-md5, and the key can be generated with dnssec-keygen. The other options shown are encryption or hashing algorithms but are not used for the scenario described.

62. A. The SSLEngine option needs to be set to On for SSL to be enabled for a given site or server. The other options are not valid. Enabling SSL is important in order to provide a level of security such that the actual data within an HTTP transaction cannot be viewed.

63. B. Squid listens on port 3128 by default. The other ports listed are valid but are not the default port for Squid. Squid proxies have sometimes been a target for attack or unauthorized use due to misconfiguration. Therefore, it's common to change the default port to something other than 3128.

64. B. The -k option enables Kerberos authentication for the net command. The -a option indicates that non-interactive mode should be used, and -l sets the log directory. There is no -b option.

65. C. The directory /etc/pam.d stores configuration files for individual PAM-aware services. Each service typically has its own file, which is managed for that service according to its usage of PAM. Of the other options, none of the directories are the default directories used for PAM.

66. A. The standard port for LDAP is 389, and that is the port on which slapd listens for connections. Port 3389 is RDP, while 3306 is MySQL. Finally, 110 is POP3.

67. C. The pam_nologin.so module facilitates a scenario whereby non-root logins are prevented when /etc/nologin exists. This module must be specified within a configuration file for a given service. For example, within the sshd PAM configuration file, the following line creates this configuration for SSH: account required pam_nologin.so.

68. C. The pam_unix.so module is used for standard login. The manpage for pam_unix.so indicates that it is for "traditional password authentication." The other modules listed are not standard PAM modules, although there is a similar pam_auth or squid_pam_auth module for Squid.

69. B. The pam_cracklib.so module enforces password strength options. The other files listed are not valid PAM modules.

70. B. PEM format is used for public and private keys with a Postfix TLS configuration. The other methods listed are valid cryptographic algorithms or systems but not for the scenario described. As with Sendmail, system administrators should take steps to secure mail servers so that the servers are not used for sending unsolicited email. For many scenarios, a full mail server like Postfix or Sendmail is not required in order to simply relay mail from a server.

71. B. The PREROUTING chain, part of the nat table, contains rules that are applied as packets arrive. A common use for this chain is to apply redirect rules. Among the other answers, REDIRECT may appear valid but is in fact a target and not a chain. The other options shown are not valid.

72. C. The iptables-save command sends the current iptables rules to STDOUT. The output can be saved to a file and then applied the next time the server is restarted. The other commands shown are not valid.

73. D. The iptables -n option causes iptables to not resolve host names or port names. The -L option lists current rules. There is no -a option.

74. D. The /etc/fail2ban directory contains configuration files related to fail2ban. The other directories shown are not valid. Other similar software such as DenyHosts may also be used but has been largely replaced by Fail2ban in many environments.

75. B. The PermitEmptyPasswords directive specifies whether empty passwords can be used for authentication. Enabling empty passwords would be a specialized use case and generally is not recommended. The other options shown are not valid.

76. C. The -P option sets the policy for a given chain in iptables. In this case, the chain is INPUT and the policy necessary is DROP.

77. B. OpenVPN listens on UDP port 1194 by default. The other combinations are not the valid OpenVPN configuration.

78. B. The DROP target silently discards packets that match the rule. An ICMP unreachable message is sent back for REJECT. In general, DROP is preferred in order to reduce the chances of denial of service (DoS) or other information-gathering issues.

79. B. The -m match limit, along with the configuration options shown including the LOG target, creates the scenario described. There will be three log entries per minute. This can be useful to prevent denial of service caused by filling up log files or overwhelming the server I/O while another attack is underway.

80. A. The INPUT chain will be used. When used with the -A option, it will append a rule to the chain. The -p option specifies the protocol, ICMP in this case; and the -j option specifies the target, ACCEPT in this case. The -P option specifies a policy and will not be used for this scenario.

81. B. The INPUT chain will be used, and a rule needs to be appended with -A. The ALL option, when specifying a protocol, means all protocols will be included in the rule. The -s option specifies the source, which in this case is a single IP. Finally, the DROP target silently discards packets. There is no BLOCK or DISCARD target, and the ACCEPT target will not block but will accept all traffic.

82. A. A rule will be appended to the INPUT chain with -A. In this case, the protocol should be specified with -p TCP and a destination port of 2222. The source address indicated, 0/0, applies the rule to all hosts. The ACCEPT target will be used.

83. B. Echoing a 1 to the /proc/sys/net/ipv4/ip_forward file enables forwarding of IP packets. This is necessary in order to utilize NAT and for other uses. There is a similar file for IPv6 at /proc/sys/net/ipv6/ip_forward. There is no /proc/sys/net/ipv4/nat file.

84. A. The logpath directive determines the log file that will be monitored for failures by fail2ban. This file is used as part of a larger configuration for a given jail. The other directives are not valid for fail2ban.

85. D. The ssh-copy-id command sends an identity to a remote server that can then be used for key-based authentication. The other commands shown are not valid.

86. B. The mailto configuration option sets the destination for emails related to sudo. The other options listed are not valid for sudo.

87. C. Port 123 is used for NTP communication by default. Port 161 is SNMP, while 139 is NetBIOS, and 194 is IRC.

88. D. The archive option, invoked with -a, is equivalent to several other options with rsync, such as recursive, preservation of groups and ownership, and others. This option is frequently used when creating backups.

89. C. Files related to SSL are typically stored in either /etc/ssl (or a subdirectory therein) or in the /etc/pki hierarchy. There is no /etc/private or /usr/share/ssl directory.

90. A. The AllowUsers directive is used to specify users who will be allowed to log in to the server. The other options shown are not valid.

91. A. The --log-prefix option specifies the string that will be prepended when a log entry is created by iptables. The other options shown are not valid for use with iptables.

92. B. The SELINUXTYPE option can be set to targeted or strict. With targeted, only specific network daemons are protected.

93. A. When Permissive is returned, SELinux is not enforcing rules but is using DAC rules. Other return outputs are Enforcing and Disabled.

94. B. The sshd.conf file is used for server configuration. On some distributions, this file is called sshd_config. The ssh.conf file is used for client configuration at the system level.

95. D. When a required module returns a failure, other modules continue to process, but the authentication ultimately fails. This is done so that logging will occur and other modules have had a chance to handle the authentication attempt. If a failure should be immediate without processing other modules, then the requisite option should be used instead of required.

96. B. The root account has UID 0 on a Linux system. Typically, service accounts have UIDs below 1000, many times below 100. Normal user accounts usually begin at UID 1000.

97. B. Although a hardware token may be available, the default option is software-based. Note also that OTP-solutions to generate a one-time passcode are similar in functionality to provide multifactor authentication.

98. D. The /etc/inittab file contains a line similar to ca:12345:ctrlaltdel:/sbin/shutdown -t1 -a -r now. Commenting out this line with a pound sign (#) will disable this key combination after restarting the system.

99. B. The directory /usr/lib/firewalld/zones/ contains predefined zones for use with firewalld. The files are copied to /etc/firewalld/zones/ when modified.

100. D. The password configuration option is set in /boot/grub/grub.conf. The other options shown for this question are not valid for the scenario.

101. B. The setenforce command is used for this purpose and can be given an argument of the number 1 or the word Enforcing to enable Enforcing mode. This can be verified with the sestatus command.

102. C. The ssh-add command is used for this purpose. The other commands shown do not exist.

103. A. The getfacl command is used to display access control list information for a file. The setfacl command is used to set this information. The other commands shown are not valid Linux commands.

104. A. By overwriting /etc/securetty with an empty echo command, root will not be able to log in at the console directly. Of the other potential answers, option C removes /etc/securetty, the effect of which is to allow root to log in from anywhere.

105. C. The file ~/.ssh/config is the appropriate location for this type of configuration information. Of the other answers, only ~/.ssh/known_hosts exists and contains public key information for hosts to which you have connected.

106. A. The -R option is used to indicate recursive behavior. Of the other options, only -v is valid and provides verbose output.

107. C. The gdisk command can be used to view GUIDs for a given partition. The other commands shown are not valid.

108. B. The -P option makes the values persistent across reboots. The other options are not valid with setsebool.

109. B. The directory /etc/apparmor.d/ is the location in which profiles are located.

110. C. DTLS, or Datagram Transport Layer Security, is used for datagram traffic. The other protocols listed are not valid.

111. B. The lastb command looks at /var/log/btmp to note bad or failed logins. The other commands shown are not valid.

112. D. The klist command shows the current tickets when using Kerberos authentication. Of the other answers, the kinit command is used to retrieve the initial ticket-granting ticket. The remaining answers are not valid commands.

113. A. The ps command can be used to help troubleshoot this. Of the other commands, the uptime command is valid but will only report broad-level CPU usage information.

114. B. The `-l` option provides a long or detailed listing of files and directories, including ownership and permissions. The `-m`, `-b`, and `-f` options are not related to the scenario described.

115. A. The `-a` option returns all booleans. The other options are not valid with `getsebool`.

116. C. The `aa-unconfined` command displays processes that are offering network ports but do not have an AppArmor profile. The other commands are not valid.

117. C. The `wheel` group can be used to restrict access to the `su` command to those accounts that are members of the group. The other groups do not exist by default.

118. C. The `chcon` command is used to change the security context.

119. A. An SSL VPN can sometimes work around firewalls that otherwise block VPN traffic. SSL-based VPNs are not typically the default in Linux.

120. A. When RSA is chosen as the key type, SHA256withRSA is the default option. Other options include SHA1withRSA, SHA512withRSA, MD5withRSA, and MD2withRSA, with MD5 and MD2 providing message digest formats. The other answers shown are not valid hashing algorithms with RSA. Notably, SHA1withEC is available as an option when ECC is selected as they key type.

121. C. An incremental backup captures only those changes since the last backup and can be used to preserve space. The other answers are all commonly used backup types. A full backup creates a backup of all files. An image typically refers to a lower-level bit-by-bit copy of a disk partition. Finally, a snapshot clone takes an image of a disk and places it in a safe location by cloning or copying the snapshot. It is also notable that an incremental backup is sometimes called a differential backup.

122. C. Of the available answers, the fact that the account is shared means it is violating a shared ID best practice. Neither integrity nor availability would normally be affected by this, and the password policy refers to things like the length and expiration of passwords.

123. B. A password set in the BIOS can be used to prevent the system from booting or handing off the boot process to a bootloader. Neither GRUB nor a root password will help with this scenario because physical access is available.

124. B. The `fprint` package is available to provide biometric authentication such as fingerprint authentication. Of the other answers, there is a `finger` command, but it should normally be disabled because it can provide information about accounts on the system.

125. A. The `-n` option to `restorecon` shows current contexts without changing them. Of the other options that are valid, `-r` changes recursively, and `-p` shows progress.

126. C. The `sudoedit` command allows a user to choose the editor of choice for editing the file. Among the other answers, `vim` and `nano` are both valid editors, but allowing them through `sudo` may have additional security ramifications. The `visudo` program is used to edit the /etc/sudoers file itself, which was not specified in this scenario.

127. D. The `ps` command shows processes. When given the `-Z` option, SELinux contexts are shown.

128. B. The `pam_tally2` module keeps track of failed logins and can be used to lock out an account after a certain number of failed attempts. Note that `pam_faillock` provides similar functionality.

129. B. Although Tunnel mode can be used for client traffic, it is most often used for site-to-site traffic, thus making Transport the correct answer for this question. Both Tunnel and Transport modes use IPSec for encapsulation.

130. C. Pseudo-terminals begin with `/dev/pty` in Linux. Standard terminals are `/dev/tty`, and the serial console begins with `/dev/ttyS`.

131. A. The command `aa-complain` is used to place profiles into complain mode. Profiles are located in `/etc/apparmor.d/`, and thus the command shown places all profiles into complain mode.

132. D. The `/var/log/secure` log file shows information about authentication and authorization. Of the other options, both `/var/log/messages` and `/var/log/kern.log` exist but do not typically contain authentication or authorization information.

133. B. The `PermitRootLogin` option is used to determine whether root can log in directly using SSH. It's typically a best practice to disable root login via SSH.

134. D. The AAA being referred to commonly for RADIUS is Authentication, Authorization, and Accounting, where Accounting is logging of dial-in attempts and other events related to the RADIUS system.

135. C. The `--runtime-to-permanent` option sets the current runtime configuration to become permanent and available on next boot.

136. D. SFTP would be the preferred option because it provides additional security over legacy FTP. In general terms, FTP usually should be disabled because credentials and other traffic are not encrypted. Among the other options, email (SMTP) such as that provided by Sendmail and Postfix provides no encryption and should be disabled if not in use. SSL by itself does not transfer files. Because the scenario did not include details of whether the transfer was over a long distance, it is difficult to tell whether USB would be appropriate. However, the use of USB devices is frequently discouraged on servers because it can be another attack vector.

137. B. Monitoring directly at the CVE website and the mailing list and other options ensures that you have the latest CVE information. While monitoring news sites and vendor sites may also reveal the CVEs, that information typically is not updated as quickly as the direct CVE site.

138. A. The `ufw allow` command is used to add rules, and SSH operates on TCP port 22.

139. C. The `auditd` daemon can be used to monitor the system for things like access or changes to files. This information is then logged for later analysis.

140. C. TACACS+ is commonly used by networking devices as a means for centralized authentication rather than storing credentials on each device or sharing credentials. Among the other answers, none provide authentication services for remote devices as specified in the scenario.

141. A. The software used to create firewalls found on most systems is iptables. Notably, later versions are called nftables, but iptables is still found on most systems in use today.

142. C. The cpio utility can work with various archive formats, one of which is HPUX-created archives. The gzip or bzip2 command likely would not be able to open or extract from the file; those are typically used for compression and not archival purposes.

143. B. The scp utility uses SSH as transport and therefore requires TCP port 22. TCP ports 20 and 21 are used for legacy FTP, while UDP/53 is used for DNS queries.

144. A. The -a option shows files and directories that begin with a dot. The other options shown are not related to this scenario.

145. A. Making a bit-level image of the partition with dd is a good idea in order to preserve any evidence of the break-in. Creating a backup using tar is a less preferred option. Examining the partition with fdisk would not reveal any relevant information, and reformatting the partition usually should not be done until the extent of the attack is understood.

146. B. The -i option specifies the identity file to use for the connection. The other options shown are valid for SSH but do not fulfill the requirements of this scenario.

147. A. The sha1sum utility can be used to create and verify checksums of files in order to ensure that the file contents have not changed. SHA1 is preferred over MD5 due to concerns over collisions and other security issues with MD5.

148. C. The -r option tells the zip command to traverse directories when creating the archive. The other options are not valid for this purpose.

149. A. The ps command, when given with arguments such as auwx, will show all processes and the owner of those processes. Combining with the grep command reveals the processes with the word *apache* in them. On other systems, this might be called httpd instead of apache, but the question specified a Debian system.

150. A. The chown command changes ownership of a file or directory, and the www-data user was specified in the question, thus making this option the only correct option for this scenario.

151. C. Non-interactive mode for sudo is triggered with the -n option. The other options are not valid for this scenario.

152. D. Telnet operates on TCP port 23. Telnet should be disabled in almost all environments because it offers no security for passwords or other traffic within the telnet session. If a legacy application requires telnet, then firewalling would be the next best option, and limiting connections only from the application itself.

153. A. The aa-disable command is used to turn off profiles used with AppArmor. The other commands shown are not valid.

154. C. The `-Z` option to `ls` is used to view the SELinux security context. The `file` command is a valid command but does not have a `-Z` option.

155. B. GnuPG can be used to provide digital signatures through its `gpg` command. The other answers shown are not valid.

156. D. The directory `/etc/apparmor.d/tunables` contains parameters and configurations that are commonly changed.

157. C. The directory `/etc/ufw` typically contains configuration information for UFW. On many systems, `/etc/default/ufw` will also contain commonly changed default configuration items.

158. B. The `ipset` project and software facilitates more effective rule management by helping to create sets of IP addresses to which common rules can be applied.

159. A. The public key should be copied to the remote host. When it is copied and the contents placed into `~/.ssh/authorized_keys`, authentication will be allowed from anyone presenting the corresponding private key.

160. C. When using octal notation, the number 4 is read, 2 is write, and 1 is execute. User, group, and other permissions appear in that order with octal notation. Therefore, 7 grants the user read-write-execute, and 5 grants read-execute for group and other.

161. C. The file `/etc/rsyslog.conf` contains configuration information for system logging. The file may be called `rsyslogd.conf` on some systems. You'll find things like which log items go to `/var/log/messages` and other logs on the system.

162. B. The `-v` option shows contexts of files listed in `/etc/sestatus.conf`. The other options are not valid for use with `sestatus`.

163. C. The `-M` option sets the maximum days for password validity, while `-m` sets the minimum days between password changes. The other options are not relevant to this scenario.

164. B. `KerberosAuthentication` is the option within the SSH server configuration that controls whether users can authenticate using Kerberos.

165. A. The `-t` option, along with the table name, limits output to just the specified table rather than all. The other options are not valid for use with `iptables-save`.

166. C. Sometimes called privileged ports, well-known ports are considered to be those ports under 1024. These ports are usually made available by system daemons and system-level services.

167. C. Individual configuration files for various log file rotation policies are found in `/etc/logrotate.d`. This directory is included from the primary configuration file `/etc/logrotate.conf`.

168. C. Just as the `tail -f` command will continuously update the display as new content is added, so too does the `-f` option display new entries for `journalctl`. The `-t` option shows messages for the given `syslog` identifier. There is no `-tail` or `-l` option.

169. D. The pam_limits.so module is responsible for enforcement of limits such as those mentioned in the question as well as several others like the maximum size of files, memory usage, and so on. The other modules listed are not valid.

170. D. There are multiple ways to specify log levels and debugging for slapd, including by keyword, by integer, or, as shown in the question, by hex. All the values shown are valid for loglevel. No debugging is 0, trace is 1, stats logging is 256 or 512 depending on type, and packets sent and received is integer 16 or hex 0x10.

171. C. The port for LDAPS or LDAP over SSL is 636. Port 389 is standard, non-SSL, LDAP. Port 443 is used for HTTPS, and 3128 is used for Squid proxies.

172. B. The pam_listfiles.so module is used to create scenarios whereby you can create files that control authentication and authorization through the PAM system. The other files are not valid for the scenario described.

173. B. The -t option sets the key type for ssh-keygen. The other options do not set the key type, but may be valid for other purposes.

Chapter 4: Linux Troubleshooting and Diagnostics

1. C. SATA disks are addressed as /dev/sdX, just like a SCSI disk. /dev/hdX is a traditional ATA disk. The other options do not exist.

2. B. The lsusb command is used to obtain a basic list of USB devices on a system. The other commands are not valid. In the case of answer D, the ls command is valid, but there is no --usb option.

3. C. The keyword single given on the Linux kernel command line will boot the system into single user mode. The other options are not valid.

4. B. Checking to ensure that the disk is detected in the BIOS is a good first step in troubleshooting. Answer A, unplugging the disk, won't help it to be detected. Restarting the web server won't help detect the disk, and the disk-detect command does not exist.

5. A. The ls command from within the grub > prompt will show the available partitions in a format such as (hd0,1).

6. A. With cable select, ATA drives will be detected in the order in which they are plugged in on the cable from the motherboard. It's likely that the drives need to be swapped physically on the cable.

7. D. Of the options presented, running dmesg is a common way to find out the location to which the kernel has assigned the drive. Rebooting the system is not a good option, although it would work. There is no such thing as /var/log/usb.log; and the location of the drive may change regardless of port, depending on how the drive may be detected in the system.

8. A. SCSI supports 7 to 15 devices per bus, depending on the type of SCSI.

9. D. The `ldconfig` command updates the current shared library cache and list. `ldconfig` reads `/etc/ld.so.conf` and incorporates any changes found within it. The other commands listed as options for this question do not exist.

10. B. The `upgrade` option for `apt-get` will upgrade the system to the latest version of software for packages already installed. The `apt-update` command does not exist, nor does the `-U` option to dpkg. The `apt-cache` command is used to work with the package cache.

11. C. The `yum install` command will install a given package. The `update` option will update a package. The other options listed do not exist.

12. B. The `export` command is used to set environment variables in bash. The other commands are not valid for this purpose.

13. C. Configuration files related to the repositories for Yum are located in `/etc/yum.repos.d`. Of the other options, `/etc/yum.conf` is a file and not a directory, and the other directories do not exist.

14. D. The `ldd` command will list the libraries on which the command's argument depends and can be helpful for solving GCC compatibility issues.

15. B. Swap space is used when there is insufficient RAM memory on a system.

16. B. The `/etc/lib` directory is not typically associated with library files and does not typically exist on a Linux system unless manually created. The other options either contain system libraries or can be used for that purpose.

17. C. The `apt-get update` command will cause the package cache to be updated by retrieving the latest package list from the package sources. There is no `cache-update` option or `update` option to `apt-cache`. The `upgrade` option is used to update the system's packages and not the cache.

18. C. The file `sources.list` located in `/etc/apt` contains the list of repositories for Debian packages. The other file locations do not exist by default.

19. B. The `pvcreate` command initializes a physical partition for future use as a logical volume with LVM.

20. C. The `lvcreate` command is used to create logical volumes with LVM. The `pvcreate` command initializes physical volumes prior to creating logical volumes. The commands in the other two options for this question do not exist.

21. A. Physical volumes are initialized first, followed by volume group creation, and then logical volume creation.

22. D. The `search` option performs a search of various fields such as the package name and description.

23. B. The `rpm -q kernel` command will show the kernel version. You can also use `uname -r` for the same purpose.

24. A. The `exclude` option can be used to exclude certain packages. The argument accepts wildcards, and therefore excluding all `kernel*` updates will create the desired behavior.

25. B. The partition type 0x83 should be created for a normal Linux partition. Type 82 is used for swap, while 84 is an OS/2 partition. There is no L type.

26. B. The `-s` option to dpkg searches for the given package and provides information about its current status on the system. The `apt-cache` command is not used for this purpose, and the `-i` option for dpkg installs a package. The `apt-info` command does not exist.

27. C. The `lvmdiskscan` command looks for physical volumes that have been initialized for use with LVM.

28. A. The `-i` option to dpkg will install a previously downloaded package. The other commands don't exist, and the `-U` option for dpkg does not exist.

29. B. The `env` command will print the current environment variables from Bash. The `printenv` command will also perform the same operation. The other commands listed in this question do not exist.

30. B. While the `ps auwx` command combined with `grep` will provide information on the running Apache instances, it will provide much more information than is required or useful for this problem. The `pgrep` command provides only the process IDs and therefore meets the criteria presented in the question.

31. D. The `free` command displays overall memory usage for both RAM and swap and can be used to determine when additional memory might be needed.

32. A. The `uptime` command shows basic information such as that described along with the number of users logged into the system and the current time. The bash command is a shell environment, and the `ls` command will not display the required information.

33. D. The `screen` command starts a new terminal that can be disconnected and reconnected as needed. Processes running from within the `screen` session do not know that they are running in a `screen` session and therefore meet the criteria needed to satisfy this question. The `fg` and `bg` commands will not meet the criteria, and the `kill` command will stop a process.

34. B. The `nice` command, when run without arguments, will output the priority for the currently logged in user, which is normally 0. The `renice` command can be used to change the priority of running processes. The other two commands shown as options for this question do not exist.

35. C. The `jobs` built-in command shows the list of jobs running in the background. Its output includes a job number and the status of the job.

36. C. The `killall` command is used to terminate processes using their name.

37. A. The `-i` option to `df` produces information on inodes across all filesystems. The `ls -i` option will produce inode listings but only for the current directory. The `-i` option is invalid for du, and dm does not exist as a command.

38. C. The -y option will attempt to repair automatically, essentially answering y or yes instead of prompting. Of the other options, only -V is valid and will produce verbose output.

39. B. The `tune2fs` command can be used for this purpose but should be used with care because it can result in data corruption.

40. B. The `mkswap` command formats a swap partition. The `fdisk` command is used to create the partition but not format it. The other two options do not exist.

41. A. The `du` command will report on disk usage in a recursive manner, unlike the other commands shown here.

42. C. The `usrquota` option will enable user-level quotas on the given mount point. This is typically set within `/etc/fstab`.

43. D. The -c option creates the files for the first time. The -f option is used to force checking, -u is used for user quotas, and -m is used to not attempt remounting read-only.

44. D. The -r test determines whether a given file exists and can be read by the current user. The -e test only checks to see if the file exists, while -s determines if the file exists and has a size greater than zero. There is no -a file test.

45. D. The `allow-guest` option changes the behavior of guest login for LightDM. And disallowing guest login would generally make the computer somewhat more secure, although if someone has physical access to the device, they might be able to get access in other ways.

46. C. The `xhost` command is used to control access to the X server. A host is added with the + sign and removed by preceding it with the - sign.

47. D. Setting a user's shell to `/bin/false` will prevent them from logging in interactively to the system, such as with SSH. The other options shown for this question are all valid shells and would allow an interactive login.

48. C. The `journalctl` command is used for this purpose; and the `--disk-usage` option displays the disk space used by journal log files, which are typically stored in `/var/log/journal`.

49. A. The `ifconfig` command will be used for this purpose and requires the addition of the -a option because the adapter is currently down. The `ifup` command can be used to bring up an interface but does not display information by default. The `netstat` command displays information about the network but not with the -n option.

50. D. Private IP addresses are found within the 10.0.0.0/8, 172.16.0.0/12, and 192.168.0.0/16 ranges, thus making an address in the 143 range a public IP.

51. C. The `route` command is used for this purpose, and adding a route is done with the add option. The default gateway is added using the `default gw` keywords followed by the IP of the gateway and the adapter.

52. A. The host command enables changing of the query type with the -t option. Using ns as the type will query for the nameservers for a given domain. There is no all type, and the other options are also invalid.

53. B. The -I option enables the choice of interface. A lowercase -i option sets the interval, while -a indicates an audible ping. Finally, -t enables a TTL-based ping only.

54. A. The host or dig command can be used for this purpose by setting the type to mx. The mx type will query for the mail exchanger for the given domain. There is no smtp type.

55. A. The -T option causes traceroute to use TCP packets. This option, which requires root privileges, can be helpful for situations where a firewall may be blocking traceroute traffic. The -i option chooses the interface, while -s chooses the source address. A lowercase -t option sets the Type of Service (ToS) flag.

56. A. The ip command with the monitor option/subcommand will display netlink messages as they arrive. There is no netlink subcommand for ip, and the route command will not work for this purpose.

57. A. The @ symbol is used to indicate a server to which the query will be sent directly. This can be quite useful for troubleshooting resolution problems by sending the query directly to an authoritative name server for the domain. Of the other options, -t sets the type, and the remaining options are not valid.

58. A. The getent command is used for working with NSS databases, and getent hosts will display the available hosts using the databases configured in /etc/nsswitch.conf.

59. C. The configuration option is called nameserver, and the value for the option is the IP address of the desired nameserver. There are several options that affect how name resolution is performed, such as the number of attempts and timeout. See resolv.conf(5) for more information.

60. A. The route command can be used for this purpose; the syntax includes the network range, denoted with the -net option, followed by the word netmask and the masked bits, followed by the word gw and the IP of the gateway. The other options shown are invalid for a variety of reasons including missing keywords and options and order.

61. A. The netstat command is used for this purpose, and the -a option displays all sockets, listening and non-listening. Note that it's frequently helpful to add the -n option, or combine them as in netstat -an, in order to prevent name lookup. Doing so can significantly improve performance of the command.

62. A. The correct format is IP address followed by canonical hostname followed by any aliases for the host. You can use entries in /etc/hosts to override DNS lookups, which can be useful to prevent those names from resolving or to provide a different resolution.

63. C. The ifconfig command for configuring interfaces begins with the device followed by the IP address, which is then followed by the netmask keyword and the netmask to add. Because this is a /24, the netmask is 255.255.255.0.

64. B. The `ip route` command can be used for this purpose, and its syntax uses a change command and the `via` keyword. The same operation could be completed with the `route` command but would require deleting the existing gateway first and then re-adding a new default gateway.

65. C. Secure Shell, or SSH, operates on TCP port 22 by default. TCP/23 is used for telnet, TCP/25 is SMTP, and TCP/2200 is not associated with a well-known service.

66. B. The `nc` command is used to start `netcat`, and the `-l` option causes it to listen. The `-p` option is used to specify the port on which `netcat` will listen. The `-s` option specifies the local source address and is not used for this scenario.

67. A. The `soa` type is used to query for Start of Authority records for a domain. Note that in many cases, `dig` will attempt to look up the domain within a given command and may not appear to have had an error. For example, when running option D (`dig -t auth example.com`), you will receive information about `example.com`, and there will be a line in the output that `dig` has ignored the invalid type `auth`.

68. A. The `search` option is used for this purpose and can be provided with multiple domain names, each separated by a space or tab. The `domain` option is valid within `/etc/resolv.conf` but does not allow for multiple domain names.

69. A. The `route` command can be used for this purpose; and in the scenario described, a `reject` destination is used for the route. The other options shown are invalid because they use invalid options to the `route` command.

70. B. The `tracepath` command provides the Maximum Transmission Unit (MTU) of the hops, where possible. Both `traceroute` and `tracepath` can be used internally or externally, and both provide IPv6 capabilities. Certain options with the `traceroute` command can require root privileges, but not enough information was given in the question for that to have been the correct option.

71. D. The `-c` option provides the count of the number of pings to send. The `-n` option specifies numeric output only, while `-p` specifies the pattern to use for the packet content. Finally, the `-t` option sets the TTL.

72. B. NXDOMAIN is the status for a nonexistent domain or host: basically, the host for which the query was sent does not exist. A normal status when there has not been an error is "NOERROR."

73. A. The `ip route flush cache` command should be executed after changing the routes. The other commands shown for this question are not valid.

74. A. SPF records are stored in the `txt` record type in DNS, thereby making `-t txt` the correct option for this. Of the other answers, only `-t mx` is valid and returns the mail exchangers for the given domain.

75. C. The only viable possibility of those listed is that ICMP traffic is blocked. TCP traffic is obviously passing because of the ability to get there using HTTP, and DNS must also be working.

76. C. The G signifies a gateway within the route table.

77. A. The axfr type is a zone transfer, and the @ symbol signifies the server to which the query will be sent. There is no xfer type. Option B is just a normal query for the domain sent to the specified server.

78. A. If /etc/nologin exists, users will be prevented from logging in to the system. The root user can still log in, assuming that root logins are enabled within the SSH configuration.

79. B. The find command will be used for this purpose, and the permission can be described as 4000 to indicate the presence of the setuid bit. The -type option can be used for changing the type of object to be returned but is not relevant for the scenario described.

80. A. The nmap command is used to scan for open ports. It will scan for open TCP ports to the address or addresses specified. The other commands shown do not scan for open ports to external (off-host) IP addresses.

81. B. The format is username (or other specifier) followed by hard or soft, depending on the limit type, and then the keyword followed by the value for that given keyword.

82. B. The lsof command can be used for this purpose; with the -i option, it will display the network ports along with their process. The netstat command will display network ports but not the process with the -a option. The ps command is used for processes but not network ports. Finally, there is no netlist command.

83. A. Setting -P0 will cause no ping requests to precede the scan and is useful for the scenario described. There is a -s option, but it is not used for this purpose. The other options are not valid.

84. C. The maxlogins parameter is used to control the number of simultaneous logins for a given account.

85. A. The -s option sets the type of scan and, when followed by an uppercase S, sets the option to SYN. The T option is a Connect() scan. There is no Y option or -type option for nmap.

86. D. The find command will be used for this purpose, and the -perm option is needed, specifically as the 2000 permission to indicate setgid. Note the use of / to indicate that the entire server will be searched. The grep command shown cannot be used for this purpose because it looks for the presence of the string setgid within files located in the current directory only.

87. D. The -p option to iostat displays information on devices and partitions. The -c option shows CPU utilization, and -d shows device utilization. There is no -a option.

88. D. The vmstat command is used to display extended information about performance including blocks in and out. The iptraf command is used to provide network-level monitoring, and the other two commands listed are not valid.

89. B. The w command shows various useful information including load average, logged-in users, and other uptime information. The uptime command does not show who is currently logged in. There is no swap or sysinfo command.

90. B. Pressing Shift+F within top enables you to choose which columns display as well as the sort order for the columns. In the scenario described, you can view the processes using the highest amount of memory.

91. C. Cacti is a graphing tool that uses scripts for gathering performance data as well as SNMP. The graphs can help to visualize performance of networks and systems alike. The pstree command is used to show a treelike structure of processes.

92. B. The -e option causes swapon to skip those partitions that do not exist. The other options are not valid for this scenario.

93. A. The -f option forces fsck to run on an otherwise clean filesystem. This can be helpful for times when you suspect there is an error on the filesystem and need to verify as part of the troubleshooting process. This can also be helpful to prepare the filesystem for conversion, such as might be the case with a tool like btrfs-convert.

94. A. The swapoff command deactivates swap space, thereby making it unavailable as virtual memory on the system. The other commands shown as options are not valid.

95. C. The --show option displays information about the swap spaces on the computer, including how much swap is currently being used. The -a option activates all swap spaces. There is no --list option, and -h displays help.

96. C. The pvdisplay command shows information about a given physical volume. You can use pvdisplay to view the device on which the PV is built along with the extent size of the PV. The other commands shown are not valid.

97. A. The vgscan command looks for both physical volumes and volume groups related to an LVM configuration. The vgscan command is run at system startup but can also be run manually. The other commands are not valid.

98. C. The pvscan command displays a list of physical volumes on a given server. The PVs displayed are those that have been initialized with pvcreate for use with LVM.

99. C. The ip command defaults to the inet family if not otherwise specified with the -f option. The command will attempt to guess the correct family and fall back to inet. The other families listed as options for this command are not valid for use with the ip command.

100. D. The -n option causes route to use numeric values only, performing no name resolution. This option is useful for the scenario described. The -e option causes the output to be in netstat format. There is no -d or -f option for the route command.

101. A. Because you're working with MAC addresses, the arp command will be used. The -d option removes or deletes an ARP entry, which would be appropriate here so that the MAC address resolution occurs again. The netstat command will not be used for this purpose. The hostname and dig commands work with name resolution but not for MAC addresses or the ARP table.

102. B. The `-o` option removes newlines from the output, thereby making the output more suitable for the `grep` command. The `-l` option specifies the number of loops for the `ip addr flush` command. The `-f` option specifies the protocol family. There is no `-n` option.

103. A. The `-s` option creates an ARP table entry. The `-d` option removes an entry. The `-c` and `--add` options do not exist.

104. C. The `-D` option lists the interfaces on a given computer. The `-d` option dumps compiled matching code, and `-i` selects an interface. There is no `-a` option.

105. B. The `-R` option requires an attempt at name resolution be performed. The `-n` option does the opposite: it disables name resolution. There is no `-b` or `-a` option.

106. B. The `mtr` command provides a unique way to view real-time information about each hop in a route between hosts. Both the `traceroute` and `route` commands are valid, but the options shown for each are not. There is no `liveroute` command.

107. A. The `--delay` option sets the interval between checks of array health. The argument value is in seconds. The other options shown are not valid.

108. C. The `!H` sequence indicates host unreachable. Network unreachable is `!N`.

109. A. The `-m` option specifies how the packet should be marked or tagged. The `-a` option is an audible ping, and `-p` enables specification of custom padding. There is no `-k` option.

110. B. The `-r` option displays a report including CPU time and exit status about the just-completed `fsck` operation. The `-f` option forces whatever operation is being requested, `-s` serializes `fsck` operations, and `-l` creates an exclusive flock.

111. D. The file `/proc/meminfo` provides a wealth of information about memory usage and utilization. Much of this information is displayed by various commands, but the canonical source for those commands is usually found in this file. Of the other options, only `/proc/cpuinfo` is valid, and that file provides information on the CPU(s) for the computer.

112. D. An Xmas scan is available using the `-sX` mode of `nmap`. The `-sT` mode is a TCP connect, and `-sS` is TCP SYN. There is no `-sP` option.

113. A. The `-s` option sets the snapshot length, or snaplen, of the capture instead of its default of 65,535 bytes. The `-l` option provides line buffering, `-c` stops after the indicated count of packets are received, and `-d` dumps compiled packet-matching code into a format that is readable.

114. D. There is no port for ICMP. The protocol does not use ports.

115. B. The `-B` option changes the format, and `T` sets the scale to terabytes. The other options do not exist.

116. C. The `-c` option checks for bad blocks. The `-b` option sets the block size. There is no `-a` or `-d` option.

117. C. The `-U` option shows latency. Of the other options, `-d` is used for debugging, `-L` suppresses multicast loopback packets, and `-i` sets the interval between packets.

118. B. The `iperf` command can be used to measure throughput and can be used for troubleshooting latency issues. The other options are not valid commands.

119. C. The `itop` command displays information about interrupt usage in real time, with a display that is somewhat like the `top` command. The other options shown for this question are not valid commands.

120. B. The `ibstat` command shows information about Infiniband devices. The other commands are not valid.

121. A. The `renice` command is used to change priorities. The lower the number, the higher the priority. The correct syntax is shown in option A. Option B will set the priority lower. Options C and D are invalid syntax.

122. D. The `-n` option is used with `netstat` to prevent hostname lookups, which can slow the output. The other options do not perform the required task.

123. B. The `pidof` command shows all of the processes associated with the given argument. In this case, option B shows the correct syntax. The `ps` command shown in other options is a valid command but not with the syntax shown.

124. A. The number 1, or `SIGHUP`, is the signal that sends a hangup to the process. The other options shown are valid signals but not for the purpose described.

125. D. The `sysctl` command can be used for changing parameters within the running kernel. The changes are not saved between reboots, though, and need to be reapplied if the system is restarted. The other commands shown are not valid.

126. C. The `-i` option sets the byte-to-inode ratio. The `-b` option sets the block size, `-r` sets the filesystem revision, and there is no `-u` option for `mke2fs`.

127. C. The `/sys/class/fc_host` directory contains information on HBA adapter ports on the system. The other options are not valid directories.

128. B. The `account` module interface is where access verification occurs. Among the other options, the `auth` and `password` interfaces are used for different purposes, and there is no `policy` interface.

129. A. The default policy should be deny. A deny-by-default policy discards packets. It's notable that a reject policy might also be used, which would send a reject back to the sender. The other options are not appropriate for the task described.

130. C. The `-l` option displays ownership information including user and group owners of a file or directory. The `-o` option only shows the user but does not display the group. The other options shown are not valid for this purpose.

131. B. The program should be created to use local sockets for communication. Socket-based programs do not need to incorporate network or protocol information, thus making them preferred over a network-based program for the purpose described. If the program needed network connectivity, then option A would be appropriate. The other options are not appropriate for this scenario.

132. C. The `buffers` column shows the amount of RAM allocated to kernel buffers. `Cache` indicates page cache usage, and `shared` usually indicates `tmpfs` usage.

133. C. The `nmcli` command provides a command-line interface into NetworkManager. The other options shown are not valid commands.

134. A. The `iftop` command is used to display real-time network usage through an interface that is reminiscent of the `top` command. The other options given are not valid commands.

135. C. The `iptraf` command shows cumulative network usage in real time for a given interface. The other options shown are not valid.

136. C. The `cfq` scheduler is the default for Linux systems. Of the other options shown, `deadline` and `noop` are valid but are not the default. There is no `iqueue` I/O scheduler.

137. D. The `ipset` command can be used for the purpose described. It's worth noting that you could create a separate `iptables` rule for each IP and rule, but doing so would be less efficient than using an `ipset` group and having a single rule applied to that group.

138. A. The `tcptraceroute` command should be used for this purpose. This command attempts to connect to the destination on the TCP port specified. This method is preferred over a simple ping because ICMP may be filtered, thus giving an inaccurate diagnosis. The other commands would not be used for this purpose.

139. C. The `tshark` command enables capture of network traffic into a file. The other commands shown are not valid.

140. C. The `whois` command is used for lookups of domains and IP addresses, among other things, and would be used for this purpose. The other commands are not valid for this purpose.

141. D. The `ioping` command sends requests to a given disk and records the time taken for the request. Of the other commands, `fdisk` is valid but would not be used to determine performance-related issues. The other commands are not valid.

142. C. The `partprobe` command causes a partition update for the kernel. The other options are not valid commands.

143. A. The `sar` command can be used to display a wide variety of performance-related information, including that captured over time. The other commands are not valid.

144. A. The `-a` option shows all available parameters. The other options shown are not valid with `sysctl`.

145. C. A state of D means uninterruptible sleep. There is no state for debug or dead processes, and interruptible sleep has a state of S.

146. B. The file /etc/default/keyboard contains information for keyboard mapping. The other options shown are not valid.

147. C. The default port is 631. The other ports listed for options are not used for CUPS.

148. B. The -R option changes ownership in a recursive manner. The other options are not valid for this purpose. The -f option exists for chown but changes the output to be silent.

149. D. The ausearch command can be used to find recent violations of an SELinux policy. The other commands are not valid.

150. C. The dmesg command shows the kernel ring buffer and is a primary tool to determine whether the system has detected a new piece of hardware. The other options are not valid.

151. A. The signal number or symbolic name can be used and is prefaced with a single dash (-) as shown in option A. The other options are not valid for the purpose required in the question.

152. A. Execute permissions for directories inherit, so the top-level directory must not allow the "other" permission to execute, which is needed for a directory listing within a subdirectory.

153. B. The default size for ioping is 4 KB.

154. A. The I/O scheduler in use is found in /sys/block/<device>/queue/scheduler. The other options are not valid locations for this scenario.

155. D. The -n option prevents hostname lookups from occurring with iftop. This is helpful for reducing the amount of noise or unnecessary information displayed within the iftop output. The other options do not accomplish the task required.

156. B. The server command, when run within the nslookup interface, will set the server to which the query will be sent. The other options shown are not valid for this purpose.

157. D. A user would need write and execute permissions in order to write into a directory for which they are not the owner and do not have group ownership.

158. C. LDAP can be used for external authentication scenarios with Linux and is frequently used to provide authentication in an integrated environment with Microsoft Windows and Active Directory. Of the other options, neither SSL nor SSH provides the external authentication, although SSH may be able to integrate with other authentication means.

159. B. The ulimit command shows the various limits that apply to a given user, including file size limitations. The other options are not valid.

160. A. The permissions should be 755 in order for a user to execute the script. The other options won't work for the purpose described or are too permissive.

161. C. The `chattr` command is used to change file attributes including making them immutable. The other commands are not valid.

162. A. UIDs less than 1,000, not including 0, are typically used by service accounts. This is not required, but is done by convention.

163. B. The `groups` command is used to retrieve a list of groups. The other commands are not valid.

164. A. The `swapon` command activates the swap space for use. The other commands are not valid.

165. D. The size of the request can be set using the `-s` option for `ioping`. The other options shown are not valid with `ioping`.

166. C. Looking for access vector cache (AVC) messages within the `ausearch` command can reveal information about policy violations. It's typical to also include `USER_AVC` within the query. The other options shown are not valid.

167. C. The `dmidecode` command shows extended information about hardware within a Linux system. The other options shown are not valid commands.

168. B. The `fail` option to `mdadm` indicates that the disk has failed. The other options shown are not valid.

169. C. The `-H` option suppresses the legal disclaimer when possible. The other options do not complete the task described in this scenario.

170. B. The `-i` option sets the interface for `iftop`. The other options shown are not valid for the required task.

171. B. The file `/sys/class/scsi_host/hostN/scan` is used for this purpose, where N is the adapter number. The other paths are not valid for the purpose described in this scenario.

172. B. The `/etc/shadow` file stores encrypted passwords. The `/etc/passwd` file does not store encrypted passwords, and the other options are not valid.

173. B. The `lsattr` command can be used to show extended attribute information about a file, such as whether the file is immutable. The other options shown are not valid.

174. A. The `size` and `rss` columns within `ps` output are helpful for determining memory usage for a given process. The other options are not valid for process-level troubleshooting.

175. C. `SIGKILL` corresponds with signal number 9. The other numbers shown are valid signal numbers but are not `SIGKILL`.

176. D. The `IN` class, or Internet class, is the default type of class queried with the `host` command. This can be changed by using the `-c` option for the `host` command.

177. A. The routing table is displayed with the `-r` option. The other options do not display the routing table.

178. C. The `-s` option displays summary output for the arguments given. The other options shown do not accomplish the required task.

179. B. The `ps` command lists processes, and using `grep` for the state of Z will show zombie processes. Of the other options, there is a `-Z` option for `ps` but it is not used for the purpose described.

180. A. The `lshw` command shows all hardware within a system, giving detailed information about many aspects of that hardware. The other commands shown are not valid.

181. B. The `-c` option sets the number of requests to send with `ioping`. The other options given are not valid for use with `ioping`.

182. B. The R state indicates a process is running. The other options do not indicate a running state.

Chapter 5: Automation and Scripting

1. A. The `echo` command is used to send output from a Bash script. The other options are not valid commands.

2. A. Ansible is agentless, using SSH and Python for orchestration. Puppet does have an agentless mode but typically uses agents for orchestration. The others are not valid orchestration packages.

3. B. The `env` command executes a command and enables a custom environment for that command execution. The `set` command changes environment variables but does not change variables for the single command execution, as specified in the scenario. The other options are not valid commands.

4. B. The `pull` command in git fetches the changes and incorporates them into the current working copy. The `fetch` command only retrieves but does not incorporate the changes. The other options are not valid `git` subcommands.

5. B. Infrastructure as code typically means managing infrastructure components using some of the same tools that developers would use, such as source code management along with programs or scripts and automation for deployments and configuration changes.

6. A. The `chmod` command will be used for this solution. The answer granting 700 enables execute privileges for the owner. The other options have incorrect syntax or inappropriate permissions for the scenario described.

7. A. The `source` command adds functions found in the file argument to the current shell. The `source` command is frequently used for software installs to ensure that the environment is set up properly prior to execution of the install scripts.

8. D. The character sequence `#!/bin/bash` invokes the commands that follow as a Bash script.

9. C. The greater-than sign is used to redirect output to a file and will overwrite the file if it already exists. The other characters do not fulfill the requirements of this scenario.

10. A. Creating a git repository requires creating the directory, changing the current working directory to the new directory, and then running `git init --bare`. The other commands will not create an empty git repository.

11. B. The term *inventory* is most often used in orchestration to refer to the collection of devices under management.

12. D. A backslash is used to escape characters such as a single quote in a Bash script. The other characters will not achieve the desired result.

13. A. An exit code of 0 indicates that the script did not encounter an error. This exit code is generally associated with a successful execution of a program in Linux.

14. A. Shell expansion, or, more accurately, brace expansion, can be used to create the output shown. The other options will not produce output as shown.

15. C. The pound sign (#) is used to indicate that what follows is a comment and will not be executed for the remainder of the line. The other options are valid comment styles in other languages but not for a Bash script.

16. D. No special extension is necessary for a Bash script to be executed. The extension .sh shown as an option is a common extension that you will see for shell scripts of any variety, but the extension isn't required.

17. C. The `merge` command incorporates changes to a previously cloned git repository. The `push` command is valid but not used for this purpose. The other commands are not valid.

18. A. An agent is software that runs on clients and listens for commands from the server in an orchestration architecture.

19. C. Infrastructure automation is the term most closely associated with adding (and removing) servers in response to load and demand.

20. C. When executed as part of a function, the `local` command can be used to create a local variable in a Bash script.

21. A. The `clone` command retrieves a copy of the repository for local use. The `checkout` and `co` commands are used with Subversion and not with git.

22. D. The $0 parameter contains the name of the script being called. The other answers do not fulfill the requirements of this scenario.

23. B. The `printenv` command can be used to print the contents of the current shell environment such as environment variables. The other options shown are not valid commands.

24. B. A single equal sign is used for string comparison in a Bash script. Of the other answers, -ne is valid but is used when comparing integers. The string *eq* would be an operator if preceded by a single dash, as in -eq. In that case, -eq is used for integer comparison.

25. B. A `while` loop that evaluates boolean `true` will accomplish the task described. The other options given are syntactically incorrect in various ways.

26. B. The `git checkout` command switches the working copy to the specified branch and points the `HEAD` toward that branch. The other commands shown as options are not valid with git.

27. C. The `export` command adds a variable to the current environment and is frequently used for the scenario described. The other options are not valid commands.

28. B. The current contents of the `PATH` variable, or any other shell environment variable, can be displayed using the `echo` command. Variables in Bash use a $ as part of the identifier. Therefore, any option without the $ would not work.

29. A. The $() sequence executes a command within a subshell, which is helpful for ensuring that global variables in a Bash script cannot be modified. The other sequences shown are not valid for the scenario described.

30. B. Managing configuration with orchestration is described in this scenario, so option B is the closest response.

31. B. The `-u` option or `--unset` will remove a variable from the environment. The other options are not valid with the `env` command.

32. C. The double-ampersand metacharacter executes the right-hand command only if the first command exits with a successful exit code. A single ampersand sends the command into the background, thus making option B incorrect. A pipe character executes the second command but does so regardless of the success or failure of the first command, thus making option D incorrect.

33. B. Two greater-than signs append output to the specified destination. Option A includes only one greater-than sign, which overwrites rather than appends output. The pipe character in option C does not send output to a file, and option D does not work for the purpose described.

34. D. File globbing is the process of expansion of special characters, which is required for this scenario. In this case, the negation character is the caret, thus making option D correct.

35. B. The `.gitignore` file is used to store files that will not be versioned.

36. C. The `for` loop should be used for this purpose because it iterates through a list. An `until` loop would require additional code, thus making it a less-preferable construct for the purpose described. There is no `do` loop or `foreach` loop in Bash, thus making those options incorrect.

37. C. Command substitution can be accomplished using backquotes or $(). These two methods are substantially but not completely equivalent.

38. C. The `git log` command is used to show a commit history. The other commands shown are not valid with `git`.

39. A. The `-m` option enables a message to be included in the commit, thereby alleviating the need to go into an editor to create the commit message. The other options shown do not accomplish the required task.

40. B. Build automation is the most appropriate name for kicking off the compilation of software on commit.

41. A. In this scenario, STDIN redirection is accomplished with a less-than sign to take the contents of `customers.sql` and send those contents into the `mysql` command. It's also likely that the `mysql` command would have things like `-u` for the username and `-p` to prompt for the password, but those were not relevant to the scenario and are not required in all circumstances. The other options shown are not valid for the purpose described. Options B and C take output from the `mysql` command, while option D is an invalid character sequence.

42. C. More than likely you have not executed `git push` to send the code to the server. Of the other options, you do not need to send commit IDs to teammates and there is nothing to indicate that you have been having problems committing the code itself.

43. B. The `-R` option performs a recursive change to the targets identified by the `chmod` command. The other options do not perform recursive changes for chmod.

44. D. The closing parenthesis is used to denote a case; when preceded by an asterisk, the default case is indicated.

45. B. The character sequence `fi`, which is the `if` statement backward, indicates the end of an `if` conditional within a Bash script. The other sequences shown as options may be used in other languages.

46. D. The `master` branch is the branch created by default within a git repository. The other names shown can be used but are not the default.

47. B. The pipe character sends, or pipes, the output from one command into another and is commonly used in a Linux environment for creating complex command sequences, whether through scripting or directly on the command line. The other options shown are not used for the purpose described in the scenario.

48. B. The `git status` command is used to show the current state of the working copy, displaying things like untracked files, files staged for commit, and so on. The other options shown are not valid for the scenario.

49. B. The `-n` option suppresses the trailing newline character from the `echo` command and is quite useful in scripting scenarios. The other options are not valid for the command.

50. A. The inventory of an infrastructure contains things like the version of software installed on clients.

51. C. Redirecting STDERR is accomplished with the character sequence `2>`. The plain greater-than sign redirects STDOUT. The other character sequences shown as options are not valid for the purpose described.

52. A. The `git config` command will be used for this purpose, and the parameter is `user.email`.

53. B. The `readonly` command displays the list of read-only variables that have been declared in the current session. The other commands listed for this question do not exist.

54. D. The `set` command can be used for a variety of purposes to change how the shell environment works. One such option is `-C`, which prevents output redirection such as that done with > from overwriting a file if the file already exists.

55. C. The `file` command can be used to determine which type of file is being used. This can be particularly helpful for files without extensions, where you are unsure if you should view the contents of the file. Option A, `grep`, is used to look within files but would not be helpful in this case. The `telnet` and `export` commands are not used for this purpose.

56. B. The `history` command will display your command history, including commands from the current session. You can specify how many lines of history to display, as shown in the answer for this question. Note that `.bash_history` will not show the current session's history.

57. A. Preceding the command with a ! will search history and execute the specified command. For example, `!vi` will start your last vi session.

58. A. The `type` built-in command returns the location that the shell will use in order to run the given command. The `find` command cannot be used for this purpose, and the other commands do not exist.

59. C. The `source` command is used to execute commands from a file. A typical use case is to create functions or variables that are then available for use within the current session. The other commands listed do not exist.

60. B. While it's true that every user has a `.bash_logout`, the file exists in their home directory and therefore can be edited by the user. Therefore, to ensure that the required command is executed at logout, the file `/etc/bash.bash_logout` must be used.

61. B. The `env -u` command will unset an environment variable for the current session. The `unset` command can also be used for this purpose.

62. A. The `env` command, when used as `#!/usr/bin/env bash`, will determine the location of the bash interpreter automatically. This makes the resulting script more portable for systems where bash may not be located in `/bin/`.

63. B. The `PS1` variable usually has its default set in `/etc/profile` and is used as the shell prompt. Users can customize the prompt to include hostname, working directory, and other elements.

64. C. The `$1` variable is automatically available within bash scripts and represents the first command-line argument. The `$0` variable is the script itself. The other variables listed in this question do not exist by default.

65. B. The seq command is used to print a sequence of numbers in a variety of formats. The answer for this question provides a starting point (0), an increment (1), and the final number (5), thus resulting in six numbers being displayed as output.

66. D. The exec command executes the command given as its argument and will then exit the shell. The source command does not exit the shell.

67. C. The read command awaits user input and places that input into the specified variable. The exec command is used to execute commands, and the other options are not valid for the purpose described.

68. A. Parentheses are used to denote a function, such as myFunction(). The parentheses are optional but are then followed by curly braces containing the commands to be executed when the function is called.

69. C. The sequence esac, which is case spelled backward, is used to indicate that a case statement has ended. Of the other options, the done statement is used for termination of certain loops in Bash.

70. C. The -p option displays declare statements in a way that the commands are fully qualified and could then be used as input for another command, through either piping or redirection to a script.

71. C. Square brackets are used to denote the beginning and end of the test portion of a while loop in a shell script. Other languages generally use parentheses for this purpose.

72. B. The test built-in will return true and can be used to test for the value existence of a variable not being null. Note that the behavior of the test built-in differs depending on the number of arguments.

73. C. The HOME environment variable, set automatically to the user's home directory, is consulted when the command cd ~ is entered. The other paths beginning with HOME do not exist by default, and the MAILPATH environment variable shown contains a list of locations where mail is checked when using the shell interactively.

74. B. The git log command will be used for this purpose, with an option of --follow and the filename/path to follow through history.

75. A. Parameters and other facts about the clients are also called *attributes* in an orchestration.

76. C. The integer comparison -eq is used for comparing integers within Bash scripts. The other answers are not valid for Bash script comparison.

77. C. The semicolon metacharacter chains multiple commands together but does not use the output from one command as input to the next. If the output needs to be sent into the next command, the pipe character (option D) is used. A single ampersand places a task in the background, thus making option A incorrect; and a greater-than sign redirects standard output, making option B incorrect as well.

78. A. The `\a` escape sequence, when used with the `echo` command, sounds an alert or bell. The `\b` option is a backspace. The `\c` option indicates that `echo` should not produce any additional output. There is no `\d` option for `echo`.

79. D. It is important to note that there cannot be any spaces between the variable name and the equal sign. Likewise, there cannot be any spaces between the equal sign and the contents of the variable. This makes answer D the only correct option.

80. A. The provided answer performs command substitution and places the value from the resulting command into a variable. Note the use of +%s formatting on the date, which then formats the output as seconds since the epoch, as specified in the question. Option C will provide the date within the `DATE` variable but will not format it as specified.

81. B. In shell scripts, the commands to execute begin at the do keyword and end at the done keyword. Other languages generally use either curly braces or tabs.

82. A. The `-r` option to `declare` will create or mark the variable as read-only. The `-p` option prints output in a format that can be reused. The `-x` option declares the variable for export.

83. C. The `LC_TIME` environment variable is used to control the display and behavior of the date and time and can be changed to a different locale in order to achieve the desired display and behavior of date and time formatting. The other options shown for this question do not exist.

84. A. The `-i` option shows interface information in a table-like format. Information such as transmit and receive bytes as well as the MTU for the interface and other information are shown. The `-r` option shows routes, while `-l` shows listening sockets. There is no `-t` option.

85. C. The Ctrl+C key combination kills a shell script that you are running interactively. The other key combinations may have an effect but not within this context or for the desired behavior.

86. C. Shell scripting syntax uses the format shown, with square brackets around the condition to the tested and double equal signs for a string test. Variables are preceded by a dollar sign as shown.

87. A. The syntax for setting the PATH separates the new path with a colon, as shown in the correct option. A primary difference between the correct and incorrect options for this question was in how the actual specified path was shown.

88. B. The `--abort` option attempts to roll back a problematic merge. The other options shown do not exist as options to the `git merge` command.

89. A. The `GIT_DIR` environment variable can be used to change the default location away from the `./.git` directory in which a new repository would normally be created. The other options are not used by git as environment variables.

90. B. The `\t` escape sequence adds a horizontal tab. The other characters may have different meaning and so are not valid for this question. For example, `\a` is alert or bell.

91. C. The double-asterisk sequence has special meaning and indicates that the file will be ignored in all directories.

92. A. The scenario requires alternation. Therefore, square brackets will be used to indicate the beginning of the sequence. After the brackets, a single asterisk indicates a wildcard. The other options will not work for the scenario described.

93. B. The git remote command will be used for this purpose; and, when given the show option and the remote name (origin, in this case), additional information about that remote will be displayed. The command is useful for displaying information about the destination for pushed code.

94. D. The $# character sequence contains the number of command-line arguments that were passed to a shell script. The other options shown are not predefined by Bash.

95. B. The TMOUT variable can be set in a given user's shell, and they will be logged out after the value given (in seconds) of inactivity. The other environment variables listed here do not exist.

96. C. The line will output the contents of the NUM variable. The comment occurs after the command on the line, and only code after the # appears is ignored.

97. A. Using the --origin or -o option enables the name to be changed instead of the default of origin. The other choices are not options with git clone.

98. D. The steal column shows the percentage of time that was spent waiting due to the hypervisor stealing cycles for another virtual processor and can be used with infrastructure automation to indicate that additional CPU resources need to be deployed.

99. C. The LC_ALL variable can be used to set environment variables for the locale and will override others. This can be used when there is a need for a temporary change. The other variables listed here are not used for this purpose and are not created by default.

100. A. A procedure is one or more commands that are executed on a client node as part of infrastructure automation.

101. C. Double semicolons are used to indicate the end of an individual clause within a Bash script. The other sequences shown do not accomplish the task described.

102. C. The unalias command is used to remove a previously defined alias. The rm command will remove regular files but not aliases. The other commands do not exist.

103. B. The -e option checks to ensure that a file exists and is typically used in the context of a conditional within a shell script. The other options may work within shell scripts but are not tests for file existence.

104. C. Setting LANG=C is an alias for POSIX compatibility and will cause programs to bypass locale translations. The other options shown for LANG are not valid.

105. A. The --list option shows the current configuration parameters for git. The other options do not exist as options for the git config command.

106. B. The number 2 indicates STDERR redirection, and double greater-than signs indicate that the output will be appended rather than overwriting.

107. A. A file with a `.yml` extension usually contains YAML. The question also gave a hint of infrastructure as code, where many tools use YAML for configuration and procedures.

108. A. The passwd file will be sent to STDOUT, where it will be captured and sent into the `cut` command. The `cut` command will separate the contents of the file line-by-line using a colon as a delimiter. The first field will be sent to STDOUT and placed into a file called `users.txt`.

109. C. The `shift` command moves positional parameters down by one. This can be helpful for complex scenarios with several command-line arguments, each containing an option.

110. D. The `--no-commit` option should be added to `git pull` to prevent the merge from being automatically committed.

111. A. Like the `for` loop, the commands within an `until` loop are delineated with `do` and `done`.

112. B. An exit code of 1 indicates a general error. The exit code of 0 indicates success, and 255 is out of range. There is no -1 exit code for Bash.

113. B. The `./configure` pattern is typically used to invoke a configure script. Option A might work, but the `build` directory is typically not in the path.

114. A. The `-a` option, when added to `git commit`, automatically commits previously known files. The `-c` option invokes the editor for the commit, and the other options do not exist.

115. C. The `LC_MONETARY` variable is used by certain programs to determine the localization for currency.

116. D. The `TZ` environment variable is used for this purpose, and the general format is as shown, thus making option D the correct answer.

117. A. Array creation in a shell script involves parentheses when used in this manner. You can also use square brackets to define individual elements, as in `ARRAY[0] = "val1"`.

118. C. The `-lt` operator is used to test for "less than" conditions within a script. The other operators are not valid for use in a shell script.

119. C. The `for` loop construct in this case will require the variable name `LIST` to be preceded with a dollar sign ($), thus making option C correct. The other options will not work for the purpose described.

120. C. The `elif` keyword is used to create an alternative execution path within a shell script. The other constructs, such as `else if` and `elsif`, are used in other languages.

121. C. The `.git` directory is used for storage of metadata for the repository.

122. B. The character sequence shown in option B is the correct sequence to redirect both STDERR and STDOUT. Of the other options shown, option A will redirect only STDERR. The other options shown are not valid.

123. D. The double-pipe metacharacter executes the right-hand command only if the first command fails. A single ampersand sends the command into the background, thus making option B incorrect. The double-ampersand metacharacter executes the second command, but only if the first command succeeds, thus making option C incorrect.

124. C. The git checkout command switches the location to which HEAD is pointing. By adding the -b option, the branch is also created.

125. D. Both while and until loops execute until a condition changes. The while loop stops when the condition is no longer true, and an until loop executes until the condition is true.

126. A. Comparing integers is typically accomplished using the binary comparison operators like -gt, -eq, and so on. Option B is incorrect because the > operator is used in square brackets. There is no -gta operator or gt operator, making both option C and option D incorrect.

127. C. SSH is typically used for communication between nodes in an agentless orchestration. Less common would be a protocol such as HTTPS. The other protocols shown as options would not be used for agentless orchestration.

128. C. Variable or parameter expansion is accomplished using ${ } wrapped around the parameter name.

Chapter 6: Practice Exam

1. B. Current interrupt (IRQ) assignments are contained in the file /proc/interrupts. Therefore, viewing the contents of the file with a command such as cat will work. There is no view command, thus making answer A incorrect. Likewise, there is no /dev/irq file, making answers C and D incorrect.

2. D. Configuration files for udev are found in /etc/udev, which makes answer D correct. The other options do not exist.

3. A. The modprobe command loads the module and its dependencies, if applicable. The lsmod command is used to list currently loaded modules, making answer B incorrect. The insmod command will load a given module but not its dependencies. Answer D, rmmod, is used to remove a module from memory.

4. A. The Shift key, if pressed when control has first been handed to GRUB, will cause the GRUB menu to be displayed.

5. D. The dmesg command displays the contents of the kernel ring buffer. On many Linux distributions, this log is also saved to /var/log/dmesg. The other options shown for this question are not valid commands.

6. A. The listing shows a symbolic linked file located in the current directory, linked to .configs/fetchmail/.fetchmailrc. The file is owned by the root user and root group and was created on July, 8, 2014.

7. B. The `systemctl` command is used to work with services and targets. The `list-units` command is used to list targets. The other commands are not used for this purpose or do not exist with the required option.

8. C. The `-nn` option displays both numbers and device names, thus making answer C correct. The `-n` option (answer B) displays only numbers. The other two options do not exist.

9. C. Out of the options given, the `systemctl status` command and option are the most appropriate. The `telinit` and `sysctl` commands are not used for this purpose. Likewise, the `--ls` option is not valid for `systemctl`.

10. D. The partition containing `/var` should be the largest for a mail server because mail spools are stored within this hierarchy. The `/etc/` hierarchy is usually small, as is `/usr/bin`. The `/mail` directory does not exist by default.

11. B. The `deplist` option displays the dependencies for the given package. The `list` option displays information about a specific package, while the other two options are not valid.

12. A. The `-ivh` options will install a file using `rpm`, displaying both verbose output and hash marks for progress. The other options presented do not exist or do not accomplish the specified task.

13. A. The `apt-cache` command is used to work with the package cache, and the `search` option is used to search the cache for the supplied argument, in this case `zsh`. The `apt-get` command is used to work with packages themselves, while the `apt-search` command does not exist.

14. A. The `-V` or `--verify` option will check the files in a given package against versions (or checksums) in the package database. If no files have been altered, then no output is produced. Note that output may be produced for files that are changed during installation or for other reasons. Note also the use of an uppercase V for this option as opposed to the lowercase v for `verbose`.

15. D. The `top` command is used to continuously monitor things like CPU and memory usage, and the `-p` option monitors a single process. By using the runquotes with the `pidof` command, the process ID is provided as input to the `-p` option. It's worth noting that this only works if there's a single instance of the process.

16. A. The `-g` option displays the progress of the dump. The other options listed do not exist.

17. C. The `debugfs` command can be used for this purpose. When the filesystem is opened with –c, it opens in catastrophic mode, meaning that it will be read-only and will not read inodes when opening.

18. C. The `xwininfo` command displays information about a given window within an X session. The other commands listed for this answer are not valid.

19. C. The file `/etc/localtime`, which can be an actual file or a symbolic link, is used to indicate the local time zone. The other files listed as options do not exist.

20. D. Within the /usr/share/zoneinfo hierarchy, you will find information on the various regions and time zones available. The files within this hierarchy can be symlinked to /etc/localtime.

21. A. The /etc/skel directory contains files that are automatically copied to a user's home directory when that user is created. The other directories listed for this question do not exist by default.

22. B. The atq command shows a list of jobs that have been scheduled with the at command. The other commands don't exist, with the exception of option D, which shows the at command but with an invalid option (--jobs).

23. B. UTF-8 provides multibyte character encoding and is generally accepted as the standard for encoding moving forward. ISO-8859 is single-byte encoded. The other answers are not valid.

24. C. LDAP over SSL (LDAPS) operates on port 636. Port 53 is used for DNS; port 389 is used for normal, non-SSL LDAP; and port 443 is used for HTTP over SSL.

25. B. The chage command can be used for this purpose, and the -E option accepts days since 1/1/1970. There is no -e option to passwd, and -l for usermod will not perform the action described. There is no chguser command.

26. A. The -i option for SSH is followed by the private key to use for authentication. Doing so implies that the public key is in the authorized_keys file on the remote host. The -k option disables the sending of GSSAPI credentials, while -f is used to request backgrounding of SSH. There is no --key option.

27. A. The -n option facilitates the scenario described and will exit non-zero rather than prompting. The -i option sets the login name and is not valid for this scenario. The -q and --noprompt options do not exist.

28. A. Single-user mode is typically runlevel 1. In runlevel 1, no network services are started. Runlevel 2 has networking but typically not services. Runlevel 5 is full multiuser with networking, and runlevel 6 is reboot.

29. B. The free command shows current memory usage for both RAM and swap space, including total available, current amount used, and current amount free. The other commands shown as options do not exist.

30. A. The df command displays information on disk usage and can help with planning disk utilization over time. For example, if you note that the disk utilization is increasing significantly, preparations can be made to bring more disk online or even to change the log-rotation schedule such that logs are rotated faster, thereby freeing up space.

31. A. The sar command can be used for this purpose and when provided with numbers in the format displayed, will update every X seconds for Y executions.

32. C. The -m option causes the disk-related statistics to use megabytes as the scale rather than the default kilobytes.

33. A. The `mkinitrd` command is used on older systems to create the initial RAM disk. The initial RAM disk is used to load, some might say preload, essential modules for things like disks and other vital components needed for booting.

34. D. A bzImage can mean that bzip was used to compress the image but can also mean simply "Big zImage" and compressed with gzip. bzImage is typically used for kernel images that can go above the 512 K limit that normally applies to a zImage.

35. A. The `-r` option repairs the filesystem, while the `-y` option causes `fsck` to assume Yes instead of prompting. The `-v` option is verbosity. There is no `-m` or `-x` option for `fsck`.

36. A. The `default.target` is the default target unit that is activated by `systemd` on boot. The default target then starts other services based on the dependencies.

37. B. The `mkswap` command is used to format a swap partition. The other commands are not valid.

38. B. A filesystem with the word `defaults` for its mount options will be mounted read-write (`rw`), `suid`, with the ability to have executables (`exec`). The filesystem will be auto-mounted (`auto`), but users will not be able to mount it (`nouser`). Character and block special devices will be interpreted (`dev`), and operations on the disk will be performed in an asynchronous manner (`async`).

39. C. The `fstrim` command is used to remove blocks that are not in use. The `fstrim` command is frequently used in a SAN configuration to give back unused storage to the SAN. The `fstrim` command can also be used with solid-state drives for the same purpose. The other commands shown are not valid.

40. A. The `--create` option enables creation of a RAID array that will use `md`. The typical argument is the `/dev/mdN` device. The other options listed are not valid for `mdadm`.

41. B. The `lvcreate` command is used to create a logical volume from previously created physical devices and volume groups. Using `lvcreate` is the final of three steps in the process for using LVM prior to actually using the logical volume.

42. A. The `ss` command provides many of the same functions as `netstat` but can show some extended information, such as memory allocation for a given socket. The `free` command shows memory usage but not by socket, and the other two commands do not exist.

43. D. The `-f` option is a flood ping. This will effectively cause the interface to send and receive large amounts of traffic, usually making it easier to find on a switch. The `-a` option is an audible ping, emitting a sound on `ping`. The `-c` option sends a certain count of pings, and there is no `-e` option.

44. C. The `bs` option is used to specify block size. Various suffixes are possible, such as M, which is equivalent to megabytes, and K, which is equivalent to kilobytes.

45. B. The `--size-only` option examines whether the files being synchronized are the same size. This can be helpful for situations where there may be significant time skew or other issues preventing the normal differencing mechanisms from working properly. The other options shown are not valid for `rsync`.

46. A. The lowest-priority number wins for MX records, thereby making 0 the highest-priority MX record for the domain.

47. D. DNS typically uses UDP port 53 except for zone transfers, in which case TCP port 53 is used due to the size of the request for most zones.

48. D. The `axfr` type can be used with `dig` to request a zone transfer. The client from which you request the zone transfer will need to be authorized to initiate a transfer.

49. D. The file `/etc/exports` contains definitions of filesystems to be shared using NFS. The other files are not valid for use with NFS.

50. B. The `max-lease-time` directive, followed by the number of seconds, specifies the amount of time that a given host can have a lease before it is purged. The other options shown are not valid in a `dhcpd.conf` configuration file.

51. A. Within `nsswitch.conf`, the `passwd` line contains information about authentication. The format is as shown in the correct answer. Local authentication is accomplished using the `files` keyword for the normal `passwd` file. There is typically a similar line called `shadow`, assuming that the server is using shadow passwords. The `shadow` line follows a similar format.

52. D. The `ssh-keygen` command generates a public and private key pair that can be used for user authentication between a client and server. The other commands shown are not valid.

53. D. The file `authorized_keys` contains keys that can then be used for authentication when the corresponding private key is sent by the client. The other files are not valid.

54. D. A logical location to begin troubleshooting is within the system BIOS or firmware to ensure that the drive is being detected by the computer.

55. B. The `export` command is used for this purpose and accepts a `name=value` pair, as shown in the answer. The other commands are not valid, with the exception of the `echo` command, which will simply echo the argument to the console.

56. C. The `HISTFILESIZE` option configures the number of commands to keep in the history file. The other variables are not valid within bash.

57. C. The `awk` command shown can be used for this purpose. The `-F` option sets the field separator, and the `OFS` option sets the output field separator.

58. B. The `git clone` command will clone into a different directory if that directory is passed on the command line, as shown in option B. The other options shown are not valid git clone syntax.

59. A. The `export` command is necessary so that any variables that are manually defined in your current session become available to child processes. The `source` command executes the file and can be used for the purpose described but requires an additional argument. The `let` and `def` commands are not valid.

60. C. The source command is the functional equivalent of a single dot (.). The set command exists but is not used for this purpose. The other commands are not valid.

61. A. The correct syntax is as shown. Note that a semicolon is required when the commands are included on one line, as shown in the answer.

62. B. The -f option sets the days between expiration and disabled for an account. The -g option is used to set the group ID, while -e is used to set the overall expiration date.

63. C. The -r option to the crontab command removes all cron entries for a given user. The -l option lists cron jobs, while the -e edits the crontab. There is no -d option.

64. D. The journalctl command is used to view and parse log file entries on systemd-based systems that maintain logs in a special format. The logger command can be used to create log entries, and the other commands shown do not exist.

65. C. The lpr syslog facility sends messages from the lp subsystem to syslog. The auth facility is used for security-related messages. The other listed options are not syslog facilities.

66. D. Standard LDAP traffic is TCP port 389 on the server. TCP port 25 is SMTP, 443 is HTTPS, and 143 is IMAP.

67. C. When connecting to an alternate port, you can use the -p option to set the port or use a colon to separate the host from the port.

68. D. The -p option preserves permissions. The -x option extracts while -z unzips with gzip. The -v option is verbose.

69. B. The -i option tells patch to ignore whitespace. This might be necessary when the patch file doesn't match exactly what's needed. The -p option sets the level of directory for the patch, while -e informs patch to interpret as an ed script. There is no -w option for patch.

70. C. LUKS encryption is the default mode for the dm-crypt command. Other modes include plain, loopaes, and tcrypt.

71. B. The -r option reverses the journal, displaying the newest entries first. The -n option shows the most recent N events, -f is follow, and -b tells journalctl to show a message from a specific boot ID.

72. D. The emergency target can be used in situations where rescue mode cannot recover the system. The other targets are not valid.

73. A. As specified in the question, you need to remove both group and user ownership, therefore both -g and -o are needed. The other options are not valid, although you can remove individual options from an archive process with --no-g and --no-o, which would be equivalent to removing the -g and -o options from the command.

74. B. The -r option bypasses the routing tables and enables sending packets directly using an interface. The -A option is adaptive ping, while -b enables sending pings to a broadcast address. The -q option is quiet output.

75. B. The `-b` option makes a copy of the original file before patching. This can be particularly useful in a scripted scenario where several files are patched in succession. The `-d` option causes a change directory prior to patching, while `-c` tells `patch` to interpret the patch file as a normal diff file. The `-s` option causes `patch` to work in silent mode.

76. C. Orchestration software can use an agent, which is described as part of the question, or the orchestration software could also be agentless, not requiring special software to be installed on each client machine.

77. B. The `\r` escape sequence is a carriage return, and `\n` is newline. The `\c` sequence invokes a control character and is not related to this question.

78. A. The `-f` file test checks to see if the file exists and is useful in a scripting scenario as described.

79. C. By invoking a shell specifically for the commands in the script, you can execute the contents of the script. Option A requires the execute bit to be set. The other options won't work.

80. A. The `ls-files` command will be used for this purpose, and `-i` or `--ignored` will be used, along with a required exclusion pattern, thus making option A correct. Option B is missing the required exclusion pattern.

81. A. Redirecting input from a file uses the less-than sign. Option B takes the output from `script.sh` and sends it to `file.txt`. Option C tries to use `file.txt` as input but without any way to send the contents to `STDOUT`. Option D executes `script.sh` and sends the contents to `file.txt`, which is opposite of the scenario.

82. B. The `-c` option sets the maximum mount count. The `-C` option sets the current number of mounts. The `-b` and `-a` options do not exist.

83. D. The `-f` option, also known as `fake`, is helpful for situations where you need to debug the mount process or when you need to add an entry to `/etc/mtab` for a previously mounted filesystem. The `-l` option shows labels, and `-v` is `verbose`. There is no `-q` option.

84. A. The `netstat` command can be used for this purpose, and the `-r` option displays the current routes. The addition of `-n` prevents DNS lookups, which can help with performance.

85. A. The `ps` command provides information on processor and memory usage for individual processes. You can use this information to predict capacity.

86. C. The `wa` statistic shows time spent waiting for I/O and can be used to measure or find a bottleneck related to disk. The `us` statistic is time spent on userspace processes, while `sy` is time spent on kernel processes. There is no statistic called `io` within `vmstat`.

87. A. Load average with the `uptime` command is displayed in 1-, 5-, and 15-minute increments.

88. A. The `-a` option displays all values and their current settings for `sysctl`. The `-b` option is binary and displays values without any newlines. The `-d` option is an alias for `-h`, which displays help. There is no `-c` option.

89. B. The `SIGTERM` signal is the default signal sent with the `systemctl kill` command.

90. C. The `ldconfig` command is used to work with the library cache, and the `-p` option prints the directories and libraries in the cache. The `-C` option informs `ldconfig` to use a different cache. The `ldd` command prints the library dependencies for a given command, but the options given don't exist for `ldd`.

Index

A

\a escape sequence, 174
aa-complain command, 115
aa-disable command, 119
aa-unconfined command, 113
AAA (Authentication, Authorization, Accounting) services, 116
--abort option for merge conflicts, 176
access control lists
    files, 111
    policies, 149
    Squid, 73–74
accounts
    disabling, 196
    expiration, 69, 96, 190
    information on, 98
    locking, 115
    PAM, 149
acl command, 73
active-backup mode for network bonding, 30
active/passive mode for network bonding, 30
addresses. *See* IP addresses
age limits for passwords, 121
agent orchestration, 164, 198
agentless orchestration, 183
alerts, escape sequences for, 174
aliased commands, 178
aliases for email, 66
allow-guest=false option, 135
AllowUsers directive, 108
alsamixer command, 82
anaconda and kickstart, 31
Ansible package, 162
Apache servers
    configuration file, 77
    restarting, 75
    SSL private keys, 83
AppArmor
    processes, 113
    profiles, 115, 119
    settings, 119
appending output
    to files, 167
    to STDOUT, 78

apt-cache search command, 51, 188
apt-get update command, 52, 130
apt-get upgrade command, 48, 129
archive mode for rsync command, 71
arguments, number of, 177
arp command, 144–145
arrays
    creating, 25, 181, 192
    RAID, 24, 26, 156
at now command, 62
atq command, 189
atrm command, 63
attributes for files, 154, 156
audio, mixer volumes, 82
auditd daemon, 117
ausearch command, 152
authentication
    biometric, 114
    Kerberos, 104, 112, 121
    keys, 190, 194
    LDAP, 122, 154
    logs, 115
    mechanisms, 194
    network components, 117
    PAM, 122
    rndc, 103
    server UIDs and GIDs, 64
Authentication, Authorization, Accounting (AAA) services, 116
authoritative name servers, querying, 16
authorization
    logs, 115
    PAM, 122
authorized_keys file, 98
autofs automounter, 70
automatic logouts, 177
automation
    build, 168, 180
    configuration management, 166
    infrastructure, 165, 178
    inventory attributes, 174
automount options, 70
AVC messages, 155
awk command, 195

B

background tasks, viewing, 133
backquotes (`) for commands, 168
backslashes (\) for escape characters, 163
backups
　extracting files from, 117
　incremental, 114
　patch command, 198
backward searches with less command, 58
bad blocks
　checking for, 147
　displaying, 23
balance-rr mode for bonding scenarios, 35
bare-metal hypervisors, 34
baseurl option for package repositories, 72
.bash_history file, 195
.bash_profile file, 60
Bash shell, invoking, 163
bcfg command, 22
bell, escape sequences for, 174
/bin/false shell, 135
BIND
　chroot scenario, 103
　reloading, 77
　server configuration, 73
　server control, 79
biometric authentication, 114
BIOS
　passwords, 114
　SATA disks, 194
blacklist information for modules, 21
blkid command
　caches, 33
　UUIDs, 11, 33
blob storage, 31
block devices, information on, 142
blocks
　removing, 25, 192
　reserved, 12
Bluetooth devices, detecting, 85
bonded-link aggregation, 33
bonding scenarios, load balancing in, 35
/boot/efi partition, 5
/boot/grub/grub.conf file, 110
/boot partition
　mounting in, 22
　size, 7
boot times for services, 76
booting
　changing order, 22
　configuration, 22
　device checking order, 12
　from HTTP and FTP, 28
　kernel ring buffer, 5
　kickstart, 35
　location, 27
　lsblk command, 72
　preventing, 114
　single-user mode, 5
　troubleshooting, 129
bootloaders
　ISO, 22
　passwords, 110
　UEFI, 22
brace expansion in echo command, 164
brctl command, 36
bridging vs. NAT, 30
btrfs filesystems, 11
buffers column for memory usage, 150
build automation, 168, 180
build files, excluding, 176
bypassing
　locale translations, 14, 179
　routing tables, 198
byte-to-inode ratio, 149
bzImage, creating, 191
bzip2 command, 103

C

caches
　Kerberos authentication, 112
　package, 52
　purging, 33
　shared libraries, 48, 129
Cacti tool, 143
caja file manager, 76
carriage returns, escape characters for, 198
case statements
　clause ends, 178
　default case, 169
　terminating, 173
cat /etc/passwd command
　contents output, 55
　description, 179
　usernames, 54
cat /proc/interrupts command, 46, 186
CentOS 7 bug-reporting tool, 78
certificate authority servers, 73
Certificate Signing Requests (CSRs), 77
certificates in Postfix TLS, 105
cfq scheduler, 150

chage command
    accounts, 96, 98
    passwords, 64, 121
chaining commands, 169, 174
change date for passwords, 64, 69
character case, converting, 83
characters
    attributes, 189
    multibyte representation, 13
    supported character sets, 32
chattr command, 154
chcon command, 113
checksums for files, 118
chgrp command
    group ownership, 94–95
    web servers, 59
chkconfig —level command, 79
chkconfig —list command, 47
chmod command
    permissions, 111
    privileges, 95
    recursive changes, 95, 169
    script execution, 162
    sticky bits, 95
chown command, 118, 152
chroot scenario with BIND, 103
CIFS (Common Internet File System), 32
clock
    setting, 15
    UTC time, 15
    working with, 14
cloning repositories, 165, 177, 195
cloud-init command, 32
cluster servers, 79
collection of devices, 163
command execution
    customized environments, 162
    on logout, 171
    in non-interactive sessions, 99
    source commands, 171
    subshells, 166
command-line interface for Network Manager, 150
commands
    aliased, 178
    arguments, 177
    backquotes, 168
    chaining, 169, 174
    executed on logout, 171
    exiting shell, 172
    from files, 171
    history, 171, 195
    kernel modules, 30
    location, 171
    multiple, 167, 182
    parameters, 172
    paths, 176
    scheduling, 62
    SQL, 168
    time to execute, 31
    user input, 172
comments
    /etc/inetd.conf file, 100
    scripts, 164
commits
    automatic, 180
    history, 168, 174
Common Internet File System (CIFS), 32
comparing
    files, 77
    integers, 174, 182
    modules, 35
    strings, 165
    variables, 176
complain mode for AppArmor profiles, 115
completed print jobs in CUPS, 67
compression
    .gz files, 72
    logs, 97
    lzma files, 94
    tar command, 102
configuration management automation, 166
connection points for USB disks, 129
connections
    hypervisors, 32
    SSH, 197
    troubleshooting, 140
    USB devices, 48
    X severs, 135
console logins by root user, 111
containers, 75
contexts
    displaying, 114
    files, 120
    SELinux, 113, 115, 119, 152
converting character case, 83
copying
    directories, 55
    files, 60, 85, 117, 189
    keys, 120
    repositories, 169
cp command
    directories, 55
    overwriting files, 55

cpio utility, 117
cron
    directory, 63
    entry lists, 65
    job execution, 62
    scheduled tasks, 96
    system-wide files, 63
    users, 62
crontab command
    entry lists, 65
    removing jobs, 196
cryptsetup command, 101
CSRs (Certificate Signing Requests), 77
Ctrl+Alt+Del keys, disabling, 110
Ctrl+C keys
    terminating daemons, 77
    terminating scripts, 175
Ctrl+Z keys for suspending daemons, 83
CUPS system
    completed print jobs, 67
    configuration, 66
    default ports, 67, 152
    restarting, 68
curl command, 80
currency-related localization, 14, 181
current default route, 199
currently mounted filesystems, 10
custom commands for kernel modules, 30
custom logs, 67
customized environments, command execution in, 162
cut command, 55
CVE process for security bulletins, 116

D

daemons
    configuration files, 81
    local servers, 149
    stopping, 81
    suspending, 83
    terminating, 77
datagram security, 112
Datagram Transport Layer Security (DTLS), 112
date command, 15
dates
    formats, 13, 175
    obtaining, 175
    setting, 15
dd command
    megabyte IO, 193
    partition images, 94, 118

Debian systems, updating, 48, 129
debugfs command, 188
debugging, enabling, 27
debugging logs for libvirt, 31
declare command, 173, 175
declaring variables, 166
default base port in VNC, 78
default branches in repositories, 169
default configuration for BIND servers, 73
default delimiters, 55
default gateways
    adding, 15, 136
    changing, 18, 138
default paths, 176
default ports
    CUPS, 67, 152
    MySQL, 82
    VNC, 78
default route, displaying, 15, 199
default.target unit, 191
default targets, displaying, 47
defaults line in /etc/fstab file, 24, 192
delimiters, setting, 81
deny policy for access control lists, 149
dependencies
    displaying, 21, 51, 186–187
    libraries, 48, 130
    loaded modules, 20
    loading, 5
depmod command
    dependencies, 20
    module comparisons, 35
detected hardware list, 157
/dev/disk/by-id directory, 24
/dev/disk/by-multipath directory, 35
/dev/disk/by-path directory, 25
/dev/disk/by-uuid directory, 33
/dev filesystem, 32
/dev/mapper directory, 26, 71
/dev/null directory, 81
/dev/nvme* directory, 70
/dev/pty device, 115
/dev/sda1 partition, 8, 94
/dev/sdX device, 50, 128
/dev/tty device, 84
devices
    boot checking order, 12
    collection of, 163
    displaying names of, 50, 187
    information on, 74
    lsmod driver display, 6
    pseudo-terminals, 115

df command
    disk utilization, 19, 190
    inodes, 134
    report scale, 147
DHCP
    configuration, 36
    leases, 194
    server system log, 71
dhcpd.conf file, 194
diff command, 77
dig command
    mail server queries, 16, 137
    server queries, 17
    Start of Authority information, 18, 139
    zone transfers, 19, 140, 193
digital signatures, 119
directories
    copying, 55
    creating, 55
    finding, 54
    large files on, 10, 134
    listing, 167
    log configuration, 121
    permissions, 153
    profiles, 112
    removing, 54
    traversal, 118
    UFW configuration, 120
disabling
    accounts, 196
    Ctrl+Alt+Del keys, 110
    hostname lookups, 148
    logging, 35
disks
    detecting, 128
    GRUB Legacy configuration file, 8
    preparing, 9
    RAM, 20–21, 191
    SATA, 50, 128, 194
    space usage, 136
    statistics, 146
    unallocated space, 30
    USB, 6, 129
    utilization display, 19, 190
DISPLAY environment variable, 60
display port setting, 75
DisplayBase option, 75
dm-crypt
    encryption, 197
    volume configuration, 101

dmesg command
    kernel ring buffer, 5, 71, 186
    logs, 35
    RAID adapters, 153
    USB disks, 129
    video cards, 83
dmidecode command, 155
dnf search command, 53
DNS
    overriding, 18
    server setting, 17, 137
    SPF records, 19, 140
    troubleshooting, 140
dnssec-keygen command, 103
do keyword
    for loops, 175
    until loops, 180
dollar signs ($)
    command execution, 166
    command-line arguments, 177
domains, information on, 13
dominfo command, 13
done keyword
    for loops, 175
    until loops, 180
dot (.) files, displaying, 117
dpkg command
    package changes, 52
    package information, 53, 132
dracut command, 21
drivers
    displaying, 36
    network interfaces, 36
DROP targets for iptables, 106
DTLS (Datagram Transport Layer Security), 112
du command
    human-friendly format, 34
    large files on directories, 10, 134
    summary output, 157
dual-homed networks, 29
dumpe2fs command, 12, 23

E

-e option for file existence, 178
e2label command, 29
EC2 instances, 32
echo command
    brace expansion, 164
    forwarding, 107
    newline characters, 169
    paths, 166
    variable display, 162

ECHO_REQUEST packets, 193
echo requests in ICMP, 147
echoing script names, 165
editing
    /etc/sudoers file, 100
    files, 114
EFI system partition, 5
efibootmgr command, 22
egrep command for finding users, 56
elif keyword, 181
email
    address changes, 170
    aliases, 66
    destinations, 26, 108
    statistics, 68
emailing logs, 97
emergency target, 197
empty passwords, 106
encrypted devices, listing, 23
encryption
    authentication passwords, 156
    dm-crypt command, 197
    group passwords, 65
Enforcing mode in SELinux, 110
enumerating hosts database, 17, 137
env command
    customized environments, 162
    displaying, 132
    environment variables, 167, 171
Environment key, 81
environment, printing, 165
environment variables
    creating, 81
    displaying, 132
    env command, 167
    HOME, 173
    PS1, 172
    removing, 171
-eq operator for integer comparisons, 174
equal signs (=)
    string comparisons, 165
    variable comparisons, 176
error corrections
    automatic, 134
    swap partition, 134
error fixes with fsck command, 8, 191
esac sequence, 173
escape sequences
    alerts, 174
    carriage return and newline, 198
    quotes, 163
/etc/apparmor.d directory, 112
/etc/apparmor.d/tunables directory, 119
/etc/apt/sources.list file, 52, 131
/etc/auto.master file, 70
/etc/bash.bash_logout file, 171
/etc/cron.allow file, 62
/etc/cron.daily directory, 63
/etc/cron.deny file, 96
/etc/crontab file, 63
/etc/crypttab file, 23
/etc/cups directory, 66
/etc/default/grub file
    changes to, 8
    timeouts, 7
/etc/default/keyboard file, 152
/etc/dhcpd.conf file, 36
/etc/exports file, 194
/etc/fail2ban directory, 106
/etc/fstab file
    defaults line, 24, 192
    device checking order, 12
    filesystem information, 10
    format, 11
    mount command, 9
/etc/grub2.cfg, 28
/etc/gshadow file, 65
/etc/hosts.allow file, 101
/etc/hosts.deny file, 99
/etc/hosts file
    correct line in, 17, 138
    hostnames, 27
    localhost addresses, 16
/etc/inetd.conf file, 100
/etc/init.d directory
    linked files, 70
    scripts, 46
/etc/inittab file
    changes to, 49
    Ctrl+Alt+Del keys, 110
    runlevels, 70, 190
/etc/issue file, 102
/etc/issue.net file, 102
/etc/lib file, 130
/etc/localtime file, 189
/etc/logrotate.conf files, 97
/etc/logrotate.d directory, 121
/etc/mdadm.conf file, 26
/etc/modprobe.conf file, 30
/etc/modprobe.d directory, 21
/etc/motd file, 102
/etc/mtab file, 10
/etc/netplan directory, 34
/etc/network directory, 27

/etc/nologin file
    login prevention, 141
    PAM for, 104
/etc/nsswitch.conf file
    authentication, 194
    group information lookups, 16
/etc/pam.d directory, 104
/etc/passwd file
    home directories, 103
    output location, 55
    user information, 61
    usernames, 54
/etc/pki directory, 108
/etc/profile.d directory, 80
/etc/rc.d directory, 70
/etc/rc.local file, 79
/etc/rcS.d directory, 80
/etc/resolv.conf file
    debugging setting, 27
    DNS servers, 17, 137
    local client services, 18, 139
/etc/rsyslog.conf file, 120
/etc/securetty file, 111
/etc/security/limits.conf file
    process limits, 141
    simultaneous logins, 142
/etc/services file, 98
/etc/shadow file
    encrypted passwords, 156
    password change dates, 69
    passwords, usernames, and UUIDs in, 64
/etc/skel directory, 60, 189
/etc/ssh_known_hosts file, 100
/etc/sshd/sshd.conf file, 100
/etc/sudoers file
    editing, 100
    email destinations, 108
    passwords, 99
/etc/sysconfig/network file, 33
/etc/sysconfig/network-scripts/ directory, 29
/etc/sysctl.conf file, 21
/etc/timezone file, 13
/etc/udev directory, 46, 186
/etc/ufw directory, 120
/etc/X11 directory, 82
/etc/X11/xorg.conf file, 60
/etc/yum.conf.d directory, 51, 130
/etc/yum.conf file, 52, 131
/etc/yum.repos.d directory, 72
ethernet bridges, creating, 36
ethtool command, 36

events, replaying, 78
exclude patterns in git command, 199
ExecStart option, 47
executable files
    location, 58
    permissions, 95
execute bit for scripts, 199
execution
    commands. *See* command execution
    scripts, 162, 164
    of services on boot, 79
existence of files, 135, 178, 198
existing files with touch command, 55
exit codes
    general errors, 180
    success, 164
expansion of variables, 183
expiration of accounts, 69, 96, 190
export command
    environment variables, 195
    libraries, 130
    variables, 166, 195
ext2 filesystems, 9
ext3 filesystems
    vs. ext2 filesystems, 9
    resizing, 31
extended hardware information, information on, 155
extensions
    determining, 170
    script execution, 164
extracting files from backups, 117

F

fail option for RAID arrays, 156
fail2ban system
    configuration, 106
    log file locations, 107
failed login attempts
    account locking, 115
    listing, 112
FAT filesystem for cluster servers, 79
fdisk command, 9
fg command, 56
FHS (Filesystem Hierarchy Standard)
    mount points for removable media, 10
    site-specific data, 9
fi keyword, 169
FibreChannel HBA, 149
file command, 170

file extensions
    determining, 170
    script execution, 164
files
    access control lists, 111
    appending output to, 167
    attributes, 154, 156
    backups, 198
    checksums, 118
    commands from, 171
    committing, 180
    comparing, 77
    contents, 72
    contexts, 120
    copying, 60, 85, 117, 189
    creating, 135
    editing, 114
    existence, 135, 178, 198
    inode index numbers, 58–59
    linked, 70
    listing, 54, 167
    matching, 177
    modifying, 103
    moving, 57
    output to, 7
    overwriting, 55
    owned by users, 66
    ownership, 112, 118, 152
    permissions, 112
    print queues, 67
    relative paths, 30
    removing, 84, 102
    searches, 141–142
    size, 154, 193
    symlinks, 58
    transferring, 116
    uncompressing, 72, 94, 102
Filesystem Hierarchy Standard (FHS)
    mount points for removable media, 10
    site-specific data, 9
filesystems
    checking, 12
    cluster servers, 79
    information on, 10
    labels, 29
    remounting, 11
    shared by NFS, 194
    size, 31
    times mounted, 10–11
    type setting, 23
    unmounting, 73
    unreachable, 27
    verification, 24

find command
    directories, 54
    files, 141–142
    files owned by users, 66
    inode numbers, 59
    modified files, 57
    users invoking sudo command, 57
finding zombie processes, 157
firewall-cmd command, 116
firewalld, zones for, 110
firewalls
    LDAP, 196
    Netfilter, 117
    NTP, 108
    SNMP traffic, 68
for loops
    list iteration, 167, 181
    marking, 175
foreground, bringing commands to, 56
formats for dates and times, 13, 175
formatting printing, 84
forwarding, enabling, 107
fprint package, 114
free command for memory usage, 133, 150, 190
fsck command
    cleaned filesystems, 143
    disk statistics, 146
    error fixes, 8, 191
    filesystem checking, 12
    inodes, 134
    root check skipping, 33
fstrim command, 25, 192
FTP, booting from, 28
functions
    adding, 163
    available at login, 60
    example, 196
    parentheses for, 173

G

G flag for route tables, 140
gateways, default
    adding, 15, 136
    changing, 18, 138
gdisk command
    GUID partition tables, 111
    partition names, 12
general errors, exit codes for, 180
getenforce command, 109
getent command
    hosts database, 17, 137
    users, 96

getfacl command, 111
getsebool command, 113
GIDs and UIDs, 64
git checkout command, 166, 182
git clone command, 195
git commit command, 180
git config command
    configuration parameters, 179
    email addresses, 170
GIT_DIR environment variable, 176
.git directory for repository metadata, 182
git log command, 168, 174
git ls-files command, 199
git merge command, 176
git pull command
    positional parameters, 180
    shared repositories, 180
git push command, 168
git remote show origin command, 177
git status command, 169
.gitignore file, 167
GnuPG key pairs, 100
gpg command
    digital signatures, 119
    key pairs, 100
    public keyrings, 101
GPIO interface, 76
graphics cards configuration information, 60
grep command
    file contents, 72
    system log, 71
groupadd command, 80
groupdel command, 65
groupmod command, 62
groups
    adding, 80
    encrypted password information, 65
    IP addresses, 150
    lookup information, 16
    membership lists, 155
    names, 62
    ownership, 94–95
    printers, 68
    removing, 65
    su command access, 113
    for users, 64
grub-install command
    alternate directories, 23
    MBR, 8
GRUB installed on MBR, 7–8
GRUB Legacy configuration file, 8
GRUB menu, 5, 186
grub-mkconfig command, 8

GRUB2 configuration files
    new, 6
    timeouts, 7
grub2-install command, 7
grub2-mkconfig command
    booting location, 27
    output to files, 7
grubx64.efi file, 23
guest logins, preventing, 135
GUID partition tables, information on, 111
gunzip command, 72
.gz files, 72
gzip command, 103

H

hangup signals for processes, 148
HAProxy server 400 response, 76
hard drives
    detecting, 128
    preparing, 9
hard links, 58
hardware
    information on, 155
    listing, 157
hardware clock
    setting, 15
    UTC time, 15
    working with, 14
hashing algorithms for PKI, 113
head command, 54, 56
HEAD location, 166
HISTFILESIZE option, 195
history
    commands, 171, 195
    commits, 168, 174
    performance data, 151
hmac-md5 algorithm, 103
home directories
    changing, 64
    chroot, 103
    copying files, 60
    creating, 63
HOME environment variable, 173
horizontal tabs, 176
host command
    authoritative name servers, 16
    authorization name servers, 136
    class type, 157
hostname characters, 27
hostname lookups
    disabling, 148
    preventing, 153

hostnamectl set-chassis command, 78
hosts
    caches, 100
    database enumeration, 17, 137
    SSH, 111
    unreachable, 146
hotplug devices, USB, 47
HTTP 405 status code with TraceEnable, 85
http_access directive, 74
HTTP, booting from, 28
hwclock command for hardware clock
    setting, 15
    UTC time, 15
    working with, 14
hypervisors
    connections, 32
    Type 1, 34

I

ibstat command, 148
ICMP
    echo requests, 147
    interface for, 16, 136
    iptables rules, 107
    ports, 98
iconv command, 32
id command, 65
id_rsa file, 99
IDs
    processes, 27, 132, 148
    SATA disks, 128
    shared, 114
    usernames, 80
if conditionals
    end character, 169
    file existence, 135
ifconfig command, 136
iftop command
    hostname lookups, 153
    interface setting, 156
    network usage, 150
images for partitions, 94, 118
IN class for host command, 157
incremental backups, 114
inet protocols
    default, 26
    ip command, 144
InfiniBand devices, information on, 148
informational messages, 66
infrastructure as code, 162
infrastructure automation, 165, 178

inheriting permissions, 111
init command, 46
initialization files, shell execution without, 60
initializing partitions, 7, 131
inode index numbers
    printing, 58
    searching for files by, 59
inodes
    byte-to-inode ratio, 149
    partitions, 134
input, user, 172
INPUT chain policies, 106
insert mode for Vi editor, 57
insmod command, 21
install command, make command targets, 72
installing
    kernel, 20, 30
    packages, 48, 53, 129, 132
    virtual machines, 33
integers, comparing, 174, 182
interactive logins, 135
interactive mode for NTP servers, 67
interfaces
    displaying, 145
    ICMP packets, 16
    iftop, 156
    information on, 136
    netstat display of, 175
    Raspberry Pi, 76
interpreter location, 171
interrupts, monitoring, 147
inventories
    automated infrastructure, 174
    device collections, 163
invoking Bash shell, 163
IO, scheduling, 150, 153
ioping command
    latency, 151
    request setting, 158
    request size, 153, 155
iostat command
    involuntary wait scenario, 178
    megabyte display, 191
    partition information, 19, 142
IP addresses
    groups, 150
    NTP servers, 66
    ownership, 151
    private, 136
ip command
    default protocol, 26
    newlines, 145
    protocol family, 144

ip monitor command, 16, 137
ip route change command
    commands following, 19
    default gateways, 18, 138
ip route flush cache command, 19, 140
iperf command, 147
ipset command
    groups, 150
    iptables, 120
iptables
    ICMP traffic, 107
    INPUT chain, 106
    ipset software, 120
    log entry limits, 106
    Netfilter, 117
    PREROUTING chain, 105
    rules, 105–107
    targets, 106, 108
    UFW configuration, 120
iptables-save command
    rules, 105
    table name, 121
iptraf command, 150
IPv6 localhost addresses, 16
IRQ assignments, viewing, 46, 186
ISOLINUX bootloader, 22
itop command, 147
iw dev command, 71
iwconfig command, 26, 83

J

JAVA_PATH environment variable, 195
JavaScript Object Notation (JSON) format, 28
jobs
    background tasks, 133
    removing, 63, 196
    scheduled, 189
journalctl command
    disk space, 136
    log entries, 96, 121
    log-file entries, 196
    reverse output, 197
journald.conf file, 97
journaling in ext3 filesystems, 9
JSON (JavaScript Object Notation) format, 28

K

Kerberos authentication
    enabling, 104
    SSH, 121
    ticket caches, 112

KerberosAuthentication option, 121
kern facility, 96
kernel
    installing, 30
    message logs, 96
    parameters, 148
    udev events, 70
    updating, 52, 131
    upgrading, 69
    version, 52, 131
kernel-install command, 30
kernel modules
    custom commands, 30
    installing, 20
    loaded, 5
    location, 28
kernel ring buffer
    clearing, 71
    kernel panic messages, 28
    viewing, 5, 186
keyrings in gpg, 101
keys and key pairs
    Apache servers, 83
    authentication, 190, 194
    certificate authority servers, 73
    GnuPG, 100
    layout, 29
    LUKS, 101
    mapping, 152
    Postfix TLS, 105
    sending, 100
    SSH, 98–99, 107, 118, 120, 194
    ssh-agent, 110
kickstart
    and anaconda, 31
    booting, 35
kill command
    BIND reloading, 77
    processes, 56–57, 148
killall command, 133
killing processes, 133, 200
klist command, 112
kmag command, 61

L

labels for filesystems, 29
LACP protocol, 33
LANG environment variable, 14, 179
large files on directories, 10, 134
last command for logs, 68
lastb command for failed login attempts, 112

latency
    diagnosing, 151
    ping command, 147
LC_ALL environment variable, 14, 178
LC_MONETARY environment variable, 14, 181
LC_TIME environment variable, 13, 175
LDAP
    authentication, 122, 154
    ports, 122, 189, 196
ldconfig command, 48, 129, 200
ldd command, 48
leases, DHCP, 194
legal disclaimer information, suppressing, 156
less command, 58
/lib/systemd/system folder, 49
libraries
    dependencies, 48, 130
    printing, 200
    shared, 48, 51, 129, 200
    storage, 130
LIBVIRT_DEBUG, 31
libvirt for debugging logs, 31
limits
    PAM, 122
    password age, 121
    processes, 141
    simultaneous logins, 142
    users, 99
lines, printing, 54
linked files, 70
links cache wireless device status, 71
links for shared libraries, 48, 129
--list option for configuration parameters, 179
ln command
    symlinks, 58
    time zones, 14
load average, 133, 142, 200
load balancing in bonding scenarios, 35
loaded modules, displaying
    currently loaded, 20
    kernel, 5
loading modules and dependencies, 5
local authentication for encrypted passwords, 156
local client services, enabling, 18, 139
local command for variables, 165
local servers, daemons on, 149
local time zones, 13
local variables, indicating, 165
local# facilities for custom logs, 67
locale
    currency, 181
    translations bypassing, 14, 179
    variable reconfiguration, 14, 178
localectl command, 29
localhost in IPv6, 16
locate command for database updates, 59
locking accounts, 115
locking out password-based logins, 63
--log-prefix option for iptables, 108
logged-in users, 68–69, 142
logical volumes
    creating, 7, 131, 192
    directories, 71
    information on, 26
    logical creation order, 8
logins
    3D acceleration, 75
    console, 111
    environment, 101
    interactive, 135
    preventing, 104, 141
    simultaneous, 142
    user information, 73
logouts
    commands executed on, 171
    processes running after, 85
    users, 177
logpath option, 107
logrotate command, 121
logrotate configuration file, 97
logs and log files
    authentication and authorization, 115
    compression, 97
    custom, 67
    disabling, 35
    emailing, 97
    entry display, 120–121
    entry limits, 106
    entry parsing, 196
    journals, 97
    kernel messages, 96
    last command, 68
    locations, 107
    output from, 76
    output to, 163
    packets, 122
    systemd-journald service, 96
    watching, 94
loops
    creating, 166
    for, 167, 181
    until, 180, 182
    while, 166, 173, 181–182
lpr command
    capturing messages, 196
    print queues, 67

lpxelinux.0 file, 28
ls command
    dot files, 54, 117
    example, 50
    filters, 167
    hard links, 58
    inode index numbers, 58
    ownership, 112, 149
    partitions, 128
    permissions, 59, 112
    SELinux, 119
    symbolic links, 186
lsattr command, 156
lsblk command
    boot partitions, 72
    partition information, 36
lsdev command, 74
lshw command, 157
lsmod command
    device drivers, 6
    loaded modules, 5, 20
lsof command, 141
lspci command
    listing, 187
    numeric codes and device names, 50, 187
lsusb command
    Bluetooth devices, 85
    USB connections, 48
    USB devices, 46, 128
-lt operator, 181
LUKS
    encryption, 197
    key-derivation function, 101
LUNs
    from Fibre Channel, 25
    paths, 25
lvcreate command, 7, 131, 192
LVM
    logical volumes, 7, 131
    partitions, 7, 131
lvmdiskscan command, 8, 132
lzma extension, 94

M

MAC addresses
    new entries, 145
    removing, 144
machine type setting, 78
magnification functionality, 61
mail command for STDIN messages, 73
mail option for emailing logs, 97

mail queues
    directories, 66
    Postfix servers, 67
mail servers
    email aliases, 66
    queries, 16, 137
mail storage, 187
MAILADDR option, 26
mailstats command, 68
mailto option, 108
make command
    commands and relationships used with, 72
    targets, 72
make oldconfig command, 69
Makefile name, 72
Master Boot Record (MBR)
    GRUB on, 7–8
    partition information, 22
    primary partitions, 6
master branch in repositories, 169
matching files, 177
MATE desktop environment, 76
max-lease-time option, 194
maximum mount count, 199
maxlogins option, 142
MBR (Master Boot Record)
    GRUB on, 7–8
    partition information, 22
    primary partitions, 6
mdadm command
    arrays, 25, 192
    email, 26
    polling interval, 145
    RAID arrays, 26
/media file, 10
membership lists for groups, 155
memory usage
    displaying, 146
    free command, 133, 150, 190
    processes, 157, 200
merge command for repositories, 164
merge conflicts, rolling back, 176
messages
    capturing, 196
    informational, 66
    kernel logs, 96
    netlink, 16, 137
    repositories, 168
    for users, 102
    warning, 103
    welcome, 61
metadata in repositories, 182
mixer volumes, 82

mkdir command
    directories, 55
    repositories, 163
mke2fs command
    bad blocks, 147
    changing, 149
    filesystem type, 23
mkfs.btrfs command, 11
mkinitrd command, 20, 191
mkswap command, 134, 192
modified files, finding, 57
modifying files, 103
modinfo command, 20
modprobe command, 5
    dependencies, 21, 186
    kernel module, 20
    removing modules, 21
modules
    blacklist information, 21
    comparing, 35
    dependencies, 21, 186
    inserting, 21
    loading, 5
    removing, 21
    unloading, 6, 35
monitoring
    interrupt usage, 147
    performance, 69
    processes, 188
monitors
    configuration, 60, 81
    X11, 81
more command, 84
mount command
    /etc/fstab files, 9
    mount process simulation, 199
    partitions, 22
    USB devices, 12
    USB disks, 6
mount count maximum, 199
mount points for removable media, 10
mounted filesystems
    displaying, 32
    /etc/mtab file, 10
moving
    files, 57
    positional parameters, 180
mtr command, 145
multibyte representation, 13, 189
multipath command, 25
multiple commands, running, 167, 182

mv command
    overwriting files, 55
    text files, 57
MX records, 193
MySQL default ports, 82

N

nagios software, 69
NAME option for network
    adapters, 82
name resolution
    nmap, 145
    routes, 144
name servers
    ports, 97
    querying, 16
named.conf file, 73
names
    changing, 65
    groups, 62
    network adapters, 82
    partitions, 12
nameserver line, 17
Nano editor, 83
NAT vs. bridging, 30
nc command, 139
net command, 104
NetBIOS name service requests, 74
netcat command, 139
Netfilter firewalls, 117
netlink messages, 16, 137
netstat command
    current default route, 15, 199
    hostname lookups, 148
    interface information, 175
    routing tables, 157
    services and sockets, 17, 138
network adapter names, 82
network bonding, 30
network interfaces, drivers, 36
Network Manager, 150
networks
    component authentication, 117
    configuration, 29
    configuration saving, 33
    throughput measuring, 147
    usage displaying, 150
new files, permissions for, 95
newaliases command, 66

newlines
  echo command, 169
  escape characters, 198
  removing, 145
nice command, 133
nmap command
  name resolution, 145
  open ports, 141–142
  Xmas scans, 146
nmbd daemon, 74
nmcli command, 150
--no-commit option for shared
    repositories, 180
nocompress option for logs, 97
nohup command, 85
non-interactive mode
  command execution in, 99
  sudo command, 119
non-swap partitions, 132
NOPASSWD option, 99
--norc option for shell execution without
    initialization files, 60
nslookup command, 36, 154
NTP
  interactive mode, 67
  IP addresses, 66
  ports, 108
ntpq command, 67
numeric codes, displaying, 50, 187
NXDOMAIN message, 140

O

o command in Vi editor, 57
octal notation for permissions, 120
open ports, scanning for,
    141–142
open source package for Remote Desktop
    Protocol, 82
OpenSSH
  empty passwords, 106
  login allowing, 108
  SSH client logins, 74
openssl command
  certificate authority servers, 73
  Certificate Signing Requests, 77
OpenVPN
  network access, 74
  ports, 106
Orca screen reader, 61

orchestration
  agentless infrastructure, 183
  agents, 164, 198
  Ansible package, 162
--origin option for repositories, 177
output
  escape characters, 163
  to log files, 163
  logging, 76
  redirecting, 7, 81, 170
  variables, 177
output files, setting, 80
OVA files, 34
overwriting files, 55
OVF templates, 29
ownership
  changing, 95, 118
  deleted accounts, 66
  displaying, 112, 149
  groups, 94–95
  inherited, 152
  IP addresses, 151

P

packages
  available, 53
  caches, 52
  changes, 52
  information on, 53, 132
  installing, 48, 53, 129, 132
  repositories, 52, 72, 131
  searching for, 51, 188
  .tgz file extension, 53
  updating, 130
packets
  ICMP, 16
  logging, 122
  snapshots, 146
pager, more command for, 84
pam_cracklib.so module, 105
pam_limits.so module, 122
pam_listfiles.so module, 122
pam_nologin.so module, 104
pam_tally2 module, 115
pam_unix.so module, 105
parameters, positional, 180
parentheses () for functions, 173
parsing log-file entries, 196
parted command, 12

partition/mounted/var directory, 50, 187
partition tables, updating, 151
partitions
    changing, 12
    displaying, 128
    EFI system, 5
    GRUB Legacy configuration file, 8
    identifying, 6
    images, 94, 118
    information on, 34, 36
    initializing, 7, 131
    inodes, 134
    listing, 36
    MBR, 22
    names, 12
    non-swap, 132
    RAID arrays, 24
    swap, 6, 134, 143, 192
    UUIDs, 11
partprobe command, 151
passwd command, 64
password-based logins, locking out, 63
passwords
    age limits, 121
    boot prevention, 114
    bootloaders, 110
    change dates, 64, 69
    empty, 106
    file, 64
    local authentication, 156
    PAM authentication, 105
    recovering, 128
    skipping, 99
    strength, 105
paste command delimiters, 81
patch command for file backups, 198
patch files, whitespaces in, 197
paths
    commands, 176
    default, 176
    displaying, 166
    files, 30
    LUNs, 25
PBKDF2 function, 101
pcap format for traffic, 151
pci-0000 file, 25
PEM format, 105
performance
    CPU, 191
    graphing, 143
    historical data, 151
    monitoring, 69
    polling interval, 145

permissions
    bash scripts, 154
    directories, 153
    displaying, 94
    files, 112
    inheriting, 111
    new files, 95
    octal notation, 120
    rsync command, 198
    suid bit, 95
    symlinks, 59
    tar command, 197
    writing, 154
Permissive mode in SELinux, 109
PermitEmptyPasswords option, 106
PermitRootLogin option, 74
persistent volumes, 29
pgrep command, 132
physical volumes
    information on, 144
    logical volumes from, 8
    searches, 8, 132
pidof sshd command, 148
ping command
    bypassing routing tables, 198
    ECHO_REQUEST packets, 193
    emulating, 18, 139
    ICMP echo requests, 147
    ICMP packets, 136
    latency, 147
    packet policies, 146
    querying, 16
PKI hashing algorithms, 113
pkill command, 153
Pluggable Authentication Modules
    authorization and authentication, 122
    configuration, 104
    failed login attempts, 115
    login prevention, 104
    password authentication, 105
    password strength, 105
    policies, 149
    required, 109
    user limits, 122
policies
    INPUT chain, 106
    PAM, 149
    SELinux configuration, 109
polling interval for performance, 145
port forwarding in SSH, 76
port-to-protocol translations, 98

ports
    configuring, 97
    CUPS administrative web interface, 67
    CUPS printing daemon, 152
    FibreChannel HBA, 149
    firewalls, 68
    ICMP, 98
    LDAP, 122, 189, 196
    MySQL, 82
    name servers, 97
    NTP, 108
    open, 141–142
    OpenVPN, 106
    slapd daemon, 104
    SMTP traffic, 97
    Squid, 104
    SSH, 122, 138
    telnet, 119
    VNC, 78
    well-known, 121
positional parameters, moving, 180
Postfix
    mail queues, 67
    TLS configuration formats, 105
postqueue command, 67
pound signs (#)
    command-line arguments, 177
    comments in scripts, 164
PREROUTING chain, 105
primary partitions, 6
printenv command, 165
printer groups, 68
printf command, 84
printing
    awk command, 195
    completed print jobs, 67
    environment, 165
    formatting, 84
    inode index numbers, 58
    libraries, 200
    lines, 54
    lists, 172
    ports, 152
    print queues, 67
priority
    MX records, 193
    processes, 133, 148
private addresses, 15, 136
private keys
    Apache servers, 83
    certificate authority servers, 73
    SSH, 118, 120
    ssh-agent, 110

privileges, minimum, 95
/proc/bus/usb directory, 50
/proc filesystem, 47
/proc/meminfo file, 146
/proc/mounts file, 32
/proc/partitions file, 34
procedure infrastructure automation, 178
processes, 158
    AppArmor, 113
    hangups, 148
    IDs, 27, 132, 148
    killing, 133, 200
    limits, 141
    after logout, 85
    memory usage, 157, 200
    monitoring, 188
    priority, 133, 148
    restarting, 57, 133
    running, 158
    stopping, 56
    terminals, 84
    uninterruptible sleep, 152
.profile file for time zones, 14, 181
profiles
    AppArmor, 115, 119
    directories, 112
progress indicators, 10, 188
ps auwx command, 118
ps aux command, 112
ps command
    memory usage, 157, 200
    SELinux contexts, 115
    uninterruptible sleep, 152
    zombie processes, 157
PS1 environment variable, 172
pseudo-terminals devices, 115
public keyrings for gpg, 101
public keys in SSH, 98, 107, 120
pubring.gpg file, 101
pull command for repositories, 162
purging caches, 33
push command for network access, 74
pvcreate command, 7, 131
pvdisplay command, 25, 144
pvscan command, 144
PXE boot, 23
pxelinux.0 file, 23

Q

query destinations, changing, 154
question marks (?) with less command, 58

quotacheck command
    file creation, 135
    user quotas, 59
quotas
    enabling, 135
    usage display, 59

R

\r\n escape characters, 198
RAID arrays
    adapter detection, 153
    mdadm command, 26
    partitions, 24
    removing disks from, 156
RAM disks, 20–21, 191
Raspberry Pi interfaces, 76
raw devices, 30
rc file runlevels, 70
read command for user input, 172
read I/O requests, displaying, 34
read-only variables
    creating, 175
    displaying, 170
readonly command, 170
rebooting, 46
reconfiguring locale variables, 178
recovering passwords, 128
recursive changes in chmod command, 169
redirection
    to log files, 163
    output, 7, 81, 170
    STDERR, 56, 84, 170, 179
    STDIN, 79, 82, 182, 199
    STDOUT, 56, 84, 103, 182
regions in time zones, 13, 189
REJECT targets for iptables, 106
relative paths, 30
reloading BIND, 77
Remote Desktop Protocol, 82
remote names, obtaining, 177
remounting filesystems, 11
removable media, mount points for, 10
removing
    blocks, 25, 192
    cron jobs, 196
    directories, 54
    environment variables, 171
    files, 84, 102
    groups, 65
    jobs, 63
    MAC addresses, 144

    modules, 21
    newlines, 145
    users, 62
renice command, 148
replaying events, 78
reports scale, 147
repositories
    changes to, 164
    cloning, 177, 195
    copying, 169
    creating, 163
    default branches, 169
    file versions, 167
    messages, 168
    metadata, 182
    packages, 131
    retrieving, 165
    retrieving objects from, 162
    shared, 180
    URLs, 72
    Yum, 130
repquota command, 59
requests
    number, 158
    size, 153, 155
reserved blocks, displaying, 12
resize2fs command, 31
resizing filesystems, 31
restarting
    Apache servers, 75
    CUPS, 68
    processes, 57, 133
restorecon command, 114
rm command, 54
rmmod command, 6, 35
rndc command
    authentication, 103
    BIND name servers, 79
rolling back merges, 176
root user
    console logins, 111
    SSH logins, 116
    UIDs, 109
route add command
    DNS servers, 17, 138
    gateways, 136
    traffic prevention, 18, 139
route command
    flags, 19
    name resolution, 144
routes
    adding, 17, 138
    default, 191, 199

routing tables
    bypassing, 198
    displaying, 157
    G flag, 140
rpm command
    altered files, 51, 188
    verbose output, 51, 187
rpm kernel command, 52, 131
rpm package file output location, 48
rpm2cpio output location, 48
RSA hashing algorithms, 113
rss column for memory usage, 157
rsync command
    archive mode, 71
    file modifications, 103
    file removal, 102
    file size, 193
    options, 108
    permissions, 198
    synchronization process, 103
rsyslog command, 120
rules
    iptables, 105–107
    reloading, 75
runlevel command, 49
runlevels
    displaying, 47, 49
    rc files, 70
    setting, 79
    single user mode, 46, 190
--runtime-to-permanent option, 116

S

Samba for NetBIOS name service requests, 74
SANs (storage area networks), 9
sar command
    CPU performance, 191
    historical performance data, 151
SATA (Serial ATA) disks
    BIOS, 194
    identifiers, 50, 128
scale, report, 147
scheduled jobs, 189
scheduling
    commands, 62
    IO, 150, 153
scp command, 85, 117
screen command, 133
screen reader, Orca, 61
Screen section for graphics card and monitor configurations, 60

scripts
    directories, 27
    execute bit, 199
    execution, 162, 164
    file extensions, 164
    file removal, 84
    permissions, 154
    services, 46
    storage, 80
    terminating, 175
scrolling logs, 94
SCSI devices
    host adapter scans, 156
    support per bus, 49, 129
search line for local client services, 18, 139
searches
    files, 141–142
    package caches, 52, 131
    packages, 51, 188
    physical volumes, 8, 132
SeatDefaults for guest logins, 135
security bulletins, 116
sed command, 53
SELinux
    access denials, 155
    booleans list, 113
    configuration policies, 109
    contexts, 113, 115, 119, 152
    Enforcing mode, 110
    Permissive mode, 109
SELINUXTYPE option, 109
semicolons (;)
    case statement, 178
    chaining commands, 77, 174
seq command, 172
Serial ATA (SATA) disks
    BIOS, 194
    identifiers, 50, 128
server command for query destinations, 36, 154
servers
    containers, 75
    queries, 17
    site-specific data, 94
service accounts UIDs, 155
service apache2 restart command, 75
service reload command, 81
service status command, 77
service units, listing, 50, 187
services
    boot times, 76
    displaying, 17, 47, 84, 100, 138
    executed on boot, 79
    loaded, 49, 187

scripts, 46
shutting down, 78
stopping, 69
sestatus command, 120
set command for output redirection, 170
setenforce command, 110
setsebool command, 111
SFTP
    file transfers, 116
    kickstart booting, 35
sha1sum utility, 118
SHA256withRSA option, 113
shared IDs, 114
shared libraries
    links and cache, 48, 129, 200
    storage, 51
shared repositories, changes to, 180
shebang lines for interpreter location, 171
shells executed without initialization files, 60
shift command for positional parameters, 180
Shift key
    GRUB menu, 5, 186
    sticky keys, 61
shim.efi bootloader, 22–23
shims for UEFI, 23
shutting down services, 78
SIGKILL signal, 157
SIGTERM signal, 200
simultaneous login limits, 142
single-user mode
    booting, 5
    passwords, 128
    runlevels, 46, 190
    setting, 49
site-specific data
    FHS, 9
    servers, 94
size
    /boot partition, 7
    dumps, 24
    files, 154, 193
    filesystems, 31
    journal logs, 97
    partitions, 12
    requests, 155
size column for memory usage, 157
slapd.conf file, 122
slapd daemon, 104
SMTP traffic ports, 97
snapshots for packets, 146

SNMP servers firewall ports, 68
sockets display, 17, 26, 138, 192
software
    updating, 129
    versions, 170
software tokens in two-factor authentication, 110
sort command for unique items, 57
sort order in top command, 143
source code, committing, 168
source command
    functions, 163
    script execution, 171
    variables, 163, 195
spawned windows in SSH sessions, 60
SPF record for DNS queries, 19, 140
Spice remote access, 79
SQL commands, reading, 168
square brackets [ ]
    file matching, 177
    while loops, 173
Squid
    access control lists, 73–74
    ports, 104
/srv directory, 9, 94
ss command
    process IDs, 27
    sockets, 26, 192
SSD disk location, 70
SSH
    agentless infrastructure orchestration, 183
    authentication keys, 190
    connections, 197
    hosts, 111
    Kerberos authentication, 121
    keys, 98–99, 107, 120, 194
    login prevention, 141
    port forwarding, 76
    ports, 122, 138
    private keys, 118
    root user logins, 74, 116
    spawned window sessions, 60
    synchronization process, 103
    ufw traffic, 116
    X session connections, 61
ssh-add command, 110
ssh-agent command, 110
ssh.conf file, 109
ssh-copy-id command, 107
ssh-keygen command, 98, 122, 194
sshd.conf file, 109

sshd_config file, 116
SSL
    certificate authority servers, 73
    configuration, 108
    private keys, 83
    VPN clients, 113
SSLCertificateKeyFile directive
    Apache servers, 83
    configuration, 104
SSLEngine option, 104
Start of Authority information, 18, 139
startup commands for udev devices, 80
STDERR, redirecting, 56, 84, 170, 179
STDIN
    mail command, 73
    redirecting, 79, 82, 182, 199
STDOUT
    appending output to, 78
    redirecting, 56, 84, 103, 182
    rpm2cpio, 48
steal column in involuntary wait scenario, 178
sticky bits, enabling, 95
sticky keys, enabling, 61
stopping
    daemons, 81
    processes, 56
    services, 69, 78
storage
    blob, 31
    host caches, 100
    libraries, 130
    mail, 187
    network configurations, 33
storage area networks (SANs), 9
strings, comparing, 165
su command
    access restrictions, 113
    login environment, 101
    non-interactive sessions, 99
subshells, command execution in, 166
substitution operation, 53
sudo command
    accounts, 96
    credentials, 190
    non-interactive mode, 119
    specific user, 99
sudoedit command, 114
suid bit for permissions, 95
summary output with du command, 157
suspending daemons, 83

swap partitions
    creating, 192
    error corrections, 134
    identifying, 6
    skipping, 143
swap space
    activating, 155
    deactivating, 143
    description, 130
    displaying, 133, 190
    information on, 143
swapoff command, 143
swapon command, 143, 155
switch support in bonded-link aggregation, 33
symlinks
    displaying, 186
    files, 28, 58
    permissions, 59
    World Wide Identifiers, 24
synchronization process in SSH, 103
/sys/block file, 153
/sys/class/fc_host directory
    FibreChannel HBA, 149
    WWN for Fibre Channel, 71
/sys/class/scsi_host/hostN/scan file, 156
sysctl command
    boot values, 21
    kernel, 148
    parameters, 152
    settings display, 20, 200
syslog level for informational messages, 66
system BIOS for hard drive detection, 128
system files, changes to, 117
system log for DHCP server, 71
system users, creating, 65
system-wide cron files, 63
systemctl command for killing
        processes, 200
systemctl daemon-reload command, 70
systemctl disable command, 69
systemctl enable command, 47
systemctl get-default command, 47
systemctl isolate command, 49
systemctl list-units command, 50
systemctl mask command, 84
systemctl restart command, 68
systemctl status command, 49, 77, 187
systemctl stop command, 81
systemd-analyze command, 76
systemd-journald service, 96

systemd system
    configuration changes, 70
    configuration files, 49
    environment variables, 81
    journal, 96
    programs to execute, 47
    service units, 187
    targets, 197
SystemMaxFileSize option, 97
systemwide time zones, 14
SysVinit service scripts, 46

T

\t escape sequence, 176
tabs
    cut command delimiter, 55
    horizontal, 176
TACACS+ authentication, 117
tail command
    lines printed, 54, 56
    logs, 94
tar command
    excluding files, 102
    packages, 53
    permissions, 197
    tar file creation, 101
    uncompressing files, 102
targets
    iptables, 106, 108
    systemd, 197
TCP
    CUPS administrative web interface portd, 67
    SMTP traffic ports, 97
    three-way handshakes, 98
    wrappers, 99
TCP SYN packets and open ports, 142
tcpdump command
    interfaces, 145
    packet snapshots, 146
tcptraceroute command, 151
telinit command, 49
telnet ports, 119
terminals for processes, 84
terminating scripts, 175
test command arguments, 173
/tftpboot directory, 23
.tgz file extension, 53
third-party logging agents, 112
three-way handshakes, 98
3D acceleration, 75
ticket caches in Kerberos authentication, 112

tilde character (~) for home directories, 173
time zones
    displaying, 13
    local, 13, 189
    regions, 13, 189
    setting, 14, 181
    systemwide, 14
timedatectl command, 13
timeouts
    GRUB2 configuration files, 7
    troubleshooting, 151
times
    command execution time, 31
    formats, 13, 175
    setting, 15
timestamps, changing, 55
TMOUT environment variable, 177
tokens in two-factor authentication, 110
top command
    process monitoring, 188
    sort order, 143
touch command
    existing files, 55
    login prevention, 141
tr command, 83
TraceEnable setting, 85
tracepath command, 139
traceroute command
    live updates, 145
    TCP SYN packets in, 137
    vs. tracepath, 139
    unreachable hosts, 146
traffic
    determining, 150
    pcap format, 151
    preventing, 18, 139
transferring files, 116
Transport mode for VPNs, 115
traversal of directories, 118
troubleshooting
    connections, 140
    third-party logging agents, 112
tshark command, 151
tune2fs command
    error corrections, 9, 134
    extended options, 25
    maximum mount count, 199
    times filesystems mounted, 10–11
two-factor authentication tokens, 110
Type 1 hypervisors, 34
type command, 171
TZ line, 14, 181

U

Ubuntu distribution Unity desktop, 80
udev devices
    configuration, 46, 186
    network adapter names, 82
    startup commands, 80
udev events, 70
udevadm control command, 75
udevadm monitor command, 70
udevadm trigger command, 78
UDP for OpenVPN, 106
$UDPListen option, 97
UEFI
    bootloaders, 22
    passwords, 114
    shims, 23
ufw allow command, 116
UFW configuration, 120
UIDs
    authentication servers, 64
    root account, 109
    service accounts, 155
ulimit command
    files, 154
    users, 99
umask command, 94
umount command
    remounting filesystems, 11
    unmounting filesystems, 73
    unreachable filesystems, 27
unalias command, 178
unallocated disk space, 30
uncompressing files
    .gz files, 72
    lzma files, 94
    tar command, 102
uninterruptible sleep process state, 152
Unity desktop, 80
unlink command, 84
unloading modules, 6, 35
unreachable hosts with traceroute command, 146
until loops
    beginnings and ends, 180
    vs. while, 182
update-grub command, 6
updatedb command, 59
updating
    Debian systems, 48
    kernel, 52, 131
    package caches, 52
    packages, 130
    partition tables, 151
    software, 129
    traceroute, 145
upgrading kernel, 69
uptime command for load average, 133, 200
URLs for package repositories, 72
USB devices
    Bluetooth, 85
    connection points, 129
    connections, 48
    hotplug, 47
    listing, 46, 128, 186
    mounting, 6, 12
    storage, 50
user accounts. *See* accounts
useradd command
    disabling accounts, 196
    groups, 64
    home directories, 63
    system users, 65
userdel command, 62
usermod command
    expiring accounts, 69
    home directories, 64
    password-based logins, 63
    printer groups, 68
    user names, 65
usernames
    changing, 65
    IDs, 80
    listing, 54
users
    automatic logouts, 177
    configuration files for login order, 60
    cron availability, 62
    cron scheduled tasks, 96
    files owned by, 66
    groups, 64
    information on, 65
    input by, 172
    limits, 99
    listing, 96
    logged in, 68–69, 142
    login allowing, 108
    login information, 73
    login limits, 122
    messages for, 102
    printer groups, 68
    process limits, 141
    quotas, 59, 135
    readable information, 61
    removing, 62
    system, 65
/usr/lib/firewalld/zones directory, 110

/usr/lib/modules file, 28
/usr/share/zoneinfo directory, 13, 189
usrquota command, 135
UTC time for hardware clock, 15
UTF-8 encoding for multibyte representation of characters, 13, 189
UUIDs
    obtaining, 33
    partitions, 11

V

values, displaying, 20
/var/log/kern.log file, 28
/var/log/secure file, 116
/var/qmail/queue directory, 66
/var/spool/cron/crontabs directory, 62
/var/tmp/abrt directory, 78
variables
    adding, 163
    availability, 195
    comparing, 176
    declaring, 166
    displaying contents, 162
    environment. *See* environment variables
    expansion, 183
    local, 165
    output, 177
    read-only, 170, 175
    setting, 174
verbose output in installations, 51, 187
versions
    kernel, 52, 131
    software, 170
VFS (virtual filesystem), 31
vgscan command, 144
Vi editor
    insert mode, 57
    saving work, 56
video cards, determining, 83
video devices Spice remote access, 79
<video> stanza for Spice remote access, 79
virsh command
    domain information, 13
    hypervisors, 32
virt-install tool, 33
virtual filesystem (VFS), 31
virtual machines, installing, 33
<VirtualHost> directive, 77
visudo editor, 100

vmlinux, 28
vmlinuz, 28
vmstat command
    blocks, 142
    IO wait statistics, 200
VNC
    default base port, 78
    services, 78
volumes
    creation order, 8
    information on, 25, 144
    logical, 71, 131
    persistent, 29
    searches, 132
VPNs
    SSL-based clients, 113
    Transport mode, 115

W

w command for logged in users, 68–69, 142
wa statistic for IO wait time, 200
warning messages, suppressing, 103
watching logs, 94
WAYLAND_DISPLAY environment variable, 74
Wayland sessions, 74
wc command, 54
web servers, enabling, 59
welcome message, setting, 61
Welcome section, 61
well-known ports, 121
wget command, 76
wheel group for su command access, 113
whereis command, 58
which command, 58
while loops
    description, 166
    test portion, 173, 181
    vs. until, 182
whitespaces in patch file, 197
who command, 73
whoami command, 80
whois command
    IP address ownership, 151
    legal disclaimer information, 156
wildcard matches in /etc/hosts.allow file, 101
windows, information on, 188
wireless devices
    link status, 71
    parameters, 26, 83

World Wide Identifiers (WWIDs)
  /dev/disk/by-multipath directory, 35
  symlinks, 24
:wq command in Vi editor, 56
WWN for Fibre Channel, 71

X

X server connections, 135
X sessions, SSH connections in, 61
X11Forwarding option
  SSH connections, 61
  X11 forwarding, 100
xfs_check command, 24
xfs_growfs command, 11
xfs_info command, 11
xfs_metadump command, 10, 188
xfsdump command, 24
xfsrestore command, 24
xhost command, 135
Xmas scans, 146
XML standard for OVF templates, 29
xorg.c file, 82
xrdp package, 82
xwininfo command, 188
xz command, 94

Y

YAML format
  EC2 instances, 32
  /etc/netplan directory, 34
  extension, 179
.yml extension, 179
yum deplist command, 51, 187
yum install command, 48, 129
Yum repositories, 51, 130
yum search command
  package caches, 52
  partitions, 131
0xFD partitions for RAID
  arrays, 24

Z

zip command, 118
zombie processes, finding, 157
zone transfers, 19, 140, 193
zones, firewalld, 110
zypper info command, 53

Comprehensive Online Learning Environment

Register to gain one year of FREE access to the online interactive learning environment and test bank to help you study for your CompTIA Linux+ certification exam—included with your purchase of this book!

The online test bank includes the following:

- **Practice Test** Questions to reinforce what you've learned
- **Bonus Practice Exam** to test your knowledge of the material

Go to http://www.wiley.com/go/sybextestprep to register and gain access to this comprehensive study tool package.

Register and Access the Online Test Bank

To register your book and get access to the online test bank, follow these steps:

1. Go to bit.ly/SybexTest.
2. Select your book from the list.
3. Complete the required registration information, including answering the security verification to prove book ownership. You will be emailed a PIN code.
4. Follow the directions in the email, or go to https://www.wiley.com/go/sybextestprep.
5. Enter the PIN code you received, and click the Activate PIN button.
6. On the Create an Account or Login page, enter your username and password, and click Login. A "Thank you for activating your PIN!" message will appear. If you don't have an account already, create a new account.
7. Click the Go to My Account button to add your new book to the My Products page.